Unconventional Monetary Policy and Financial Stability

Since the financial crisis of 2008–09, central bankers around the world have been forced to abandon conventional monetary policy tools in favour of unconventional policies such as quantitative easing, forward guidance, lowering the interest rate paid on bank reserves into negative territory, and pushing up prices of government bonds. Having faced a crisis in its banking sector nearly a decade earlier, Japan was a pioneer in the use of many of these tools.

Unconventional Monetary Policy and Financial Stability critically assesses the measures used by Japan and examines what they have meant for the theory and practice of economic policy. The book shows how in practice unconventional monetary policy has worked through its impact on the financial markets. The text aims to generate an understanding of why such measures were introduced and how the Japanese system has subsequently changed regarding aspects such as governance and corporate balance sheets. It provides a comprehensive study of developments in Japanese money markets with the intent to understand the impact of policy on the debt structures that appear to have caused Japan's deflation. The topics covered range from central bank communication and policymaking to international financial markets and bank balance sheets.

This text is of great interest to students and scholars of banking, international finance, financial markets, political economy, and the Japanese economy.

Alexis Stenfors is Senior Lecturer in Economics and Finance at the University of Portsmouth, UK.

Jan Toporowski is Professor of Economics and Finance at SOAS University of London, UK.

Routledge Critical Studies in Finance and Stability

Edited by Jan Toporowski, *School of Oriental and African Studies, University of London, UK*

The 2007–8 Banking Crash has induced a major and wide-ranging discussion on the subject of financial (in)stability and a need to revaluate theory and policy. The response of policy-makers to the crisis has been to refocus fiscal and monetary policy on financial stabilisation and reconstruction. However, this has been done with only vague ideas of bank recapitalisation and 'Keynesian' reflation aroused by the exigencies of the crisis, rather than the application of any systematic theory or theories of financial instability.

Routledge Critical Studies in Finance and Stability covers a range of issues in the area of finance including instability, systemic failure, financial macroeconomics in the vein of Hyman P. Minsky, Ben Bernanke and Mark Gertler, central bank operations, financial regulation, developing countries and financial crises, new portfolio theory and New International Monetary and Financial Architecture.

Financial Stability, Systems and Regulation
Jan Kregel
Edited by Felipe C. Rezende

Financialisation in Latin America
Challenges of the Export–Led Growth Model
Noemi Levy and Jorge Bustamante

Evolutionary Financial Macroeconomics
Giorgos Argitis

Unconventional Monetary Policy and Financial Stability
The Case of Japan
Edited by Alexis Stenfors and Jan Toporowski

The Political Economy of Central Banking in Emerging Economies
Edited by Mustafa Yağcı

For more information about this series, please visit www.routledge.com/series/RCSFS

Unconventional Monetary Policy and Financial Stability

The Case of Japan

**Edited by
Alexis Stenfors and
Jan Toporowski**

Routledge
Taylor & Francis Group

LONDON AND NEW YORK

First published 2021
by Routledge
2 Park Square, Milton Park, Abingdon, Oxon OX14 4RN

and by Routledge
52 Vanderbilt Avenue, New York, NY 10017

Routledge is an imprint of the Taylor & Francis Group, an informa business

British Library Cataloguing-in-Publication Data
A catalogue record for this book is available from the British Library

Library of Congress Cataloging-in-Publication Data
Names: Stenfors, Alexis, editor. | Toporowski, Jan, editor.
Title: Unconventional monetary policy and financial stability : the case of Japan / edited by Alexis Stenfors and Jan Toporowski.
Description: Abingdon, Oxon ; New York, NY : Routledge, 2020. | Series: Routledge critical studies in finance and stability | Includes bibliographical references and index.
Identifiers: LCCN 2020011205 (print) | LCCN 2020011206 (ebook) | ISBN 9780367145958 (hbk) | ISBN 9780367507251 (pbk) | ISBN 9780429032479 (ebk)
Subjects: LCSH: Banks and banking—Japan. | Monetary policy—Japan. | Finance—Japan.
Classification: LCC HG3324 .U53 2020 (print) | LCC HG3324 (ebook) | DDC 339.5/30952—dc23
LC record available at https://lccn.loc.gov/2020011205
LC ebook record available at https://lccn.loc.gov/2020011206

ISBN: 978-0-367-14595-8 (hbk)
ISBN: 978-0-429-03247-9 (ebk)

Typeset in Bembo
by Apex CoVantage, LLC

Contents

Preface

Whereas the advanced economies of the West entered a period of slow growth and disinflationary headwinds after the Global Financial Crisis (GFC) in 2008, Japan had done so much earlier, in the lost decade and occasional banking crises in the 1990s. So, Japan became a pioneer and forerunner of many of the Unconventional Monetary Policies (UMPs) that have been subsequently taken up elsewhere in Europe and North America. Indeed, it was partly in the light of such earlier Japanese experience that the subsequent policies introduced by the Fed, ECB and Bank of England were framed and adjusted.

It is, therefore, splendid to have a book focusing on the Japanese monetary experience, with a wide and expert range of contributors, both from within Japan, including the former Governor Masaaki Shirakawa, as well as outside commentators from a variety of countries and universities. The editors, Alexis Stenfors and Jan Toporowski, are to be congratulated for putting together such a stimulating collection of chapter papers.

Nevertheless, despite all the efforts that have gone into such UMP, and Abenomics more widely, the results have not been strong enough to bring about a return to the inflation target 2%. On the other hand, productivity per worker has grown since about 2000 faster than in almost any other country among the advanced economies, and unemployment has been driven down to historically very low levels. If the economy has been typified by relatively good results in output per worker and in employment, does it actually matter much if inflation has remained at, or just below, 1%, rather than at 2%? This may lessen a central banker's self-esteem, failing to hit their self-imposed target, but why would this really have any adverse effect on the ordinary person in the street? Given its ageing population and declining workforce, the Japanese experience is much better and healthier than is often realized.

One curious feature that I noted among the various stimulating chapters, was that Ayhan Nadiri, in Chapter 7, on 'Unconventional Monetary Policy Announcements and Japanese Bank Stocks', has the equity valuation of bank stocks rising after such announcements in the latter part of the period after the launch of Abenomics in 2013. In contrast, in Chapter 9, Etsuko Katsu, on 'Quantitative and Qualitative Monetary Easing, Negative Interest Rates and the Stability of the Financial System in Japan', suggests that the unconventional monetary policy worked much better to influence bank profitability and the return on equity, as well as inflationary expectations in the earlier period, whereas 'the negative interest rate policy has cast a shadow on financial intermediaries, especially outside the large urban areas', in the later years. So there seems to be something of an inconsistency in that announcements of UMP in the latter part of the period were welcomed by the stock market, but, if anything, had a negative effect subsequently on, at least some of, the banks; whereas in the earlier period, there was no significant effect on bank equity values from UMP announcements, but the policies then introduced did benefit the banks. Still, there is no reason why stock markets should necessarily be able to forecast subsequent outcomes correctly.

You will find this and many other gems of analysis when you read through this well-designed and well-timed book.

Charles A. E. Goodhart

Acknowledgements

The credit for a book like this spreads far beyond the title page. Thanks are due in the first instance to the contributors to this volume whose helpful discussions with us and willingness to revise drafts have improved the clarity of the arguments in the book. We are grateful to Andy Humphries, the editors at Routledge and Lilian Muchimba for their guidance and assistance in the editing of this volume. We record our thanks to the Great Britain Sasakawa Foundation and the Toshiba International Foundation for material support that facilitated the discussions from which this book emerged. Finally, very personal debts are owed to Maria and Anita for their patience and forbearance during our lengthy absences in the maze of Japanese monetary and financial arrangements.

Contributors

Tanweer Akram is International Economist at General Motors, Detroit, MI, USA.

Konstantin Bikas is Economist at Positive Money, London, UK.

Charles A. E. Goodhart CBE, FBA was the Norman Sosnow Professor of Banking and Finance at the London School of Economics (1985–2002, and is Emeritus Professor of Economics at the LSE since 2002). From 1997–2000 he was a member of the Bank of England's Monetary Policy Committee.

Ewa Karwowski is Senior Lecturer in Economics at the University of Hertfordshire, UK.

Etsuko Katsu is Professor in Economics at Meiji University, Tokyo, Japan.

Huiqing Li is Associate Professor at the School of National Fiscal Development in the Central University of Finance and Economics, Beijing, China.

Heather Montgomery is Senior Associate Professor at the Department of Business and Economics, International Christian University (ICU), Tokyo, Japan.

Ayhan Nadiri is Doctoral Researcher in Economics and Finance at the University of Portsmouth, UK.

Mimoza Shabani is Senior Lecturer in Financial Economics at the University of East London, UK.

Masaaki Shirakawa is the 30th Governor of the Bank of Japan (2008–2013) and Professor at Aoyama Gakuin University, Tokyo, Japan.

Alexis Stenfors is Senior Lecturer in Economics and Finance at the University of Portsmouth, UK.

Masayuki Susai is Professor at the Faculty of Economics, Nagasaki University, Japan.

Jan Toporowski is Professor of Economics and Finance at SOAS University of London, UK.

Ulrich Volz is Reader in Economics at SOAS University of London, UK.

Ho Yan Karen Wong is Assistant Professor at the Lee Shau Kee School of Business and Administration, Open University of Hong Kong.

Figures

Tables

Abbreviations

ABS	Asset-backed security
ADB	Asian Development Bank
AR	Abnormal return
ARCH	Autoregressive conditional heteroskedastic
ASEAN	Association of Southeast Asian Nations
AUD	Australian dollar
BBSW	Bank Bill Swap Rate
BKBM	Bank Bill Market Rate
BOJ	Bank of Japan
bp	Basis point
CAD	Canadian dollar
CAR	Cumulative abnormal return
CD	Certificate of Deposit
CDOR	Canadian Dollar Offered Rate
CDS	Credit default swap
CHF	Swiss franc
CIBOR	Copenhagen Interbank Offered Rate
CIP	Covered interest rate parity
CLO	Collateralised loan obligation
CLS	Continuous Linked Settlement
CME	Comprehensive Monetary Easing
CP	Commercial paper
CPI	Consumer price index
CRS	Cross-currency basis swap
CUSUM	Cumulative sum
DKK	Danish krone
DSGE	Dynamic stochastic general equilibrium
ECB	European Central Bank
EGARCH	Exponential Generalised Autoregressive Conditional Heteroskedastic
Eonia	Euro Overnight Index Average
ETF	Exchange-traded fund
EUR	Euro

EURIBOR	Euro Interbank Offered Rate
FDI	Foreign direct investment
Fed	Federal Reserve
FRA	Forward rate agreement
FX	Foreign exchange
GAFA	Google, Apple, Facebook and Amazon
GARCH	Generalised Autoregressive Conditional Heteroscedasticity
GBP	British pound
GDP	Gross domestic product
GFC	Global Financial Crisis
GFCF	Gross fixed capital formation
GMM	Generalized method of moments
GPIF	Government Pension Investment Fund
G-SIFI	Global systematically important financial institution
HFT	High-frequency trading
IMF	International Monetary Fund
IOER	Interest rate on excess reserves
IORR	Interest rate on required reserves
IRS	Interest rate swap
JBA	Japanese Bankers Association
JGB	Japanese government bond
J-REIT	Japanese real estate investment trust
JPX	Japan Exchange Group
JPY	Japanese yen
LDP	Liberal-Democratic Party
LIBOR	London Interbank Offered Rate
LSAP	Large-scale asset purchase
M	Month
M&A	Mergers and acquisitions
MDH	Mixture of Distribution Hypothesis
MMF	Money market (mutual) fund
NAV	Net asset value
NFC	Non-financial corporation
nGDP	Nominal GDP
NIBOR	Norwegian Interbank Offered Rate
NIRP	Negative Interest Rate Policy
NOK	Norwegian krone
NZD	New Zealand dollar
OECD	Organisation for Economic Co-operation and Development
OIS	Overnight index swap
OLS	Ordinary least squares
OTC	Over-the-counter
QE	Quantitative Easing
QQE	Quantitative and Qualitative Monetary Easing
ROE	Return on equity

SEK	Swedish Krona
SME	Small and medium-sized enterprises
Sonia	Sterling Overnight Interbank Average Rate
SSE	Shanghai Stock Exchange
STIBOR	Stockholm Interbank Offered Rate
TAF	Term Auction Facility
T-bill	Treasury bill
TIBOR	Tokyo Interbank Offered Rate
Tonar	Tokyo Overnight Average Rate
TOPIX	Tokyo Stock Price Index
TVP-VAR	Time-varying vector autoregressive
UMP	Unconventional monetary policy
USD	US dollar
VEC	Vector error correction
Y	Year
YCC	Yield curve control
ZIRP	Zero interest rate policy

Introduction

Alexis Stenfors and Jan Toporowski

Monetary policy is undertaken with a view to influencing the rate of inflation and the business cycle. The theory behind this is that agents adjust their production and expenditure plans in some predictable way in response to changes in monetary policy. However, this monetary transmission mechanism assumes a very basic monetary and financial system. In a complex financial system, monetary policy affects financing structures rather than production and expenditure in the real economy.

During recent decades, financial markets have undergone a remarkable transformation. The launch of the first cash-settled futures contract in 1981 by the Chicago Mercantile Exchange set the scene for the creation of a range of new financial instruments. Since, the growth in the exchange-traded and over-the-counter derivatives markets has seen little sign of slowing down. In April 2019, the daily turnover of the over-the-counter (OTC) derivatives market linked to just interest rates averaged $6.5 trillion compared to $2.7 trillion in 2016 (BIS, 2019a). The internationalisation of the markets is perhaps best illustrated by the continuing increase in the global foreign exchange (FX) market turnover – having more than trebled in size since 2014 and reaching $6.6 trillion in April 2019 (BIS, 2019b). However, the impact of financial innovation is not only visible in the ever-expanding list of derivative acronyms. The evolution has also resulted in new requirements to define, quantify and trade 'risk', and ultimately how to manage and mitigate it. In parallel, technological advances have led to the emergence of a series of new electronic trading venues, and a surge in algorithmic and high-frequency trading (HFT). The Japanese financial markets have not been on the sidelines of these developments. According to estimates by the Japanese Financial Services Agency, HFT accounted for around 70% of all orders submitted to the Tokyo Stock Exchange in 2016 (Reuters, 2017). The persistent rise in passive investing and the exchange-traded fund (ETF) markets have also come to transform the traditional stock markets. Institutional changes in the financial markets have also been reflected in the (often global) concentration of the banking sector and the emergence of a range of new shadow banking activities. Furthermore, as a result of crises (the financial crisis of 2008–09 and the Eurozone sovereign debt crisis) and a string of highly publicised banking and trading scandals (concerning LIBOR and FX in particular), the regulatory and supervisory architecture has been subject to a restructuring process that is still ongoing.

Following such ground-breaking changes, it is only logical that the role of central banks in general, and their monetary policy in particular, should also be subject to change or, at least, debate. A couple of decades ago, debates among academics and policymakers largely involved institutional arrangements, such as central bank independence, inflation targeting and newly created bodies equipped to monitor financial conduct and stability. From this perspective, the severity of the financial crisis of 2008–09 acted as a trigger point. Central banks around the world were forced to resort to extraordinary policy measures to safeguard the financial system and fight deflationary pressures amid the economic slowdown.

Japan, in this respect, has taken the unconventional monetary policy and financial stability measures to an extreme unknown in North America and Europe and, as in those regions, ultimately with the aim to recover the dynamism of the Japanese economy.

Some of these measures can be traced back to stem from the Japanese banking crisis during the 1990s. Japan became a pioneer not only with its zero interest rate policy (ZIRP) but also with quantitative easing (QE). At the time, such measures were seen as radical and confined to the unique case of Japan. It was not until the aftermath of the financial crisis of 2008–09 that ultra-low interest rates and large-scale asset purchases became the norm in several other advanced economies.

With the launch of Abenomics in 2013, Japan embarked upon a quantitative easing programme of historic proportions. When, in 2016, the Bank of Japan adopted negative interest rates, several other central banks had already started to test the 'zero lower bound'. Again, however, Japan went further with the inclusion of a yield curve control policy that aimed to maintain long-term government bond yields at 0%. Moreover, the central bank started purchasing exchange-traded funds (ETFs) already in 2010 and significantly increased the volume in 2016. Measures to boost and stabilise domestic stock markets through such interventions only serve to confirm the role of the Bank of Japan as the boldest central bank in recent history.

To sum up, Japan has been at the forefront, and in many cases further than any other country in terms of its monetary policy. Understanding the effects and the effectiveness of the Japanese policy response is of high urgency, given the extraordinary measures that policymakers in other economies have taken and are still pursuing since the financial crisis of 2008–09. Importantly, the sluggish growth and problems with labour productivity in many developed economies (which bear similarities to the economic situation in Japan) make an assessment of Japan's reform efforts highly policy relevant to the other OECD (Organisation for Economic Co-operation and Development) countries. The case of Japan can no longer be seen as unique.

This book assesses those measures critically and examines what they mean for economic dynamics and the theory and practice of economic policy. The overall main aim is to generate a deeper understanding of why such measures were introduced, and how the Japanese system, as a result, has changed regarding governance, financial markets and the financial system as a whole.

Overall, the book is a study of developments in Japanese money and financial markets with the intent to understand the impact of policy on the debt structures that appear to have caused Japan's deflation. This impact is still poorly understood because the usual approach to economic policy is to treat the real economy as the object of policy (since features of the real economy, such as inflation, unemployment and real economy disequilibria are supposed to enter the objective function of policymakers) with the credit system acting as channels of policy transmission. In this view, policy ineffectiveness is treated as a breakdown or blockage in a transmission mechanism that is presumed rather than observed. In its latest incarnation, the purpose of structural reforms is to make markets, and banking and financial markets in particular, respond more effectively to monetary policy. Thus, the approach in this book, assessing the outcomes of the current reforms, is unique since the book does not start from the usual assumption that the economy and more generally society are merely the objects of policymaking. Instead, the impact of unconventional measures is assessed from a holistic view based on the evaluation of socio-economic structures in which there is a core financial system.

The book contains nine chapters. Each chapter addresses a different part (or parts) of the monetary transmission mechanism from the perspective of the unconventional policy measures by the Bank of Japan.

Chapter 1, 'The Japan Premium and the First Stage of the Monetary Transmission Mechanism', is written by Alexis Stenfors. For the first stage of the monetary transmission mechanism to function properly, changes, or expected changes, in the official central bank interest rates ought to be reflected in interbank money market rates. Thus, high and volatile money market risk premia tend to signal a disturbance or breakdown of the mechanism. This may seriously impact the ability of central banks to conduct conventional monetary policy. Elevated risk premia were not only visible during the financial crisis of 2007–08, but already during the Japanese banking crisis in the late 1990s. This chapter, however, shows how the functioning of the first stage of the monetary transmission mechanism no longer tells a consistent story. Using money market benchmarks and the covered interest rate parity (CIP) as a lens, the chapter critically examines a string of distinct, but closely interconnected, assumptions and misperceptions underpinning theoretical assumptions. By doing so, it not only sheds some fresh light on recent financial market 'puzzles' but also on the so-called Japan Premium during the 1990s.

Chapter 2 is written by Masaaki Shirakawa. Entitled 'The Foreign Currency Swap Market: A Perspective from Policymakers', the chapter draws from the author's long professional experience at the Bank of Japan (culminating with the role as governor during 2008–2013). Despite the fact that the foreign currency swap market is a critical market linking funding markets in various currencies, its importance is still underappreciated. Assuming that a well-functioning foreign exchange swap market exists, the covered interest parity should hold in theory. However, it does not hold in practice. After exploring factors inhibiting interest rate arbitrage, this chapter evaluates how public policy should cope with this market failure and examines various policy measures to address this. Finally, the implications of such actions for financial markets and policymaking are examined.

Chapter 3 is written by Heather Montgomery and Ulrich Voltz. The chapter, entitled 'The Effectiveness of Unconventional Monetary Policy on Japanese Bank Lending', focuses on the bank lending channel of the monetary transmission mechanism. Thus, whereas the emphasis in Chapter 1 and Chapter 2 is on the interest rate channel, or the first stage of the transmission mechanism more generally, Chapter 3 focuses on the credit channel (Bernanke and Gertler, 1995). Since the financial crisis of 2007–08, central bankers around the world have been forced to abandon the conventional monetary policy tools in favour of unconventional policies, such as quantitative easing, forward guidance and even lowering the interest rate paid on bank reserves into negative territory. Japan, which faced a crisis in its banking sector and came up against the theoretical zero lower bound on interest rates nearly a decade earlier, has been a pioneer in the use of many of these unconventional policy tools. Using a panel of bi-annual data on 147 Japanese banks' balance sheets and financial statements over the period 2000–2015, the chapter is an investigation into the effectiveness of Japan's bold experiment with unconventional monetary policy on the bank lending channel of monetary policy transmission. The empirical results show that unconventional monetary policy has significant effects through the bank lending channel, although the impact on bank lending is quantitatively small. However, contrary to the predictions of banking theory, the impact of quantitative easing seems to come predominantly through undercapitalised banks. Put differently, the policy appears to encourage risk-taking behaviour, but by the 'wrong' banks. The chapter, therefore, raises questions as to the appropriateness of the policy implementation and the long-term implications of the policy for the banking sector and the Japanese economy as a whole.

In Chapter 4, 'Japanese Banks in the International Money Markets', Mimoza Shabani, Alexis Stenfors and Jan Toporowski investigate the behaviour of Japanese banks, with emphasis on international expansion and the growing use of foreign exchange swaps and cross-currency basis swaps. The chapter considers the fundamental difference between foreign exchange swaps as derivative instruments, and as money market instruments. It argues that swaps essentially are money market instruments that have gradually replaced the official money market. This transformation is particularly relevant for Japan, where policies to revive growth and exit the deflationary era, coupled with the uncertainty with regards to the development of the currency and bond market, encouraged large Japanese banks to take more risk and to diversify abroad. The Bank of Japan's monetary policies gave Japanese banks the liquidity to finance that expansion abroad. But this could only be done by converting that liquidity into the US dollars required for that expansion abroad. However, the establishment of the foreign exchange swap network (to which the Bank of Japan belongs) during the global financial crisis has highlighted the importance of the Federal Reserve with its control over the world's reserve currency. The new institutional setup formalises an arrangement whereby the Federal Reserve has an ability to act opportunistically, whereas the Bank of Japan is dependent on its foreign exchange reserve to be able to do so. The chapter stresses the limitation of targeting short-term domestic interest rates, since policy rates of interest in the interbank market are marginal to credit and financing decisions made in US dollar foreign exchange swap markets. Paradoxically, because of the crucial role of the US dollar, the monetary policy of the US Federal Reserve might be even more important for Japanese banks than the monetary policy of the Bank of Japan.

Chapter 5 is co-authored by Konstantin Bikas, Ewa Karwowski and Mimoza Shabani. Entitled 'The Japanese Balance Sheet Recession 20 Years On: Abenomics – Economic Revival or Corporate Financialisation?', it examines another route of the credit channel. Here, the starting point is what Koo (2011) refers to as the 'balance sheet recession', in other words, the high levels of debt and low investment rates of Japanese non-financial corporations (NFCs) since the 1990s stock exchange and real estate market collapse. Acknowledging that economic growth during the bubble era was primarily driven by corporate investment, this chapter assesses the impact of Abenomics on the balance sheets of Japanese NFCs. Enthusiasm for the wide-reaching Abenomics programme was fuelled by IMF's (International Monetary Fund's) approval, and its partial success has been well documented. However, some policy elements of Abenomics have also been identified as an inherently neoliberal (Robinson, 2017). This raises the question of whether the recent policy measures are more inclined to stimulate a US-style corporate financialisation process rather than to end the Japanese balance sheet recession. The authors explore this using flow of funds data, and conduct an analysis of Japanese firms' income sources and their balance sheets. Their finding can be summarised as follows. Corporate liabilities have, on the one hand, decreased since the peak in the mid-1990s, and the balance sheet recession appears, indeed, to be over. At the same time, however, there is little evidence pointing towards Japanese corporations having become increasingly financialised. Financial assets continue to make up a limited share of total NFC assets. Cash holdings have increased sharply, and firms appear have become 'over-capitalised'. Indeed, this trend has been reinforced since the launch of Abenomics. Thus, Abenomics has neither led to a sustainable recovery in firms' spending nor to their financialisation.

The interest rate channel of the monetary transmission mechanism is further explored in Chapter 6. The chapter by Tanweer Akram and Huiqing Li is entitled 'An Analysis of the Impact of the Bank of Japan's Monetary Policy on Japanese Government Bonds' Low Nominal Yields'. The yields of Japanese government bonds' (JGBs) have been remarkably low for several decades. Many analysts are puzzled by this phenomenon because the country has the highest government debt/GDP ratio among major advanced economies. According to the loanable funds doctrine, the increasing supply of bonds, spurred by government borrowing, should result in higher government bond yields. Following Keynes (1930, 1936), this chapter shows that the Bank of Japan's highly accommodative monetary policy is primarily responsible for keeping JGBs' yields low for an extended period. The low short-term interest rate, set by the Bank of Japan, has been largely responsible for keeping long-term JGB nominal yields subdued despite chronically large deficits ratios and elevated government debt ratios. Moreover, since early 2016, the central bank has directly targeted the ten-year interest rate on JGBs. Combined with other measures undertaken by the central bank, the authors conclude not only that the Bank of Japan is the primary driver of the long-term interest rate on JGBs but also that fears of dramatic spikes in yields are misplaced.

In Chapter 7, 'Unconventional Monetary Policy Announcements and Japanese Bank Stocks', Ayhan Nadiri assesses the impact of unconventional monetary policy announcements by the Bank of Japan on Japanese bank stock returns. Monetary policy decisions are intended to affect prices in financial markets and, ultimately, the activity in the economy as a whole. The stock market, in this respect, plays an important role as a barometer for how a central bank announcement is interpreted by market participants. Overall, tighter monetary policy should have a negative impact on asset prices, whereas a looser monetary policy would imply the opposite. However, expectations also play a crucial role, and share prices of banks might be affected very differently from those of financial corporations (Ricci, 2014). After all, banks act as intermediaries in the financial system and monetary policy decisions are supposed to filter through to the real economy *via* financial markets. At the same time, bank earnings are highly dependent on the level of interest rates and the shape of the yield curve. Indeed, as Nakajima (2011) points out, banks are particularly susceptible to *unconventional* monetary policy decisions. This chapter focuses on 12 key unconventional monetary policy announcements by the Bank of Japan during 1999 and 2016. A short-horizon event study is then conducted in order to measure the cumulative abnormal returns (CARs) of 82 Japanese banks around these announcements. The results indicate that during 1999–2012, very few banks' stocks showed statistically significant reactions to unconventional monetary policy announcements. Notably, this includes announcements during and in the immediate aftermath of the global financial crisis. By contrast, since the launch of Abenomics in 2013, a clear majority of the sample responds to such announcements. Thus, from the perspective of the stock market, the monetary transmission mechanism differs sharply between the pre-Abenomics and the post-Abenomics periods.

Chapter 8 is co-authored by Masayuki Susai and Ho Yan Karen Wong and is entitled 'Bank of Japan and the ETF Market'. The surge in passive investing and exchange-traded funds (ETFs) is a worldwide phenomenon. However, whereas other major central banks have left the stock markets to their own devices from a monetary policy perspective, the Bank of Japan has intervened in the ETF market since 2010 – as a way to support and stabilise the stock market. The programme has expanded progressively and, currently, the annual ETF purchase by the central bank stands at ¥6 trillion. By February 2017, the Bank of Japan owned 67% of ETFs in the Japanese market. Thus, the BOJ has become a key participant in the equity market and one of the ten leading shareholders in 40% of listed companies in Japan. In this chapter, the authors empirically explore the impact of the interventions on stock market prices and volatility during 2010–2018, using a dataset covering ETFs, stock market indices and futures contracts. They find that interventions by the Bank of Japan have a significantly positive influence on stock market indices – and that the intervention volume plays a crucial role. Moreover, they document that the central bank has managed to reduce stock market volatility as a result of the regular ETF purchases. This is particularly evident since August 2016. Not only the volatility but also the persistence of the volatility has been reduced through these stock market interventions.

Chapter 9 by Etsuko Katsu is entitled 'Quantitative and Qualitative Monetary Easing, Negative Interest Rates and the Stability of the Financial System in Japan'. The chapter first provides a historical overview of the Bank of Japan's monetary policy since the 1990s. It then goes into depth to investigate how Governor Kuroda's unconventional monetary policy, including negative interest rates, affects financial markets and the behaviour of financial institutions – particularly from the perspective of financial stability and monetary and fiscal policy coordination. Quantitative and Qualitative Monetary Easing (QQE) is shown to have had a significant and immediate impact in helping to increase expected inflation, rebalance bank holdings from risk-free to riskier bonds and spur bank lending. However, the author finds that the negative interest rate policy introduced in February 2016 came to have a negative impact on the financial system.

References

Bernanke, B. S. and Gertler, M. (1995) Inside the black box: The credit channel of monetary policy transmission, *Journal of Economic Perspectives*, 9 (4), 27–48.

BIS (2019a) *Triennial Central Bank Survey: OTC Interest Rate Derivatives Turnover in April 2019*, 16 September. Available from: www.bis.org/statistics/rpfx19_ir.pdf [Accessed 13 September 2019].

BIS (2019b) *Triennial Central Bank Survey: Foreign Exchange Turnover in April 2019*, 16 September. Available from: www.bis.org/statistics/rpfx19_fx.pdf [Accessed 13 September 2019].

Keynes, J. M. (1930) *A Treatise on Money: The Applied Theory of Money*. London: Macmillan.

Keynes, J. M. (2007 [1936]) *The General Theory of Employment, Interest, and Money*. New York: Macmillan.

Koo, C. R. (2011) The world in balance sheet recession: Causes, cure and politics, *Real-World Economics Review*, 58, 19–37.

Nakajima, J. (2011) Monetary policy transmission under zero interest rates: An extended time-varying parameter vector autoregression approach, *IMES Discussion Paper Series*, No. 11-E-08, Institute for Monetary and Economic Studies, Bank of Japan.

Reuters (2017) Japan passes law to tighten regulations on high-frequency trading, *Reuters*, 19 May. Available from: www.reuters.com/article/us-japan-regulations-hft/japan-passes-law-to-tighten-regulations-on-high-frequency-trading-idUSKCN18F0UG [Accessed 13 September 2019].

Ricci, O. (2014) The impact of monetary policy announcements on the stock price of large European banks during the financial crisis, *Journal of Banking & Finance*, 5 (2), 245–255.

Robinson, G. (2017) Pragmatic financialisation: The role of the Japanese Post Office, *New Political Economy*, 22 (1), 61–75.

1 The Japan Premium and the first stage of the monetary transmission mechanism

Alexis Stenfors

1 Introduction

Japan has taken unconventional monetary policy and financial stability measures to the extreme – ultimately with the aim to recover the dynamism of the Japanese economy. In order to understand the logic underpinning these measures, it is necessary to study the history and process which resulted in them being adopted. Put differently, why were conventional policy measures inadequate?

This chapter focuses on the interest rate channel and the first stage of the monetary transmission mechanism, which is central to the traditional view of central banking. Namely, if the central bank changes the official interest rate, banks will adjust their interest rates accordingly. Coupled with the expectations of future central bank interest rate changes, and a host of other factors influencing markets, interest rates with longer maturities are also to be affected. Ultimately, the central bank monetary policy decision should have an impact on banks, businesses, households and variables in the economy as a whole – such as inflation, employment and output. Central banks do not determine at which interest rate banks lend to each other, or, indeed, to other agents in the economy. The first stage of the monetary transmission mechanism is therefore crucial, as it involves the immediate response to a central bank decision by banks and other financial market participants.

A breakdown of the first stage of the monetary transmission mechanism is serious, as it seriously undermines the ability of central banks to conduct monetary policy or even influence expectations by market participants. Consequently, variables and indicators used to measure and decompose risks in the interbank market are crucial for central bankers. For Japan, this became evident during the Japanese banking crisis – when the strains in the interbank market triggered the so-called Japan Premium. The market turmoil that started in August 2007 came to have a similar effect, albeit on an international scale. Both episodes resulted in significant central bank and government intervention to rescue the financial system – in other words, to restore the functioning of the first stage of the monetary transmission mechanism.

This chapter studies the evolution of Japanese money market risk premia during the last two decades. It shows that traditional ways to measure the functioning of the first stage of the monetary transmission mechanism no longer tell a consistent story. Using money market benchmarks and the covered interest rate parity as a lens, the chapter critically examines a string of distinct, but closely interconnected, assumptions and misperceptions underpinning theoretical assumptions. By doing so, it not only sheds some fresh light on current financial market 'puzzles' but also on the Japan Premium during the 1990s.

The chapter is structured as follows. Section 2 gives a historical background of money market risk premia from the emergence of the Japan Premium until today. Section 3 studies the market micro-foundations of the short-term money markets, and their implications. Section 4 concludes.

2   Money market risk premia and the covered interest rate parity

2.1   The Japan Premium era

The monetary transmission mechanism is the process by which central banks, through their monetary policy decisions, influence market interest rates and expectations – and ultimately credit and price formation in the economy as a whole. Seen from a different perspective, the process is also the key channel through which a money market interest rate, such as the interbank deposit rate, is generated. On the one hand, the level is affected by the official central bank rate. On the other hand, it is influenced by the borrowing and lending activity of market participants – and their expectations.

The London Interbank Offered Rate (LIBOR) and equivalent benchmarks tend to be used as market indicators for at which interest rate interbank deposits are traded. If LIBOR deviates substantially and systematically from the risk-free rate derived from the official central bank rate, it signals that the monetary transmission mechanism is severely impaired. From this viewpoint, the mechanism appears to have worked reasonably well until the outbreak of the financial crisis of 2007–08. LIBOR tended to track official central bank interest rates, and the expectations of future changes in them, very closely. In other words, LIBOR could be relied upon as a benchmark in models for monetary policy decisions.

One major exception to this was the Japanese banking crisis in the 1990s. Up until August 1995, when Hyogo Bank defaulted, Japanese authorities had intervened by arranging the merger of an insolvent bank with a solvent acquiring bank. The first commercial bank failure in Japan resulted in the so-called Japan Premium, which highlighted the increasing inability of Japanese banks to access unsecured funds in foreign currencies. Before the Hyogo collapse, the Japanese government had intervened when needed to prevent potential failures of financial institutions, by arranging a merger of the insolvent bank with a solvent bank. With such a policy framework, Japanese banks had, therefore, been perceived to be solvent and safe by financial market participants. When the authorities failed to save Hyogo Bank, however, this perception radically changed – resulting in a premium on Japanese banks' borrowing costs. Indeed, as Spiegel (2001) notes, the *trigger* for this premium to emerge was a change in government policy.

The Japan Premium was reflected in two financial market indicators in particular: the TIBOR-LIBOR spread and the CRS spread.

The LIBOR is a benchmark for the short-term interbank money market in which large banks can borrow from each other in major currencies. The TIBOR (Tokyo Interbank Offered Rate) is a similar benchmark set in Tokyo. The Japanese yen LIBOR and TIBOR are interbank money market benchmarks for yen deposits. They should theoretically reflect not only the current and expected future official rate of the Bank of Japan, but also incorporate credit and liquidity risk (Stenfors, 2013). The TIBOR panel mainly consisted of Japanese banks, whereas the London-based LIBOR mainly included European and American banks. Hence, a higher TIBOR could be seen as a reflection of the increased funding cost (i.e. perceived creditworthiness and ability to access liquidity) of Japanese banks compared to that of their foreign peers. The individual LIBOR submissions by the few large Japanese banks that were part of the panel in London were consistently higher and thus mostly omitted from the calculation of the LIBOR average. This left the Japanese yen LIBOR fixing largely in the hands of non-Japanese banks without funding issues. Figure 1.1 shows the 3-month Japanese yen LIBOR and TIBOR, the TIBOR-LIBOR spread and Mutan (the

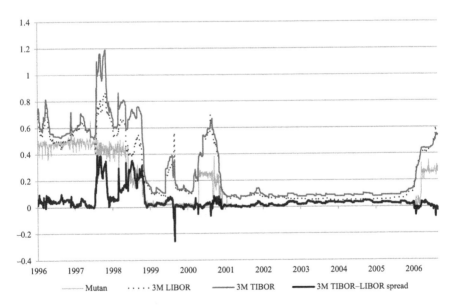

Figure 1.1 3M TIBOR-LIBOR spread (%) 01.05.1996–29.12.2006

Source: Bloomberg and author's own calculations

uncollateralised overnight call rate) from 1 May 1996 to 29 December 2006. As can be seen, the TIBOR–LIBOR spread for Japanese yen widened sharply during the crisis period. Hence, the jump in the TIBOR–LIBOR spread could be said to have originated in higher perceived credit risk directly leading to funding liquidity risk that the benchmarks were supposed to express.

However, overall market liquidity in Japanese yen was not affected in the same way. Transactions in yen between non-Japanese banks continued normally, and despite becoming considerably more volatile, market illiquidity did not force foreign banks to liquidate yen-denominated assets on a large scale. As such, market indicators did not point towards a 'Japanese yen crisis', but a 'Japanese banking crisis'.

The Japan Premium was also noticed in the foreign exchange swap and cross-currency swap markets. According to the covered interest rate parity (CIP), interest rate differentials between two currencies should be perfectly reflected in the foreign exchange swap price. Otherwise, arbitrage would be possible. In terms of Japanese yen against US dollars, this can be expressed as:

$$e^{t_i i_t^\$} = e^{t_i i_t^\yen} \frac{S^{\$/\yen}}{F_t^{\$/\yen}} \tag{1}$$

where $i_t^\$$ is the continuously compounded US interest rate (typically expressed in the US dollar LIBOR), and $i_t^\yen$ the yen interest rate (such as yen LIBOR) for maturity t. $S^{\$/\yen}$ and $F_t^{\$/\yen}$ represent the FX spot and forward rates between the currencies respectively.

In log-terms, the continuously compounded forward premium, ρ_t, is equal to the interest rate differential between Japanese yen and US dollars:

$$\rho_t \equiv \frac{1}{t}\left(F_t^{\$/\yen} - S^{\$/\yen}\right) = i_t^\yen - i_i^\$ \tag{2}$$

This particular kind of arbitrage, it was assumed, had ensured that the deviation from the CIP had tended to be close to zero. Following the market convention, interbank foreign exchange swaps are generally quoted against US dollars. Deviations from the CIP are therefore normally measured as the difference between the *implied* interest rate (using the US dollar interest rate and the foreign exchange transactions) and the benchmark interest rate for the counter currency.

Although Japanese banks were offered ample liquidity in yen from domestic sources (notably the Bank of Japan), they needed foreign currency funding as a result of large-scale investments made abroad during previous boom years. Since the Bank of Japan could not offer US dollar reserves, and the Eurocurrency markets dried up for the Japanese banks (being perceived as less creditworthy), they had to turn to the FX swap markets. In this way, they could use their yen liquidity to swap them into US dollars, which they required. When

Japanese banks headed for this last funding avenue, the CIP-deviations became more substantial, indicating that, for traders holding Japanese yen, swapping them to US dollars (or other foreign currencies through dollars) would be much more expensive than stated in the Eurodollar market.

Equation (1) can be rearranged to depict the difference between the implied interest rate (via the base currency interest rate and the FX market) and the direct interest rate in the counter currency – typically referred to as the 'cross-currency basis'.

In terms of Japanese yen against US dollars, the continuously compounded cross-currency basis, x_t, can be seen as the CIP-deviation between the two currencies for maturity t:

$$e^{t i_t^{\$}} = e^{t i_t^{¥} + t x_t} \frac{S^{\$/¥}}{F_t^{\$/¥}} \tag{3}$$

In logs, the cross-currency basis is expressed as:

$$x_t = i_t^{\$} - \left(i_t^{¥} - \rho_t \right) \tag{4}$$

This expression is useful when studying the cross-currency basis swap (CRS) market, which is closely related to the FX swap market. Although the turnover in the FX market is phenomenally large, they tend to have a short maturity. A CRS, by contrast, can have a maturity of 10 years or longer. Since the floating rate index for a CRS typically is the 3-month LIBOR, the instrument can be viewed as a market price for a string of 3-month CIP-deviations for a specific maturity.

A CRS is a floating-floating interest rate swap, where cashflows are exchanged between two counterparties periodically, and a notional amount in two currencies at the start and maturity of the contract. For instance, in terms of Japanese yen against US dollars, LIBORs would be used to determine the floating rate coupons (which often are 3 months). The price of the CRS is expressed in the 'basis', where the counterparties agree to exchange floating cashflows in one currency against floating cashflows in another currency. For instance, a 1-year USD/JPY CRS trading at cross-currency basis price of $x_t^{XCCY} = -20$ indicates that counterparties are prepared to borrow (lend) US dollars at 3-month USD LIBOR against lending (borrowing) Japanese yen at 3-month JPY LIBOR minus 20 basis points for one year.

It can be shown that such a CRS can be deconstructed into a zero-coupon fixed-fixed cross-currency swap in US dollars against Japanese yen, and two fixed-for-floating interest rate swaps (IRS) in the two currencies:

$$e^{t i_t^{IRS(\$)}} = e^{t i_t^{IRS(¥)} + t x_t^{XCCY}} \frac{S^{\$/¥}}{F_t^{\$/¥}} \tag{5}$$

Figure 1.2 JPY CRSs against USD (bps) 30.6.1997–29.12.2006
Source: Bloomberg.

The forward premium is:

$$\rho_t \equiv \frac{1}{t}\left(F_t^{\$/¥} - S^{\$/¥}\right) = i_t^{IRS(¥)} - x_t^{XCCY} - i_i^{IRS(\$)} \tag{6}$$

Thus, the CRS market essentially provides us with a yield curve for current and expected future deviations from the CIP. Figure 1.2 shows the 1-year, 2-year, 5-year and 10-year CRSs for Japanese yen against US dollars from 30 June 1997 to 29 December 2006. The prices illustrate the difficulty of Japanese banks to access funding in US dollars during the crisis period.

2.2 The Zero Premium era

The Japanese government responded to the banking crisis (i.e. to reduce the Japan Premium) through a range of measures and reforms. Two laws for financial stability were passed in February 1998, allowing the Deposit Insurance Corporation to use ¥30 trillion of public money to bail out troubled banks and to strengthen depositor protection (Montgomery and Shimizutani, 2009). In October 1998, laws were passed which gave authorities better tools to deal with bank failures, rather than relying on finding suitable healthy banks to take over failed banks. The regulations also provided more funds for bank resolution, and a total of ¥60 trillion (12% of GDP) of government funds were made available to strengthen the Japanese banking sector (Kanaya and Woo, 2000). Furthermore, Long Term Credit Bank of Japan and Nippon Credit Bank were nationalised, a second round of capital injections of around ¥15 trillion was provided to a total of 15 banks in 1999 and the banking sector went through a wave of mergers and restructuring. To sum up, the Japanese banking crisis resulted in the Japan Premium and was followed by profound changes in the Japanese banking system. Then, after a series of bank capital injections and reforms initiated by the government, the premium (both regarding the TIBOR-LIBOR spread and the CIP-deviation) disappeared around March 1999.

As Spiegel (2001) points out, the Japan Premium was directly affected by the financial strength of the borrowing Japanese banks. However, it was also affected by the policy of the Bank of Japan (or ultimately the Ministry of Finance) through its ability or desire to act as Lender of Last Resort, and also its willingness (and ability) to shield unsecured creditors from losses. The offshore premium faced by a Japanese borrowing bank was, therefore, a function of both the actual economic characteristics of that bank and the expectations in the market concerning government intervention in the event of its insolvency. Indeed, Peek and Rosengren (1999) found empirical evidence that the Japan Premium played a significant role in the shaping of government policy towards the banking sector. Actions to strengthen supervision increased the premium; government announcements that occurred in the absence of concrete steps appeared to be ineffective, whereas injections of funds into the banking system decreased the Japan Premium.

Renewed uncertainty with regards to the banking sector caused the Japan Premium to reappear in 2001, albeit minimally.[1] Nonetheless, 'normality' was rather quickly restored and risk premia in Japan and elsewhere remained low up until 2007. Indeed, market participants not active in the Japanese yen market – or having no memory of the Japanese banking crisis – had, until 2007, become used to minimal deviations of the LIBOR from the official, and expected future, central bank rate (and minimal CIP-deviations). Access to liquidity was easy, and central bank operations became increasingly transparent and predictable. Reoccurring year-end liquidity issues could be easily dismissed as temporary and were smoothed out by sufficient central bank liquidity measures. Central bankers, in turn, having grown accustomed to a seemingly liquid, transparent and well-functioning money market more or less without credit and liquidity issues for a decade, could rely on the first stage of the monetary transmission mechanism and LIBOR to keep money market rates in the range set by monetary policy. Monetary policy could focus instead on channels affecting output and inflation and on increasing transparency and minimising monetary policy surprises.

2.3   The Dollar Premium era

For market participants, central bankers and the public alike, this symmetry came to an abrupt end with the demise of the US subprime mortgage market and the advent of the financial crisis of 2007–08. When, on 9 August 2007, the French bank BNP Paribas froze redemptions for three investment funds, citing its inability to value structured products, the asset-backed mortgage credit risk associated with subprime lending quickly came to affect the global uncollateralised money market (Brunnermeier, 2009; Khandani and Lo, 2007). Central banks acted swiftly, with the European Central Bank (ECB) injecting €95 billion and the Federal Reserve $24 billion overnight. On 17 August, the Federal Reserve broadened the type of collateral accepted, increased the lending horizon to 30 days and lowered the discount window by 0.5% to 5.75%. However, the measure was not deemed a success. The 7,000 or so banks that could borrow at the discount window were historically reluctant to do so because of the stigma associated with it. Using the discount window would signal desperation and hence a lack of creditworthiness in the market. A series of write-downs in October and November 2007 pushed up the total loss in the mortgage market. When the Federal Reserve realised that rate cuts announced during the autumn did not filter through the monetary transmission mechanism, it introduced the Term Auction Facility (TAF) where banks could borrow from the Federal Reserve without using the discount window. However, uncertainty returned, and in March 2008 the Federal Reserve took new measures by expanding the TAF, and by introducing the new Term Securities Lending Facility. A loan package to Bear Stearns through JP Morgan and a new Primary Dealers Credit Facility was also announced.

As the crisis spread to other countries, central banks found themselves in a difficult position as their monetary policy lost its purchase on the money markets. Decomposing LIBOR had become almost synonymous with assessing the effectiveness of central bank policy in dealing with the crisis. Theoretically, LIBOR (or TIBOR) should not only reflect current and expected future risk-free interest rates, but also credit and liquidity risk. Should banks face credit constraints, these ought to be reflected in the individual LIBOR submissions and result in a higher average reported LIBOR. The standard technique, at the time, was to quantify each of these components. By assuming that LIBOR was a reflection of the offshore money market, and taking the overnight index swap (OIS) market prices as given and representing the risk-free interest rate for a given maturity, it simply became a task of allocating the difference between the two variables into the appropriate credit and/or liquidity components making up the spread (see, for instance, McAndrews et al., 2008). In fact, if a measure for credit risk could be agreed upon, the remaining component could be regarded as 'non-credit', or liquidity risk. This was the approach taken by the Bank of England (2007) in an indicative decomposition of LIBOR. In principle, credit default swap (CDS) spreads should reflect the probability of default of the reference entity, the loss given default and some compensation for uncertainty about these factors. By assuming that investors recover 40% of their deposits in the event of default, and by ignoring any liquidity effects in the CDS market itself, an implied (risk-neutral) probability of default for the underlying security is derived. Then, using the OIS as a measure of the risk-free interest rate and adding the credit risk, they arrive at an interest rate that includes credit risk. The residual premium from the LIBOR–OIS spread is the 'non-credit premium', or simply speaking the 'liquidity premium'. Following this logic, the results showed that during the beginning of the market turbulence, liquidity issues played a critical role whereas credit issues were less significant.[2]

Thus, at the height of the financial crisis, credit, market and liquidity risk rose significantly and became reflected in the LIBOR-OIS spreads and its equivalents in other financial centres (see Figure 1.3). These indicated that the difference between the funding costs of large banks and the risk-free rate had increased significantly. As can be seen, however, the reaction in the Japanese yen market was considerably less pronounced.

Moreover, whereas the Eurozone sovereign debt crisis prompted renewed fears in the international money markets, the yen market seemed completely immune. Indeed, the TIBOR-LIBOR spread (as an indicator for the 'old' Japan Premium) now turned *negative* (see Figure 1.4). Counterparty risk increased as banks became reluctant to lend to each other. This suggested that non-Japanese banks found it more difficult to fund themselves than their Japanese counterparts – resulting in a reverse Japan Premium and reflecting a perception of Japan as a relative 'safe haven'.

The financial crisis of 2007–08 also led to substantial, lasting and volatile deviations from the CIP that had hitherto held (with the notable exception of the Japanese banking crisis). This time, however, the markets pointed towards a specific 'Dollar Premium' indicating that the relative demand for US dollars rose compared to other currencies. As such, they were showing that the problems in the money markets were not only bank-specific (such as with the Japan Premium), but also currency-specific (affecting the US dollar more than other currencies). Nonetheless, as with the LIBOR-OIS and TIBOR-LIBOR spreads, the impact on the Japanese yen market was, initially, relatively less severe. As Figure 1.5 shows, the 1-year CRS spread, as measured against US dollars, turned negative as soon as the crisis broke out. The differences were largest for shorter maturities, up to and including three months, and exceptionally so in the aftermath of the Lehman bankruptcy.

Domestic liquidity injections were not sufficient to reduce the CIP-deviation – echoing the situation during the Japanese banking crisis. As only the Federal Reserve could offer US dollar liquidity, an international policy response was therefore required. Unprecedentedly, FX swap lines were set up between the Federal Reserve and a range of major central banks (including the Bank of Japan). Hereby, US dollars could be channelled to banks in countries where the demand was particularly severe (Baba and Packer, 2009; McGuire and von Peter, 2009). As can be seen from Figure 1.5, this measure prompted a decrease in the CIP-deviations in 2009.

However, as the euro sovereign debt crisis gained momentum during the spring of 2010, the global financial crisis entered into a new phase. Risk premia started to widen again, after an extended period of narrowing that followed the central banks' injections of vast amounts of liquidity into the banking systems in the aftermath of the Lehman Brothers collapse. Also, both the FX swap and the

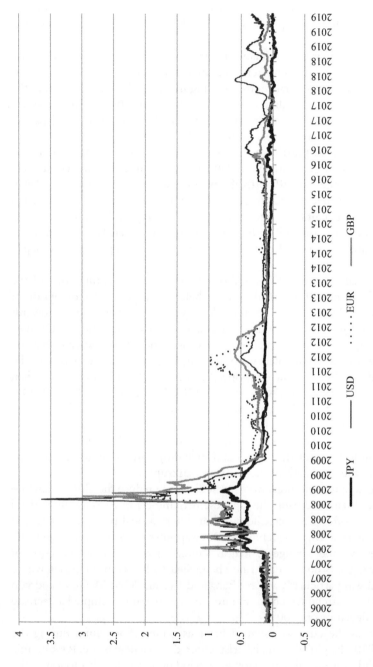

Figure 1.3 3M money market risk premia (%) 03.06.2006–30.09.2019

Sources: Bloomberg, authors' own calculations.

Notes: USD = 3M LIBOR – 3M OIS, JPY = 3M LIBOR – 3M Tonar, GBP = 3M LIBOR – 3M Sonia, EUR = 3M EURIBOR – 3M Eonia.

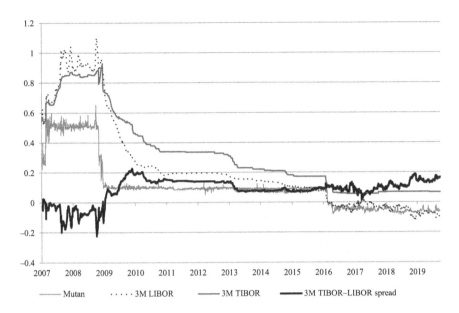

Figure 1.4 3M TIBOR–LIBOR spread (%) 03.01.2007–30.09.2019

Sources: Bloomberg and authors' own calculations.

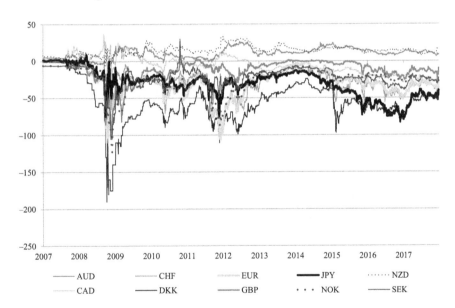

Figure 1.5 1-year CRS against USD (bps) 2007–2018

Source: Bloomberg.

Note: the floating rate benchmark used is the 3-month USD LIBOR and the 3-month benchmark in the other currency (plus/minus the premium expressed in basis points). The 3-month benchmarks for the other currencies are: AUD: Bank Bill Swap Rate (BBSW); CAD: Canadian Dollar Offered Rate (CDOR); CHF: LIBOR; DKK: Copenhagen Interbank Offered Rate (CIBOR); EUR: Euro Interbank Offered Rate (EURIBOR); GBP: LIBOR; JPY: LIBOR; NOK: Norwegian Interbank Offered Rate (NIBOR); NZD: Bank Bill Market Rate (BKBM); and SEK: Stockholm Interbank Offered Rate (STIBOR).

CRS markets started to indicate severe strains in the interbank lending market for dollars again. European banks had significantly increased their activities in the US since the launch of the euro. These strains reflected difficulties the banks faced in funding those positions. With the European Central Bank unable to offer dollars, and the Federal Reserve unable to lend dollars directly to European banks, dollar swap lines were re-introduced on 9 May 2010 (Kaltenbrunner et al., 2010).

2.4 The Premium puzzle era

During the financial crisis of 2007–08, it became apparent that the Japanese banking sector was in considerably better shape than that of the US or indeed the major European countries. This was not only reflected in the LIBOR-OIS, or the CRS spreads, but also in bank CDS spreads. As can be seen in Figure 1.6, which depicts CDS spreads of Japanese and major banks, financial market participants perceived the 'Big 3' Japanese banks as relatively creditworthy

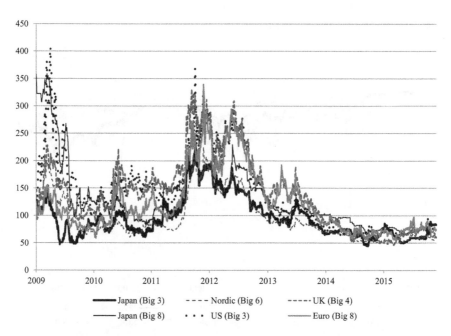

Figure 1.6 Median of Japanese and major bank CDS spreads (bps) 01.01.2009–25.11.2015

Sources: Datastream, Bloomberg and author's calculations.

Notes: Japan (Big 8): Aozora Bank, BTM UFJ, Mizuho Bank, Norinchukin Bank, Resona Bank, Shinsei Bank, Sumitomo Mitsui Banking Corp., Sumitomo Mitsui Trust Bank; Japan (Big 3): BTM UFJ, Mizuho Bank, Sumitomo Mitsui Banking Corp.; Nordic (Big 6): DNB, Nordea, SEB, Svenska Handelsbanken, Swedbank and Den Danske Bank; US (Big 3): Bank of America, Citi and JP Morgan Chase; UK (Big 4): Barclays, HSBC, Lloyds Bank, RBS; Euro (Big 8): BNP, Commerzbank, Crédit Agricole, Deutsche Bank, ING, Société Générale, UBS.

during and in the aftermath of the crisis. Only the large Nordic banks (having also experienced and revived from a severe banking crisis in recent times) were regarded as equally safe.

The extraordinary monetary policy measures introduced by central banks across the globe resulted in a significant fall in CDS spreads during 2009. Perceived probabilities of default continued to fall until the advent of the Eurozone crisis in 2010 when the trend reversed sharply. Whereas the CDS spreads of large banks have recovered since, and LIBOR-OIS spreads mostly returned to 'normal' (see Figure 1.3), another critical indicator has begun to deviate much more sharply: the CRS spread. Looking at Figure 1.5, we can see that the premium paid to access US dollar funding (not least via Japanese yen) has increased at an alarming rate since mid-2014. In fact, despite extraordinary monetary policy measures by central banks across the world since the financial crisis of 2007–08, the US Dollar Premium derived from the FX swap and CRS markets indicate continuing or even elevated stress in the international monetary system.

The historical background just discussed shows how, during the case of the era of the Japan Premium and the Dollar Premium, subsequent policy measures by central banks, governments and regulators were aimed at restoring health in the banking system and overall financial stability – and, in this way, at reducing the risk premia. Rather than disappearing in recent years, however, the Dollar Premium derived from the FX and CRS markets indicate continuing (or even elevated) stress.

Overall, it has become evident that traditional ways to measure the functioning of the first stage of the monetary transmission mechanism no longer tell a consistent story – particularly with regards to the CIP.

3   Uncovering the CIP puzzle from a market micro-foundation perspective

The failure of the CIP during times of severe stress in the financial system is not wholly surprising – whether it relates to the Japanese banking crisis, the financial crisis of 2007–08 or the Eurozone sovereign debt crisis. It is continuing substantial and volatile deviations since that has resulted in this being coined the 'CIP puzzle'. In this regard, a range of explanations has emerged that stretch beyond standard reasons such as heightened credit and liquidity risk in the international financial markets (Coffey et al., 2009; Genberg et al., 2011; Griffoli and Ranaldo, 2010). Other factors have been found to be crucial in preventing arbitrage activities to eliminate the CIP-deviations fully, such as the prominent role of the US dollar in cross-border lending and its impact on the balance sheets of non-US banks (Ivashina et al., 2015; Avdjiev et al., 2019). Indeed, as noted by Sushko et al. (2016) and Borio et al. (2016), there are important cross-country variations when it comes to US dollar funding gaps. Banking systems with significant gaps, such as Japan and large Eurozone countries, tend to observe significant (negative) CIP-deviations, whereas countries on the other side of the spectrum, such as Australia, are affected less or in the opposite direction. Increasing regulation also plays a crucial role, and, hence, a range of factors might result in continuing failure of the CIP.

Regardless, however, the approach largely to emphasise frictions within the financial system, but still outside the microstructure of the financial market itself, prevents the arbitrage condition from being restored. In essence, it treats the FX components of the CIP as 'mispriced' at the outset or seeks answers as to why 'money is left on the table' and not arbitraged away as theory suggests it should. However, if we focus more closely on the micro-foundations of the CIP components, a somewhat different interpretation of events appears. Here, five points are notable.

First, according to the CIP, interest rate differentials between two currencies should be perfectly reflected in the FX forward price. Otherwise, arbitrage would be possible (see Equation 1). Typically, the FX forward price is regarded as the price that is supposed to adjust according to the prevailing interest rates in the two currencies. However, it is important to note that for most currency pairs, there is no interbank FX forward market per se. Whereas academic textbooks often describe an FX swap as a combination of an FX spot and an FX forward transaction done simultaneously but in opposite directions, the market convention is different. End users may request FX forward prices from banks. However, market makers traditionally only provide liquidity to each other in FX spot and FX swaps only (Stenfors, 2018). Hence, a more accurate depiction of the CIP would be to eliminate the FX forward component and introduce an FX swap component instead. Whereas this, in principle, does not alter anything, it serves to highlight the *dual* nature of the FX swap market. An FX swap is a foreign exchange instrument (as described earlier) as well as an interest rate instrument: a loan in one currency versus a simultaneous deposit in another currency for the same maturity and with the same counterparty. As FX swap prices essentially are interest rate differentials expressed in FX terms, it is only logical that FX swap trading desks typically are located within (or next to) interest rate trading desks rather than FX spot desks.

Second, as outlined in the previous section, the CIP is typically approached from the perspective of arbitrage activities. An arbitrageur, in this respect, is viewed as a market taker who closely studies the market from 'the outside' and immediately jumps on the opportunity of the lock-in risk-free profits if and when the situation arises. In reality, however, FX and money market trading is mainly a banking activity and involves banks simultaneously acting as both market makers and market takers in the different CIP components. Moreover, the credit risk is not symmetrically distributed among the components. In particular, FX swaps have, since the 1988 Basel Accord was put into place, involved considerably less credit risk than interbank deposits with the same maturity. As Stenfors and Lindo (2018) note, this reform resulted in deposit trading being 'penalised' at the same time as derivatives and FX swap trading were 'rewarded'. This, naturally, acted as an incentive to boost FX swap trading at the expense of interbank deposits. Superior liquidity also meant that FX swaps came to influence interbank deposit rates – rather than the other way round.

Third, the 'i' in the CIP-equation refers to the term money market and is generally expressed in LIBOR. However, LIBOR is not a market per se, but a benchmark reflecting where the banks claim the market should be trading. Problematically, very little unsecured borrowing and lending takes place between banks for maturities of, say, 3 months – which is the almost exclusively used as the 't' in the CIP (Stenfors and Lindo, 2018; Stenfors, 2019).

Fourth, despite the lack of trading underpinning LIBOR for maturities such as 3 months, the financial derivatives market referencing LIBOR is phenomenally large and liquid. In fact, it has increased substantially despite the opposite trend in the underlying market. This can be illustrated by the growth of the market in forward rate agreements (FRAs), which enable users to hedge against or speculate on changes in LIBOR. According to the BIS (2016), the daily turnover increased from around $100 billion in 1998 to $350 billion in 2007 – approximately in line with other interest rate derivatives. Despite the financial crisis of 2007–08 (and the resulting freeze in the term money market), the turnover grew to $800 billion in 2010 and almost $900 billion in 2013. However, this was not a sudden 'replacement' of deposit trading by derivatives trading. The trend towards a larger and more liquid derivatives market started several decades ago. Figure 1.7 exemplifies this by showing indicative bid-ask

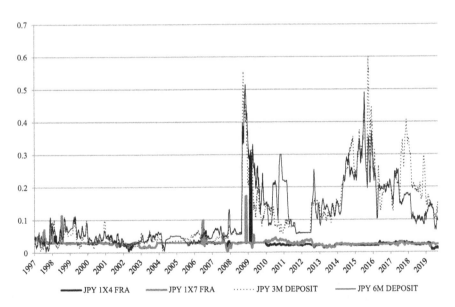

Figure 1.7 Indicative bid-ask spreads (%) 01.01.1997–30.09.2019

Sources: Bloomberg and author's calculations.

Notes: monthly 20-day M/A. Deposit rates are averages of Tokyo, London and New York closing prices.

spreads (the standard measure of price-based market liquidity) for 1X4 JPY FRAs (a contract for the 3-month JPY LIBOR in 1 month's time), 1X7 JPY FRAs (a contract for the 6-month JPY LIBOR in 1 month's time) and 3- and 6-month interbank deposit rates, respectively.

Fifth, market participants have not only gradually shifted their attention away from interbank deposits and towards FX swaps and LIBOR-indexed derivatives. The same goes with the CIP-deviation itself. As argued by Chatziantoniou et al. (2019), rather than treating CIP-deviations as anomalies that ultimately should disappear, they should be seen as prices or risk premia that can be bought and sold – most notably through the CRS market. Thus, it is the current and expected CIP-deviations in the future that drive the price development, instead of arbitrage activities preventing them from arising or eliminating them if and when they appear. Using a TVP-VAR (time-varying vector autoregressive) framework and data between 2007 and 2018, they find that CRS markets for different currency pairs are highly connected and that the level of connectedness is event-dependent. They provide evidence that countries with major overseas banking operations tend to transmit shocks to other countries via the international CRS markets, whereas typical safe-haven currencies appear to be on the receiving end of such shocks. Japan is an interesting case by being regarded both as a safe haven (particularly during the financial crisis of 2008–09) and as a country with large banks having expanded abroad (which was felt in 2015 and 2016, in particular).

4 Concluding discussion

There are a number of indicators of risk in the international (and Japanese) banking system. This chapter has, through the lens of the Japan Premium reflected in TIBOR-LIBOR, CIP-deviations and CRS spreads, illustrated how the Japanese banking crisis emerged and was solved through government intervention. After years of stability, money market risk premia surged in virtually all developed countries with the advent of the financial crisis of 2007–08. Central banks then introduced a wide range of extraordinary measures to alleviate the stress in the banking systems or, put differently, to reduce LIBOR-OIS spreads and CIP-deviations. At the present moment, these indicators do not tell a consistent story. LIBOR-OIS, TIBOR-LIBOR and bank CDS spreads suggest that credit and liquidity risks are largely absent. By contrast, CIP-deviations implied from the CRS spreads suggests that the financial markets continue to observe severe stress and funding constraints – particularly facing Japanese banks. When studying the market micro-foundations of the components of the CIP, however, a somewhat different picture emerges.

Already decades ago, the FX swap market overtook the interbank deposit market decades ago not only as a venue for hedging and speculation but also as a source of funding for banks. With regards to indicators for actual borrowing and lending, the FX swap market is the only reliable indicator among the components that make up the CIP. Hardly any activity takes place in the interbank term money market, and LIBOR is neither a market per se nor, as widely documented, unreliable. However, via other instruments and methodologies, LIBOR is, perhaps, more important than ever. It is used for mortgages, student loans and credit card debt, as well as a range of financial derivatives (including CRSs and FRAs). It is also the most widely used price to study the effectiveness and frictions within the first stage of the monetary transmission mechanism, most notably via the TIBOR-LIBOR spread, the LIBOR-OIS spread and the CIP-deviation.

Without a liquid, tradable and transparent unsecured term money market, none of these are wholly reliable indicators. In fact, that the 'LIBOR equation' could not be solved was already observed by Hanajiri (1999) when using the CIP to analyse why the Japanese Premium differed between the markets during 1997 and 1998. In theory, the Japanese Premium in the US dollar interest rate market should equal the Japanese Premium in the yen market plus the Japanese Premium in the USD/JPY FX swap market. This was not the case; or put differently, the CIP did not hold. Importantly, already here, LIBOR was regarded as the underlying liquid money market, from which FX swaps and other instruments were derived. The author also compared the US dollar LIBOR and the Eurodollar interest rates in Japan's offshore market, finding a higher rate for the latter (showing the Japan Premium). When, on the other hand, the US dollar LIBOR and the implied dollar interest rate from the TIBOR and the USD/JPY FX swaps were compared, the difference was more significant. In other words, the Japan Premium appeared to be greater in the 'tradable' money market than in LIBORs. Ito and Harada (2004) also pointed out, early on, that interbank money market benchmarks, such as LIBOR, did not serve as robust indicators of stress in the Japanese banking system during the early 2000s.

Arbitrage involves actual buying and selling, or borrowing or lending. Financial benchmarks and indicators (and particularly those involving money markets) are, however, not always tradable and can, therefore, point towards arbitrage opportunities where such, in fact, do not exist. In fact, seemingly obvious arbitrage opportunities such as deviations from the CIP can be seen as instruments in themselves, which can be 'bought and sold' according to market participants' expectations. This is important from the perspective of policymaking. On the one hand, the phenomenal growth in financial markets in recent decades has provided central banks with new and more liquid instruments to assess and, if necessary, address the functioning of the first stage of the monetary transmission mechanism. On the other hand, however, it is problematic as the vast majority of money markets involve banks and are, consequently, highly opaque. From the outside, it is tremendously difficult to obtain detailed trade data let alone sufficient information on the *actual* credit and liquidity standing of banks. The gradual disappearance of the 'actual' money market has made this even more challenging.

Notes

1 According to Ito and Harada (2004), however, the individual yen LIBOR submissions by the Japanese banks understated the perceived creditworthiness of the Japanese banks at the time. When probabilities of default, as perceived by market participants, were derived from the credit default swap (CDS) market (which was relatively new at the time), a considerably more worrying picture of bank vulnerability emerged. Consequently, the authors argued that CDS spreads were a more accurate gauge for the Japan Premium, and recommended its further use.

2 The assumption that the independent variable (i.e. LIBOR) was based upon actual transactions between banks was central to attempts to decompose money market risk premia in the aftermath of the financial crisis of 2007–08. As Stenfors (2014) points out, however, underlying risks in the banking sector might be masked should the LIBOR be manipulated or understated – as evidenced by regulatory investigations around the world in recent years.

References

Avdjiev, S., Du, W., Koch, C. and Shin, H. S. (2019) The dollar, bank leverage, and deviations from covered interest parity, *American Economic Review: Insights*, 1 (2), 193–208.

Baba, N. and Packer, F. (2009) From turmoil to crisis: Dislocations in the FX swap market before and after the failure of Lehman brothers, *BIS Working Papers*, No. 285.

Bank of England (2007) An indicative decomposition of Libor spreads, *Bank of England Quarterly Bulletin*, 47 (4), 498–499.

BIS (2016) Triennial Central Bank Survey – Foreign exchange turnover in April 2016, September 2016. Available from: http://www.bis.org/publ/rpfx16fx.pdf [Accessed 16 April 2020].

Borio, C., McCauley, R., McGuire, P. and Sushko, V. (2016) Covered interest parity lost: Understanding the cross-currency basis, *BIS Quarterly Review*, September 2016, 45–64.

Brunnermeier, M. K. (2009) Deciphering the liquidity and credit crunch 2007–2008, *Journal of Economic Perspectives*, 23 (1), 77–100.

Chatziantoniou, I., Gabauer, D. and Stenfors, A. (2019) From CIP-deviations to a market for risk premia: A dynamic investigation of cross-currency basis swaps, *Working Papers in Economics & Finance*, No. 2019-5, Portsmouth Business School.

Coffey, N., Hrung, W. B. and Sarkar, A. (2009) Capital constraints, counterparty risk, and deviations from covered interest rate parity, *Federal Reserve Bank of New York Staff Report*, No. 393.

Genberg, H., Hui, C.-H., Wong, A. and Chung, T.-K. (2011) The link between FX swaps and currency strength during the credit crisis of 2007–2008, in Cheung, Y.-W., Kakkar, V. and Ma, G. (eds.) *The Evolving Role of Asia in Global Finance*, Vol. 9, pp. 83–94. Bingley: Emerald Group Publishing Limited.

Griffoli, T. M. and Ranaldo, A. (2010) Limits to arbitrage during the crisis: Funding liquidity constraints and covered interest parity, *Swiss National Bank Working Papers*, 2010–14.

Hanajiri, T. (1999) Three Japan premiums in Autumn 1997 and Autumn 1998: Why did premiums differ between markets? *Financial Markets Department Working Paper Series*, No. 99-E-1, Bank of Japan.

Ito, T. and Harada, K. (2004) Credit derivatives as a new Japan premium, *Journal of Money, Credit and Banking*, 36 (5), 965–968.

Ivashina, V., Scharfstein, D. S. and Stein, J. S. (2015) Dollar funding and the lending behavior of global banks, *Quarterly Journal of Economics*, 130 (3), 1241–1281.

Kaltenbrunner, A., Lindo, D., Painceira, J. P. and Stenfors, A. (2010) The euro funding gap and its consequences, *Quarterly Journal of Central Banking*, 21 (2), 86–91.

Kanaya, A. and Woo, D. (2000) The Japanese banking crisis of the 1990s: Sources and lessons, *IMF Working Paper*.

Khandani, A. E. and Lo, A. W. (2007) What happened to the quants in August 2007? *Journal of Investment Management*, 5 (4), 5–54.

McAndrews, J., Sarkar, A. and Wang, Z. (2008) The effect of the term auction facility on the London inter-bank offered rate, *Federal Reserve Bank of New York Staff Reports*, No. 335.

McGuire, P. and von Peter, G. (2009) The US dollar shortage in global banking and the international policy response, *BIS Working Papers*, No. 291.

Montgomery, H. and Shimizutani, S. (2009) The effectiveness of bank recapitalization policies in Japan, *Japan and the World Economy*, 21 (2009) 1–25.

Peek, J. and Rosengren, E. S. (1999) Determinants of the Japan premium: Actions speak louder than words, *Journal of International Economics*, 52 (2), 293–305.

Spiegel, M. (2001) The return of the "Japan premium": Trouble ahead for Japanese banks? *FRBSF Economic Letter*, 2001–06.

Stenfors, A. (2013) *Determining the LIBOR: A Study of Power and Deception*, PhD dissertation, SOAS, University of London.

Stenfors, A. (2014) LIBOR deception and central bank forward (mis-)guidance: Evidence from Norway during 2007–2011, *Journal of International Financial Markets, Institutions and Money*, 32, 452–472.

Stenfors, A. (2018) Bid-ask spread determination in the FX swap market: Competition, collusion or a convention? *Journal of International Financial Markets, Institutions and Money*, 54, 78–97.

Stenfors, A. (2019) The covered interest parity puzzle and the evolution of the Japan premium, *Journal of Economic Issues*, 53 (2), 417–424.

Stenfors, A. and Lindo, D. (2018) Libor 1986–2021: The making and unmaking of 'the world's most important price', *Distinktion: Journal of Social Theory*, 19 (2), 172–190.

Sushko, V., Borio, C., McCauley, R. and McGuire, P. (2016) The failure of covered interest parity: FX hedging demand and costly balance sheets, *BIS Working Paper*, No. 590.

2 The foreign currency swap market

A perspective from policymakers

Masaaki Shirakawa

1 Introduction

The foreign currency swap market is a critical market linking funding markets in various currencies, but its importance is underappreciated in academic circles. The purpose of this chapter is to explain its importance and stimulate more research on this topic.[1] The structure of this chapter is as follows. Section 2 explains the importance of the foreign currency swap market drawing on my own experiences related to this market. Section 3 highlights some policy issues.

2 Events that affected my thinking on the foreign currency swap market

When I joined the Bank of Japan (BOJ) in 1972, I did not have a scant idea about what the foreign currency swap market and its implications for financial markets were, except an abstract understanding of the covered interest rate parity (CIP). Subsequently, I encountered several events, which opened my eyes and shaped my thinking on the foreign currency swap market and for that matter, the financial market and the financial system. The first such event was the comprehensive overhaul of foreign exchange controls that Japan instituted in 1980. The second event was Japan's severe financial crisis in 1997–1998, which taught me the importance of counterparty credit risk in the functioning of the financial market. The third event was the Global Financial Crisis, which erupted in 2007. The fourth event was the recent significant increase in deviations from the CIP, notwithstanding relative calm in financial markets. The latter two taught me the importance of the central bank's role as a lender of last resort and the institutional design of the financial market.

Japan's comprehensive overhaul of foreign exchange control

Japan's overhaul of foreign exchange control in 1980 was quite comprehensive, and it had a significant impact on financial institutions and the financial market. Various regulations of financial institutions and markets were made obsolete. One such example was the regulation of the interest rate setting in the domestic interbank funding market. Since interest rates in this market became aligned with foreign currency swap-implied US dollar funding rates, regulation of interest rates in the domestic funding market became obsolete. The other example was a separation between commercial banks and long-term credit banks, which had long characterized the postwar Japanese financial system. Prior to this overhaul, commercial banks were not allowed to issue long-term bonds, while they were allowed to have large branch networks, which enabled them to obtain retail deposits with interest rates below market rates. In contrast, long-term credit banks were allowed only a very limited number of branches, while they were allowed to issue long-term bonds, which enabled them to lend long-term money to non-financial firms. Since transactions of foreign currency swaps were completely deregulated after the overhaul of foreign exchange controls, commercial banks could now effectively raise long-term funds in the market. The liberalization of the foreign currency swap market drastically transformed the financial market landscape. Interest rate arbitrage enabled by the foreign currency swap market had a really sweeping impact.

Japan's severe financial crisis in 1997–1998

After the bursting of the bubble in the early 1990s, Japan experienced a severe financial crisis, which culminated in 1997–1998. At the time, Japanese banks faced difficulties in securing US dollars in the uncollateralized funding market. As a result, they were forced to rely on the foreign currency swap market, which essentially was a collateralized dollar funding market.

Figure 2.1 shows that Japanese banks had to pay an additional cost ("Japanese premium"). Lenders – the US and European banks – could enjoy attractive returns, but were faced with the problem of where to invest the yen proceeds. Their problem was counterparty credit risk. Instruments chosen were short-term JGBs, deposits with the BOJ and interest-bearing short-term bills issued by the BOJ. At the time, BOJ provided a huge amount of reserves to troubled financial institutions as a lender of last resort to maintain financial stability. But at the same time, BOJ had to absorb reserves from the market in order to maintain the short-term interest rate at the target level. It should be noted that interest was not paid on reserves at the time. It was ten years later, in the autumn of 2008, that Japan and the US introduced the system of paying interest on reserves. The instrument used to absorb excess reserves in 1997–1998 was the BOJ bill.

As Figure 2.2 shows, its peak amount climbed to as much as 22 trillion yen corresponding to 4% of nominal GDP. It should be noted that BOJ bills were issued to absorb the excess reserves, but they also functioned as sweeteners to facilitate Japanese banks' dollar funding by offering a good investment opportunity, free from counterparty credit risk, to foreign banks.

What I learned in terms of the foreign currency swap market during this turbulent period was that existence of counterparty credit significantly affects the

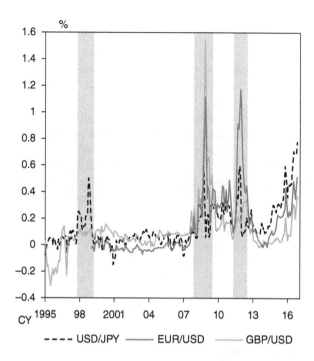

Figure 2.1 Foreign currency swap–implied US dollar funding rate (deviation from US dollar LIBOR in %)

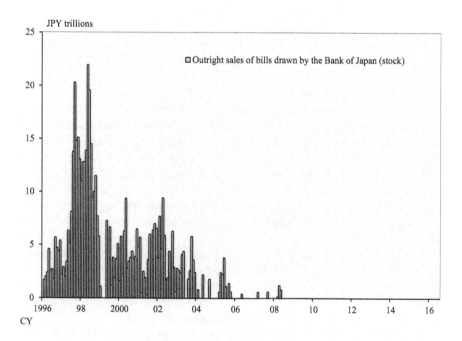

Figure 2.2 Outstanding balance of BOJ bills (JPY trillions)

activity of arbitrage. The corollary to this is that the lack of safe assets constrains the degree of arbitrage.

The Global Financial Crisis in 2007–2009

The Global Financial Crisis in 2007–2009 was a truly severe financial crisis. In particular, in the autumn of 2008, the global financial system appeared to be on the brink of collapse. The uncollateralized funding market froze, as is shown in Figure 2.1. The foreign currency swap market did not function either, because perceived counterparty risk was so huge. Against this background, a US dollar swap line was instituted between the New York Fed and major central banks in advanced economies in the autumn of 2008.

If I am asked to identify what was the most effective measure in avoiding the collapse of the financial system at the time, I would say it was the US dollar swap line with the New York Fed.

However, it has a limitation as well. The ability to borrow US dollars via this scheme was restricted to the "club members" with which the New York Fed had swap agreements. Most central banks in emerging market economies could not get access to this swap line. Duvvuri Subbarao, then Governor of the Reserve Bank of India, wrote in his memoir as follows (Subbarao, 2016, p. 286):

> We requested a similar rupee-dollar swap arrangement, but the Federal Reserve did not respond positively. Although they never said it in so many words, I believe their reluctance was either because the rupee is not a freely convertible currency or because our financial markets were not important from the US perspective.

What deters full-scale deployment of this kind of swap line? One reason is a concern for possible moral hazards created by such a network of swap lines if this becomes really comprehensive and generous. Another is that central bank swap lines inevitably are accompanied by sovereign risk. Foreign currency-providing central banks obviously weigh potential benefits against their costs. This consideration naturally involves an element of foreign policy.

The recent deviation from the covered interest rate parity

The strain in the funding market after the Global Financial Crisis gradually waned. But this did not mean that the foreign currency swap market returned to a normal situation.

As Figure 2.3 shows, we have observed a sharp deviation from the covered interest rate parity even after the acute phase of the Global Financial Crisis had passed. For example, between 2016 and 2017, the deviation increased to a level which was almost the same as the one seen during the Global Financial Crisis. We knew that the CIP does not hold perfectly based on the experiences

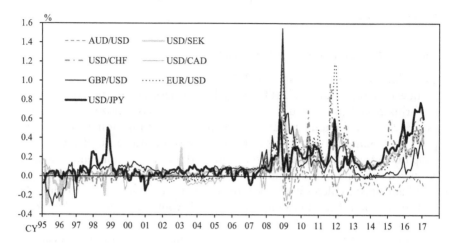

Figure 2.3 Deviations from the CIP (%)

of financial crises, as mentioned previously. How can we explain the persistent deviation from the CIP of this magnitude in a relatively benign environment?

There are several hypotheses. The first is counterparty credit risk, which is captured by replacement cost, however small it may be since the acute phase of the crisis has been over. This replacement cost is affected by the probability of default of the counterparty and volatility of the price of collateral, among others. The second is foreign exchange settlement risk due to the time difference. As long as this risk is involved, a foreign currency swap transaction is not collateralized, because the risk of failing to receive principal payment cannot be neglected. Anticipating that such risk could hamper the functioning of the foreign exchange market, central banks encouraged financial institutions to establish a mechanism that was not exposed to such settlement risk. The result was the establishment of Continuous Linked Settlement (CLS) Bank Group (CLS Bank), which started in 2002 (Caruana, 2015). This was a great achievement. It eliminated settlement risk for major currency pairs. However, settlement risk still exists for currencies of many emerging market economies. In addition, overnight foreign exchange transactions are only processed for the US dollar/Canadian dollar currency pair so far. The third hypothesis to explain the persistent deviation from CIP is the lack of risk-free assets, which was mentioned earlier.

Based on this conceptual framework, we can investigate the cause of imperfect CIP arbitrage in a benign environment by looking into the demand factor (increased demand for hedging foreign exchange risk) and the supply factor (limits to arbitrage). As a demand factor, we can point to the increased demand for hedging foreign exchange rate risk. Reflecting monetary policy divergence between the US and other economies, European and Japanese financial institutions have increased investment in US dollar-denominated assets. Hedging cost is measured by the difference between short-term interest rates in the US on the one hand and Europe and Japan on the other. As long as the long-term interest rate in the US is reasonably high, hedging demand increases because of growing investment in dollar assets. At the same time, a supply factor that limits arbitrage kicks in. In this regard, it should be noted that the cost of using the balance sheet ("the balance sheet cost") has increased due to strengthened regulation after the Global Financial Crisis. The reform measures of US money market (mutual) funds (MMFs) introduced in 2016 also affected supply capacity (Nakaso, 2017). It induced a huge fund shift from prime MMFs to "government" MMFs, which invest mostly in US Treasuries because prime MMFs invested their money in commercial paper (CP) and Certificates of Deposit (CDs) issued by non-US banks. In this environment, non-US banks could not shift to alternative dollar funding sources. As the previous analysis shows, both demand and supply factors explain imperfect arbitrage.

The next question is why the CIP deviation for the Japanese yen against the US dollar is so large compared with other currency pairs, as is shown in Figure 2.3. For example, the deviation from the CIP as of January 2017 was 0.60% for the Japanese yen, which is much higher than for the euro (0.40%), the British pound (0.24%), the Canadian dollar (0.33%), the Swiss franc (0.41%), the Swedish Krona (0.35%) and the Australian dollar (-0.10%).

The most important reason is that Japanese banks and institutional investors are aggressively expanding foreign currency assets (as is shown in Figure 2.4).

There are two reasons for this. First, the domestic lending market is expected to shrink due to demographic change. Second, the yield curve is flatter than that of the European countries, which accentuates the demand for high-yielding assets, as is shown in Figure 2.5. Incidentally, the flipside of the high cost of securing US dollars is the negative cost of securing yen by US dollar providers. Therefore, holdings of short-term JGBs by non-residents have increased, as is shown in Figure 2.6.

However, the analysis is not complete without looking into the incentives of suppliers of US dollars. One possible explanation is that global investors' demand for safe assets has increased after the Global Financial Crisis. Obviously, US Treasuries are the primary instruments to satisfy this demand. But if these are not sufficiently provided, some other assets have to fill the gap. Public debts issued by advanced countries other than the US are natural candidates. However, viewed by global investors, safe government bonds are not so abundant. There are logical reasons for this. Central banks are aggressively purchasing public debt, and not all are deemed as safe assets. A case in point is government bonds of member states of the Eurozone whose potential vulnerability was visible during the European Debt Crisis. Ironically, JGBs are filling the global gap of safe assets, even though government finances are in bad shape. First, the size of Japan's net external position is the largest in the world. Japan seems to be a fortress in the funding of foreign currency at least in the short run. Second, the size of the financial markets in yen is large in comparison to that of US dollars

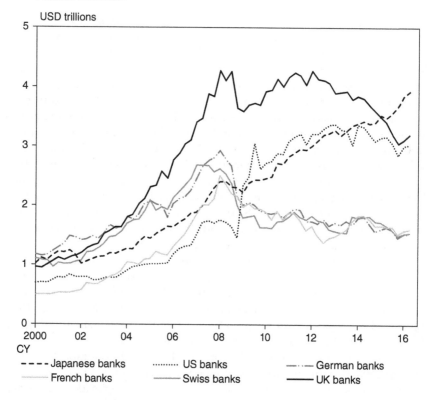

Figure 2.4 External claims by nationality of banks (USD trillions)

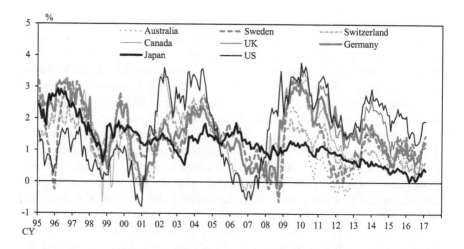

Figure 2.5 Japan's yield curve is flatter in international comparison (%)

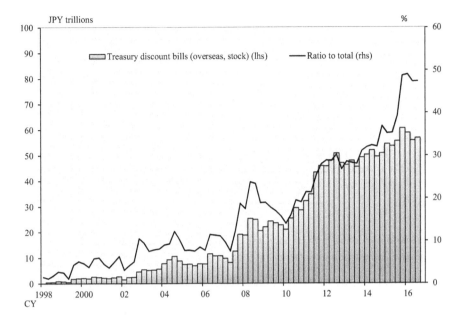

Figure 2.6 Short-term JGBs

and euros. Currency convertibility is assured, and the rule of law is respected. Specifically, when it comes to foreign currency swaps, yen as collateral tends to appreciate in the event of counterparty failure amid a global financial crisis.

3 Some policy issues

In this section, some policy issues are highlighted. The objective is to provide food for thought rather than to present the right policy.

How serious is the failure of CIP that we are now seeing?

As discussed earlier, we are witnessing the increase in the cost of securing US dollars in the foreign currency swap market or, to put it differently, the failure of CIP. Is this a serious phenomenon worthy of careful consideration? There are two opposing arguments. One is that it hampers a globally optimal allocation of capital. Even in case that the size of the additional cost of securing US dollars remains the same, its relative impact would be higher, given that global potential growth rate has declined. A counter-argument might, however, be possible. Given the sober reality that the anti-globalization movement sometimes erupts, some deterrent might be a necessary evil, if not first-best solution.

How should we evaluate the foreign currency funding arrangement?

Some forms of official funding arrangements for foreign currency are needed as a backstop in the face of a financial crisis. These arrangements could mitigate funding pressures and thus, deviations from CIP. Looking at Japan, there are currently several arrangements: BOJ's standing foreign currency swap arrangements with five major central banks (the New York Federal Reserve, the European Central Bank, the Bank of England, the Swiss National Bank and the Bank of Canada), BOJ's bilateral local currency swap arrangements with the Singapore Monetary Authority and the Reserve Bank of Australia, BOJ's cross-border collateral arrangements with Asian central banks (Thailand, Singapore, Indonesia and the Philippines) and the Ministry of Finance's Chiang-Mai Initiatives among Association of Southeast Asian Nations (ASEAN) Japan, China and Korea.

How should we avoid a "safe asset trap" in the global financial system? Triffin's dilemma in a new form

In the face of the progress of financial globalization, we need a "global safe asset" in order to maintain global financial stability. What we are observing is a tiering of global safe assets. The first tier is always public safe assets. The genuine first tier is US public debt. The quasi first tier is foreign currency risk-hedged non-US public debt. A case in point is JGBs. The second tier is private safe assets. Before the Global Financial Crisis, repos of US mortgage-backed securities were deemed as such.

In order to satisfy the increasing demand for global safe assets, issuance of US public debt has to increase. But it threatens the fiscal sustainability of the US, which eventually leads to global financial instability. This is a modern version of Triffin's dilemma. Triffin's dilemma is really daunting. We have already witnessed that a second-tier safe asset cannot be counted as a safe asset in a crisis. What about quasi first-tier safe assets? Countries whose public debt with foreign exchange risk hedging is deemed as quasi first-tier "safe" assets are also caught in the trap. The issuing cost of public debt is suppressed, which weakens fiscal discipline. A case in point is Japan. On top of that, the problem here is that "safe" is a relative concept with the emphasis on short-run movements of exchange rates as perceived by global investors. In a genuine stress situation, foreign exchange risk-hedged public debt cannot compete with US public debt.

Is it feasible for non-US banks to become truly global banks?

In order for global banks to be able to weather the storm of a financial crisis, it is critical for them to get access to US dollar funding in a truly systemic crisis. Banks of countries whose public debt is deemed as a quasi first-tier safe asset can expand their global banking business, but cannot count on the foreign currency swap market as a stable source of dollar funding in a truly systemic crisis. The fact that global investment banks are confined to US banks might be interpreted in this light. In this regard, the US is really enjoying an "exorbitant privilege."

Note

1 I greatly benefitted from the discussion with Takeshi Kimura as well as his papers (see, for instance, Iida et al., 2018). Any remaining errors are, of course, my responsibility.

References

Caruana, J. (2015) The role of the CPMI as part of the Basel process, *Keynote Speech at the CPMI 25th Anniversary Conference*. Available from: www.bis.org/speeches/sp150702.pdf [Accessed 2 November 2019].

Iida, T., Kimura, T. and Sudo, N. (2018) Deviations from covered interest rate parity and the dollar funding of global banks, *International Journal of Central Banking*, 14 (40), 275–325.

Nakaso, H. (2017) Monetary policy divergence and global financial stability: From the perspective of demand and supply of safe assets, *Speech at a Meeting Hosted by the International Bankers Association of Japan*. Available from: www.boj.or.jp/en/announcements/press/koen_2017/ko170120a.htm/ [Accessed 1 November 2019].

Subbarao, D. (2016) *Who Moved My Interest Rate: Leading the Reserve Bank Through Five Turbulent Years*. New Delhi: Penguin India.

3 The effectiveness of unconventional monetary policy on Japanese bank lending[1]

Heather Montgomery and Ulrich Volz

1 Introduction

Since the global financial crisis of 2007–2008, central bankers around the world have resorted to unconventional policies such as quantitative easing (QE), forward guidance and even lowering the interest rate paid on bank reserves into negative territory. Japan, which faced a crisis in its banking sector and came up against the theoretical zero lower bound on interest rates nearly a decade earlier, was a pioneer in the use of many of these unconventional policy tools.

Did they work? This chapter analyzes the effectiveness of Japan's bold experiment with unconventional monetary policy. Using a panel of bi-annual bank data covering the full universe of Japanese commercial banks over a 15-year period, this study analyzes the effectiveness of unconventional monetary policy – specifically QE – on the bank lending channel of monetary policy transmission. Our findings suggest that Japan's unconventional monetary policy worked: there is a bank lending channel of monetary policy transmission in Japan. Our results are robust to the inclusion of time fixed effects and generalized method of moments analysis. However, contrary to the predictions of banking theory, the effects of QE seem to come mostly through *under*capitalized banks. These findings suggest that bank balance sheet problems continue to be important factors impairing the credit channel.

The rest of this chapter is organized as follows. The next section presents an overview of unconventional monetary policies pursued by the Bank of Japan (BOJ) over the last two decades. This is followed in Section 3 by a discussion of the theoretical framework we use to inform our empirical analysis. First, we discuss the transmission channels through which monetary policy, both conventional and unconventional, are intended to work. Then we draw on existing models in the literature to derive a hypothesis about the effectiveness of unconventional monetary policy on the bank lending channel of monetary policy transmission. Section 4 discusses the empirics: the data and methodology used in the empirical analysis as well as a discussion of the results of that analysis. Section 5 concludes.

2   Japan as a pioneer of unconventional monetary policy

Japan's early experiments with unconventional monetary policy were born of necessity. In response to the recession of 1997–1998, which came on the heels of the bursting of the asset bubble in 1991 and the start of the "lost decade" of low growth, the BOJ first tried conventional monetary policy: the Bank cut the target uncollateralized, overnight inter-bank rate, the call rate, from 0.43% down to 0.25% in September 1998 and, in order to achieve that target, injected huge amounts of reserves into the banking system through open market operations.

Zero Interest Rate Policy (ZIRP): February 1999 ~

Despite the expansionary open market operations, toward the end of 1998 and early in 1999, long-term interest rates actually increased and the yen appreciated. With the call rate already at only 25 basis points, conventional monetary policy was no longer really an option. The BOJ thus embarked on its first unconventional monetary policy. Starting in February 1999, the call rate target was pushed down to zero. Then, in April 1999 at a press conference following the monetary policy committee meeting, BOJ Governor Hayami followed up with what the Bank called a "policy duration effect", what would now be considered unconditional forward guidance: a statement that the "zero rate will be maintained until deflationary concerns are dispelled". The zero rate and the bank's commitment to maintaining it came to be called ZIRP, Zero Interest Rate Policy.

Quantitative easing (QE1): March 2001 ~

ZIRP was lifted at the August 2000 monetary policy meeting and the target call rate was raised back to 25 basis points. However, with the benefit of hindsight, it seems apparent that the rate rise was premature. The decision was reversed just six months later, in February 2001, when the call rate target was lowered back down to 0.15%. The following month, in March 2001, with short-term interest rates already essentially at zero,[2] the economy still mired in deflation and output below potential, the BOJ embarked on its second experiment with unconventional monetary policy. The monetary policy instrument was changed from the policy rate, the uncollateralized, overnight, inter-bank call rate, to current account balances, essentially the level of required and excess reserves the commercial banks held on deposit at the BOJ.

Japan's bold experiment in targeting bank reserves was the world's first policy of QE. Despite much controversy and debate, even among the monetary policy board members of the Bank itself, this first round of QE, now referred to as "QE1", remained in effect for nearly six years. Over that period, the targeted balance of the BOJ's current account was raised nine times. When the policy was first announced in March 2001, reserves were targeted at 5 trillion yen, about 1 trillion yen above the required reserves of approximately 4 trillion yen. That target was raised to 6 trillion yen in August 2001 and then to a range of 10–15 trillion yen in December of the same year. When BOJ Governor Hayami was succeeded by Toshihiko Fukui in 2003, QE1 was expanded further to reach a target current account balance of 30–35 trillion yen by January 2004.[3] The January 2004 policy decision included some conditional forward guidance on how long QE would remain in place: until (1) "not only the most recently published CPI should register zero percent or above, but also that such tendency should be confirmed over a few months", and (2) the BOJ was "convinced that prospective CPI was not expected to register below zero" percent. The statement also noted that (3) although the other two conditions were the necessary condition for termination of QE, "there might be cases where the Bank would judge it appropriate to continue with quantitative easing even if they were fulfilled".

Finally, on March 9, 2006, the BOJ lifted the QE policy by a 7–1 vote, citing that the three conditions for lifting QE set out at the January 2004 monetary policy meeting had been met.[4] The BOJ's monetary policy instrument was switched from the current account balance back to the conventional monetary policy instrument, the uncollateralized overnight call rate. To assuage critics in the Ministry of Finance and Cabinet Office, the BOJ pledged that the targeted call rate would remain effectively at zero for some time: ZIRP would remain in place. Three months later, in July 2006, the BOJ made the historic decision to lift ZIRP and target a 25-basis point call rate. Interest rates in Japan had finally been normalized after more than six years of unconventional, experimental policies.

The Lehman Shock: September 2008 ~

In April 2008, after the end of Governor Fukui's term in March, Masaaki Shirakawa took over at the helm of the BOJ. Within months, the Shirakawa BOJ was facing the global financial crisis, or the "Lehman Shock" as it is sometimes referred to in Japan.

At first, the Bank pursued conventional policy by lowering interest rates. The uncollateralized, overnight call rate was lowered from 0.5% to around 0.3% in October 2008. The interest rate applied to the Complementary Lending Facility, a backstop for the BOJ to provide liquidity to financial institutions in its role as lender of last resort (the equivalent to discount window lending in the United States), was cut from 0.75% to 0.5%. A separate Complementary Deposit Facility was established for banks to deposit excess reserves and that interest rate was set at 0.1%.[5]

By December 2008, policy rates were nearly at zero in the United States. The BOJ lowered the target call rate further from 0.3% to 0.1% and the discount window interest rate applied to the Complementary Lending Facility was cut further from 0.5% to 0.3%.[6]

Comprehensive Monetary Easing (CME): October 2010 ~

In October 2010, with little room for further tweaks using conventional policy measures, the BOJ introduced a "Comprehensive Monetary Easing" (CME) policy. Under CME, Japan returned to a virtually Zero Interest Rate Policy as the call rate was lowered from 0.1% to a range between 0% and 0.1% and the BOJ announced a commitment to maintaining virtually zero interest rates until it judged that medium- to long-term price stability was "in sight".[7] The forward guidance was presumably included to try and nudge long-term rates, which remained positive despite the policy rate being near zero, lower as well.

The main element of CME, however, was the establishment of an Asset Purchase Program, through which the Bank continued to provide longer-term funds at a fixed rate and purchased Japanese government bonds (JGBs)[8] as well as less conventional assets such as commercial paper, corporate bonds, exchange-traded funds (ETFs) and even Japan real estate investment trusts (J-REITs). The combined size of the fixed rate funds provision and the Asset Purchase Program was initially set at 35 trillion yen,[9] but was later increased.[10] Despite the commitment to increased purchases of assets, BOJ Governor Shirakawa insisted that this was *not* a return to QE. The instrument of monetary policy would continue to be the short-term policy interest rate. Governor Shirakawa also reiterated previous arguments that Japan's deflation had multiple causes, only some of which could be addressed by monetary policy.

Quantitative and qualitative easing (QQE): April 2013 ~

QE returned, however, in April 2013, under Governor Shirakawa's successor at the BOJ, Haruhiko Kuroda. On December 16, 2012, Japan's Liberal-Democratic Party (LDP) won back a clear majority in the parliament, and it became apparent that the LDP's leader, Shinzo Abe, would become the next prime minister. Massive monetary expansion was promoted as the first of three "arrows" in Prime Minister Abe's economic plan, "Abenomics",[11] which he placed at the center of his political agenda. Under political pressure from the new prime minister, who even resorted to threats to change the BOJ law to limit the Bank's independence at the January 2013 monetary policy meeting, the BOJ – still under the leadership of Governor Shirakawa – introduced a hard 2% inflation target, more than doubling the previous 1% inflation "goal".

The following month, in February 2013, Prime Minister Abe nominated Kuroda to be the next Governor of the BOJ and the nomination was approved by Japan's parliament in March. At his nomination hearings, Kuroda pledged to end the "incremental" approach of the BOJ (presumably a dig at former Governor Shirakawa) and achieve the new 2% inflation target within two years. In contrast to Governor Shirakawa, who emphasized the structural causes of deflation and felt that the government shared responsibility with the Bank for ending it, Kuroda expressed confidence that the BOJ, and only the BOJ, could end Japan's deflation. Kuroda was also confident that the Bank would do so within two years.

Governor Kuroda's policy was announced as qualitative and quantitative easing, or QQE. Under QQE the main operating target of the Bank was again shifted from interest rates to the monetary base. The monetary base was to be doubled within two years and the average maturity of JGBs held by the BOJ would be lengthened.

After chairing his first monetary policy meeting in April 2013, Governor Kuroda announced at a press conference that the board had approved a massive monetary expansion to be carried out through large-scale asset purchases, mostly of JGBs, initially at a rate of about 60–70 trillion yen per year.[12] Analysts forecasted that this pace would increase the size of the BOJ's balance sheet by about 1% of GDP each month, nearly double the rate that had been set by the Federal Reserve Board of Governors (the Fed) under its program of "Large Scale Asset Purchases".[13] The maturity of the JGBs purchased by the Bank was lengthened: any maturity JGBs, up to 40 years, were included, and the average maturity of JGBs held by the Bank was to rise to about seven years,[14] a substantial lengthening from the short-term bonds purchased under conventional open market operations or even the three-year maturities purchased under CME. QQE also expanded annual purchases of risk assets such as ETFs and J-REITs by 1 trillion yen and 30 billion yen respectively.[15] At the same time, the BOJ pledged to continue QQE as long as necessary to achieve the 2% inflation target.

Since it was announced in 2013, QQE has been augmented by two other unconventional policies: the Negative Interest Rate Policy (NIRP) and Yield Curve Control, which are discussed briefly in the next sections.

QQE+ *Negative Interest Rate Policy (NIRP): January 2016 ~*

In January 2016, markets were surprised by the announcement that QQE would be supplemented with a "Negative Interest Rate Policy" (NIRP): a -0.1% interest rate on new deposits banks hold on reserve at the BOJ. The negative interest rate was applied to current accounts that financial institutions held on deposit at the BOJ in the Complementary Deposit Facility. As explained earlier, when the Complementary Deposit Facility was established in October 2008, the Bank paid an interest rate of 0.1% on deposits held there. Those funds are basically excess reserves that banks hold over and above their required reserves. Under NIRP, the interest rate paid on those excess reserves would become negative, -0.1%. Essentially the BOJ was initiating a fee charged to financial institutions that hold excess reserves on deposit at their central bank. Required reserves would continue to earn no interest. NIRP was announced on January 29, 2016, and would become effective on February 16, 2016, less than a month after it was announced, although it was actually implemented in a rather complicated three-tier system which meant that the negative interest rate was essentially only applied to banks' *new* excess reserves.

QQE+ Yield Curve Control (YCC): September 2016 ~

In September 2016, QQE and NIRP were further supplemented by a policy called "Yield Curve Control": the BOJ announced it would target a yield of less than 0% on ten-year JGBs. Outright purchases of JGBs would not increase from the current pace of 80 trillion yen annually, but the BOJ would introduce what it called "fixed-rate purchase operations": outright purchases with designated yields to prevent the long end of the JGB yield curve from deviating substantially from zero. Guidelines for purchases of other assets, such as ETFs and J-REITs, remained unchanged and the Bank reiterated its commitment to stick with its new policy of "QQE with Yield Curve Control" as long as necessary to achieve the 2% inflation target.

Despite Governor Kuroda's initial confidence in the power of monetary policy to achieve the 2% inflation target within two years, at the time of this writing, QQE remains in place, more than six years after it was implemented. Interest rates in Japan remain at or even below zero, 20 years after the introduction of ZIRP in 1999. The duration of these "unconventional" policies naturally leads to questions about how they are supposed to work and whether or not they are actually effective.

3   Theoretical framework

Conventional monetary policy transmission

Conventional monetary policy is thought to work mostly through the so-called interest rate channel. Expansionary monetary policy is usually announced as a lower target on the uncollateralized, overnight inter-bank borrowing rate, the so-called call rate in Japan, and implemented through purchases of short-term government bonds from commercial banks on the secondary market in exchange for bank reserves. The resulting increase in bank reserves means there is less demand for overnight inter-bank borrowing in order to meet reserve requirements, so the call rate does, in fact, fall toward its new lower targeted level. Since all short-term interest rates tend to move together, lower inter-bank rates are correlated with lower short-term nominal interest rates overall, and because of sticky prices, the lower short-term nominal interest rates lead to lower short-term *real* interest rates as well. The expectations hypothesis of the term structure, which states that the long rate is an average of expected future short-term rates, explains the effect of lower short-term real interest rates on real long-term interest rates. Lower long-term real rates stimulate higher investment, and higher investment eventually leads to higher aggregate demand, a.k.a. output, and therefore prices.

The theory on how conventional monetary policy works dates back to Keynes (1936). Keynes's original theory emphasized the influence of long-term real interest rates on fixed business investment, but more recent research has recognized the influence of long-term real interest rates on other types of investment, such as consumer housing (residential housing investment), as well as consumer durable expenditure (Mishkin, 1996).

Keynes's focus on long-term real interest rates was a result of his Liquidity Preference Theory, which modeled the demand for money as a function of the interest rate. In Keynes's model, the only alternative asset to money was government bonds. Later economists expanded Keynes's framework to incorporate other assets, leading to alternate channels of monetary policy transmission such as the exchange rate channel and wealth effects. In the exchange rate channel of monetary policy transmission, lower real interest rates lead to less demand for the domestic currency and therefore lead the domestic currency to depreciate, which drives up net exports and therefore aggregate demand. Wealth effects work through the effect of monetary policy on equity prices: lower real interest rates lower the discount value of future cash flows, raising equity prices, which increases wealth, stimulating consumption and therefore aggregate demand.

Some economists argue that there is plenty of empirical evidence for the traditional interest rate channel (e.g. Taylor, 1995), but Bernanke and Gertler (1995) interpret the empirical research as having had great difficulty in identifying significant effects of interest rates through the cost of capital and articulate a new channel of monetary policy transmission: the credit channel. What is often referred to as "the credit channel" is really two distinct channels of monetary policy transmission: the balance sheet channel and the bank lending channel, both of which work through financial intermediaries. Building on earlier research which emphasized the role of equity prices in transmitting monetary policy, the balance sheet channel emphasizes the role of net worth in financing. The lower the net worth of potential borrowers, the worse the adverse selection and moral hazard problems that may result in credit constraints for those borrowers. By raising equity prices and therefore the net worth of potential borrowers, expansionary monetary policy reduces the problems of adverse selection and moral hazard, thereby leading to more lending, more investment and, finally, more output. The bank lending channel focuses more on the bank side. By increasing bank reserves and deposits, expansionary monetary policy increases the quantity of bank loans available. This increase in the supply of bank loans stimulates investment and therefore aggregate demand, especially for borrowers that are dependent on bank loans for financing.

Regardless of the channel of transmission – the interest rate channel, the exchange rate channel, alternate asset price channels or the credit channels, the balance sheet channel and bank lending channel – all the theories on the non-neutrality of money discussed earlier start with a change in short-term interest rates: for expansionary monetary policy, a lowering of that short-term interest rate. But what if nominal interest rates are already at zero? How are *un*conventional monetary policies expected to affect the economy: aggregate output and inflation?

Unconventional monetary policy transmission

Unconventional monetary policies in some ways work much like conventional monetary policy. The aim of both conventional and unconventional expansionary monetary policy is to expand some components of aggregate demand other than government spending (government spending is left up to fiscal policy). The objective is to stimulate consumption, investment or net exports, thereby shrinking the output gap and, through a Phillips Curve type trade-off between output and inflation, stimulate inflation. Conventional monetary policy does this by lowering short-term interest rates, which stimulates consumption, investment and net exports through one or more of the channels of monetary policy transmission outlined previously. When short-term rates are already at zero, unconventional policies aim to stimulate consumption, investment and net exports by other means.

Zero Interest Rate Policy (ZIRP)

For example, forward guidance such as ZIRP – a pledge to maintain short-term nominal interest rates at zero until inflation is achieved – essentially aims to raise the public's inflation expectations, which brings down *real* interest rates, even if nominal rates are up against the zero lower bound. Like conventional monetary policy, forward guidance may work mostly through the interest rate channel, stimulating fixed business investment or even residential investment. But forward guidance might also work through the exchange rate channel or wealth effects leading to higher household consumption as well.

Quantitative easing (QE)

QE1 also included forward guidance but set new targets for current account balances, required and excess reserves on deposit at the central bank. QE1 was expected to work primarily through the bank lending channel of monetary policy transmission. Building up reserves makes commercial banks more liquid, which should lead to more favorable terms on loans and stimulate lending to businesses and households. This borrowing, in turn, would be used to finance new investment, which in turn would stimulate economic activity and eventually inflation in the macroeconomy.

Comprehensive Monetary Easing (CME)

Under CME, the BOJ continued with forward guidance to shape market expectations of monetary policy and inflation. The Bank also continued to supply funds to banks, although rather than targeting current account balances as under QE, CME provided banks with funds through its funds-supplying operations. The main new policy tool of CME, however, was the Asset

Purchase Program, which included the purchase of less conventional assets such as commercial paper, corporate bonds, ETFs and even J-REITs, in addition to the traditional JGBs. This was intended to compress the risk premium, making it easier for firms to finance business fixed investment through direct financing, rather than having to rely on bank loans. Purchases of risk assets by the central bank were also expected to have a wealth effect on households, stimulating household consumption.

Quantitative and qualitative easing (QQE)

QQE built upon many of the earlier policies. As with earlier policies, inflation expectations were guided by forward guidance on conditions for changes in future policy, liquidity at commercial banks was boosted by large-scale asset purchases, and the risk premium was compressed through continued direct purchases of unconventional risk assets. Thus, QQE aimed to work through all of the channels of monetary policy transmission discussed earlier: the (real) interest rate channel, the exchange rate channel, alternate asset price channels and the credit channels, the balance sheet channel and bank lending channel.

Under QQE the BOJ's asset purchases included substantially longer maturity JGBs than under conventional monetary policy. This was intended to put downward pressure directly on real *long-term* interest rates, which are more relevant to investment decisions by firms and households.

Augmenting QQE with NIRP and Yield Curve Control was intended to amplify these effects. By essentially charging banks for keeping their current account balances on deposit at the BOJ, NIRP further incentivized banks to lend out or otherwise transform their liabilities into return-bearing assets. Both NIRP and Yield Curve Control further increased the downward pressure on long-term real rates. All three of these policies aimed to give holders of JGBs – many of those being financial institutions – an incentive to move into riskier assets.

Effects on Banks

Unconventional monetary policy has negative side effects, however. Super-low interest rates in loan and corporate bond markets help keep poorly performing, unproductive companies – often referred to as "zombie" firms – alive. Observers worry about the growing monopolization of the secondary JGB market by the BOJ, especially of long-term JGBs, and the resultant disappearance of any market discipline in the bond market. The fact that long-term rates on JGBs remain low or even negative, despite the fact that Japan's public debt is now more than 230% of the country's GDP, provides some foundation for those concerns.

However, some of the biggest risks of unconventional monetary policy are felt in the banking system. With such low interest rates in place for so long, the profit margin on financial intermediation – transforming short-term deposit liabilities into longer-term loan assets – narrowed. In general, the interest rate paid on bank deposits and other liabilities cannot easily be lowered, so lower policy rates mostly affect the rates banks earn on loans and other assets, which squeezes bank profit margins. QE, which flooded the economy with liquidity, certainly eased any remaining liquidity problems at the banks, as the policy intended, but without a change in the demand for loans from client firms, banks were incentivized to make loans to riskier firms willing to pay slightly higher interest rates. However, with interest rates depressed overall, interest rates charged to even those clients may not adequately compensate for default risk. When NIRP was introduced, charging a negative interest rate on some of the banks' excess reserves, the already struggling financial sector in Japan was dealt a further blow. Some of the larger banks were able to respond by turning to non-interest income or international lending, but the majority of Japanese banks have just suffered through further downward pressure on net interest margins.

The effects of unconventional monetary policy are important not only for the health of the financial sector per se, but also because some theories about how monetary policy is transmitted to the real economy – in particular, the credit channel of monetary policy transmission – focus on financial institutions as a critical link in the chain of transmission. The profitability and capitalization of financial institutions may significantly impact the effectiveness of expansionary monetary policy in stimulating bank lending and transmitting effects to the real economy (see, for example, Kopecky and VanHoose, 2004). In the empirical analysis to follow, the heterogeneity of banks is explicitly considered and how bank health affects the transmission of monetary policy is empirically estimated.

4   Empirical analysis

Kashyap and Stein's (2000) seminal article found some of the first empirical support for the existence of the bank lending channel in an analysis of quarterly balance sheet data on US commercial banks from 1976 to 1993. Looking at Japanese data, Hosono (2006) also found evidence of a bank lending channel in Japan although in sub-sample analysis Hosono (2006) demonstrated that the effectiveness of the bank lending channel of monetary policy transmission differs between periods of monetary tightening and periods of monetary easing. The study most closely related to this one is perhaps Bowman et al. (2015) who empirically evaluated the effect of *unconventional* monetary policy in Japan, finding a positive, statistically significant, albeit quantitatively small impact of bank liquidity on lending by Japanese banks. The analysis to follow builds upon and improves on these earlier studies through its analysis of the full universe of Japanese banks over a longer time period which spans not only the first round of so-called QE1, but subsequent unconventional policy as well. Building on Montgomery and Volz (2019), the analysis here also explores concerns about the impact of these prolonged unconventional policies on the banks themselves and how that may influence policy effectiveness by incorporating bank health into the empirical analysis.

Data

To investigate the effectiveness of the BOJ's unconventional monetary policy, we use an unbalanced panel of data on 147 Japanese banks' balance sheets and financial statements over the 15-year period between 2000 and 2015[16] from the Japanese Bankers Association (JBA). The data frequency is semi-annual, as balance sheet and financial statement information is reported every September and March (note that Japan's fiscal year runs from April 1 to March 31). The final panel of data includes a total of 4,003 bank-period observations for most series. Table 3.1 reports the summary statistics.

Methodology

The baseline estimation regresses the panel of data described previously using the following reduced-form equation:

$$\Delta log\left(L_{i,t+1}\right) = \beta_0 + \beta_1 LR_{i,t} + BX_{i,t} + \varepsilon_{i,t+1} \tag{1}$$

Where:

$\Delta log\left(L_{i,t+1}\right)$ represents log change of loans for bank i at time $t+1$.

$LR_{i,t}$ represents the liquidity ratio of bank i at time t, defined as the ratio of liquid assets ("cash and due from banks" plus "call loans") divided by total assets.

$X_{i,t}$ represents a vector of control variables, including the log of total assets, the log of total deposits, the equity ratio (the ratio of bank equity to total assets) and the bad loan ratio (the ratio of bad loans to total bank equity; bad loans are defined as the sum of "loan to borrowers in legal bankruptcy", "past due loans in arrears by six months or more", "loans in arrears by three months or more and less than six months" and "restructured loans") for bank i at time t.

$\varepsilon_{i,t+1}$ represents the error term for bank i at time $(t+1)$.

Table 3.1 Summary statistics, 2000–2015

Variable name	Mean	Standard deviation	Min	Max
Loan growth (log change, %)	0.85%	5.24	−103.73%	84.43%
Liquidity ratio (%)	6.64%	3.91	1.13%	54.85%
Total assets (log, million yen)	14.67	1.23	10.38	19.12
Total deposits (log, million yen)	14.45	1.38	4.01	18.70
Equity ratio (%)	5.04%	4.93	−78.82	79.83
Bad loan ratio (%)	81.79	95.55	−612.47	1,916.83
No. of banks (*i*)	147			
No. of time periods (*t*)	30			
No. of observations	4,003			

Source: Japanese Bankers Association

In Equation (1), the main parameter of interest is β_1, the coefficient on the liquidity ratio. If monetary policy is effective, the estimate of β_1 will be positive and statistically significant, indicating that a higher bank liquidity ratio leads to higher bank loan growth.

To explore the implications of the model of commercial bank behavior presented earlier, we also estimate the following equation, which includes an indicator of whether or not banks have an excess capital cushion:

$$log\left(L_{i,t+1}\right) = \beta_0 + \beta_1 LR_{i,t} + \beta_2 LR_{i,t} xHealthyBank + BX_{i,t} + \varepsilon_{i,t+1} \qquad (2)$$

Where all variables are defined as in the previous equation and *HealthyBank* is a dummy variable that takes a value of one for banks that are meeting their capital adequacy requirements.

Thus, in Equation (2), the coefficient estimate on the liquidity ratio, β_1, still gives us an overall estimate of the effectiveness of expansionary monetary policy as measured by an increase in the liquidity ratio on bank lending. If the estimate of β_1 is positive and statistically significant, it indicates that expansionary monetary policy is effective: a higher bank liquidity ratio leads to higher bank loan growth. The new parameter of interest in Equation (2) is β_2, the coefficient on the interaction term of bank i's liquidity ratio at time t, $LR_{i,t}$, and the new *HealthyBank* dummy variable. If the estimate of β_2 is positive and statistically significant, the assumptions laid out in the theoretical framework are correct: monetary policy is effective (or, if the estimate of β_1 is also positive, then we can conclude that monetary policy is especially effective) in stimulating lending by healthy banks that are meeting their required capital adequacy ratio.

The empirical methodology used in estimating both Equations (1) and (2) starts with a simple pooled ordinary least squares (OLS) regression, then turns to balanced panel data analysis, exploring the effect of including both individual and time fixed effects. Finally, to address concerns about lagged dependent variable bias, we report the results of generalized method of moments analysis (GMM).

Results

The empirical results from the estimations of Equation (1) and (2) are reported in Table 3.2 and Table 3.3, respectively. The results reported in Table 3.2, which reports the results of empirical estimation of Equation (1), indicate that monetary policy was effective during the period of our study. For nearly all empirical methodologies – pooled OLS, panel data with individual fixed effects or time fixed effects, and for GMM – the coefficient estimate of interest is positive and highly statistically significant at the 5% or even 1% level. This suggests that banks with relatively higher liquidity ratios in a given period tend to have statistically significantly higher loan growth in the following period.

The size of the parameter estimate nearly doubles when individual bank fixed effects are accounted for in column (2), and when we address the possibility of

Table 3.2 The effect of higher bank liquidity ratios on loan growth

	Dependent variable: loan growth $\Delta log(L)_{i,t+1}$				
	Pooled OLS	Panel analysis with individual fixed effects	Panel analysis with time fixed effects	Two step system GMM	Two step difference GMM
Independent variables	(1)	(2)	(3)	(4)	(5)
Constant term	-0.00				
	(0.01)				
Liquidity ratio, $LR_{i,t}$	0.06★★	0.14★★★	0.06★★★	0.15★★	0.19
	(0.03)	(0.03)	(0.03)	(0.08)	(0.12)
Log total assets	0.00	-0.05★★★	0.00	0.00	-0.06
	(0.00)	(0.01)	(0.00)	(0.00)	(0.06)
Equity ratio, $ER_{i,t}$	0.08	0.53★★★	0.06	0.04	1.23★★
	(0.06)	(0.10)	(0.06)	(0.20)	(0.50)
Bad loan ratio	-0.01★★★	-0.01★★★	-0.00★★★	-0.00	-0.01
	(0.00)	(0.00)	(0.00)	(0.00)	(0.01)
No. obs.	2,580	2,460	2,460	4,003	2,172

Note: Standard errors are written in parenthesis below the finding, and asterisks represent significant findings at the 10%★, 5%★★ and 1%★★★ level, respectively. I = 147 (or 133), T = 33 (or 30), N = 4,003 (or 2,460).

Table 3.3 The effect of higher bank liquidity ratios on loan growth – controlling for bank health

	Dependent variable: loan growth $\Delta log(L)_{i,t+1}$				
	Pooled OLS	Pooled OLS with bank type dummies	Panel analysis with time fixed effects	Two step system GMM	Two step difference GMM
Independent variables	(1)	(2)	(3)	(4)	(5)
Constant term	-0.00	-0.01	-0.01		
	(0.01)	(0.02)	(0.01)		
Liquidity ratio, $LR_{i,t}$	0.08★★★	0.08★★★	0.08★★★	0.18★★	0.15
	(0.03)	(0.03)	(0.03)	(0.09)	(0.12)
Log total assets	0.00	0.00	0.00	0.00	-0.06
	(0.00)	(0.00)	(0.00)	(0.00)	(0.09)
Equity ratio, $ER_{i,t}$	0.15★★	0.19★★★	0.13★	0.05	1.18★★★
	(0.07)	(0.07)	(0.06)	(0.21)	(0.49)
Bad loan ratio	-0.01★★★	-0.01★★★	-0.01★★★	-0.01	-0.01
	(0.00)	(0.00)	(0.00)	(0.00)	(0.01)
Liquidity ratio x health bank dummy, $LR_{i,t}xHealthyBank$	-0.07★★	-0.07★★	-0.07★★	-0.12★	-0.07
	(0.03)	(0.03)	(0.03)	(0.07)	(0.08)
No. obs.		2,460	2,460	4,632	2,172

Note: Standard errors are written in parenthesis below the finding, and asterisks represent significant findings at the 10%★, 5%★★ and 1%★★★ level, respectively. I = 133 (or 147), T = 30 (or 33), N = 2,460 (or 4,003).

endogeneity due to a lagged dependent variable on the right-hand side through two-step system GMM analysis in column (4).

The results reported in Table 3.3, which reports the results of empirical estimation of Equation (2), largely confirm the results reported in Table 3.2. That is, the empirical results again indicate that monetary policy was effective during the period of our study. For nearly all empirical methodologies – pooled OLS, panel data with individual fixed effects or time fixed effects, and for GMM – the coefficient estimate of interest is positive and highly statistically significant at the 5% or even 1% level. This confirms that banks with relatively higher liquidity ratios in a given period tend to have statistically significantly higher loan growth in the following period. In estimating Equation (2), we are not able to include individual bank fixed effects due to multicollinearity with the *HealthyBank* dummy variable, but as in Table 3.2, the size of the parameter estimate on the liquidity ratio nearly doubles when we address the possibility of endogeneity due to a lagged dependent variable on the right-hand side through two-step system GMM analysis (column (4)).

What is new in Equation (2) and the empirical results reported in Table 3.3, is the interaction term of each individual bank's liquidity ratio at time *t* and the *HealthyBank* dummy variable. Contrary to the implications of our theoretical model, the coefficient estimate on the interaction term is highly statistically significantly *negative*. This indicates that monetary policy was effective overall, but was relatively less effective at stimulating lending by healthy banks that were meeting their regulatory capital ratio requirement. Or, alternatively, the results suggest that although monetary policy was effective overall, the lending stimulated by providing banks with higher liquidity was mostly lending by sick, undercapitalized banks.

5 Conclusions

Two decades after the introduction of ZIRP in 1999, and with QQE in place for more than six years now, the BOJ is still far from achieving its 2% inflation target. The efficacy of its unconventional monetary policies is therefore under scrutiny for good reason. The empirical results presented in this chapter indicate that unconventional monetary policy has significant effects through the bank lending channel, although the impact on bank lending is quantitatively small. Interestingly, the unconventional expansionary monetary policy seems to be particularly encouraging increased lending from sick, undercapitalized banks.

For sure, we have only looked at one transmission channel of unconventional monetary policy, and hence our analysis is not suited to give a comprehensive assessment of the BOJ's monetary policies. While our empirical analysis suggests that the bank lending channel of monetary policy transmission has been working in Japan, the effects on bank lending appear small. This begs the questions whether the benefits of such policies outweigh the costs inflicted through its unintended side effects, including possible distortion in asset valuations, financial markets and the corporate sector. In particular, our findings suggest that QE works through sick, undercapitalized banks, which raises questions whether QE may actually perpetuate weaknesses in the banking sector. This raises concerns as to the appropriateness of the policy implementation and the long-term implications of the policy for the banking sector and macroeconomy as a whole.

Notes

1 The authors are grateful for receiving excellent comments on a presentation of an earlier version of this chapter at the Third Annual Conference of the Japan Economy Network at the University of Zurich in September 2018, especially from our discussant Andrea Barbon, as well as from Kenji Aramaki, Katrin Assenmacher-Wesche, Andrew Filardo, Stefan Gerlach and Toshitaka Sekine. We also thank Alexis Stenfors and Jan Toporowski for thoughtful comments. Heather Montgomery gratefully acknowledges support from MEXT Kaken Grant #18K01621. Ulrich Volz would like to acknowledge support for this research through a Meiji Jingu research grant. The usual disclaimer applies.
2 During most of QE1, in particular after the increase in targeted current account balances to 6 trillion yen in September 2001, the uncollateralized, overnight call rate remained below even its level during ZIRP.
3 The policy announcement also expanded the assets to be purchased to include asset-backed securities (ABSs) that passed certain screening, and forward guidance on how long QE would remain in place.
4 In retrospect, many observers feel QE1 may have been lifted too soon. In March 20016, inflation as measured by the CPI and what in Japan is called "core core CPI" (the CPI excluding food and energy prices) remained negative. Core CPI (the CPI excluding food prices) was positive in November and December of 2005, but had turned negative again in January 2006. Part of the decline may have been due to revisions to the base year and weighting.
5 This prepared a framework for implementing the Negative Interest Rate Policy, or NIRP, a few years later, as in the following discussion.
6 In addition to adjustments to interest rates, in December 2008 the Bank established "Special Funds-Supplying Operations to Facilitate Corporate Financing" under which the Bank provided financial institutions with unlimited funds at the current policy rate as long as banks provided corporate debt as collateral. Initially, only debt with credit ratings of A or higher were accepted, but the criteria were later expanded to include BBB-rated debt. This first special operation was originally set to expire in March 2009, but it was eventually extended into March 2010. In December 2009, a 10 trillion yen, three-month "Funds-Supplying Operation against Pooled Collateral". was implemented. In March 2010 the operation was expanded to 20 trillion yen and in August 2010 a separate 10 trillion yen, six-month Funds Supplying Operation, was introduced, bringing the total covered by these operations to 30 trillion yen.
7 The definition of medium- to long-term price stability had been introduced in March 2006 under Governor Fukui and then clarified in December 2009 under Governor Shirakawa to mean a positive range of 2% or lower with a midpoint of around 1%. In February 2012, forward guidance was further strengthened by announcing a "goal" (*medo* in Japanese, which is distinct from a "target", but stronger than the previous "understanding") of 1% inflation and a statement that the virtually Zero Interest Rate Policy and Asset Purchase Program would continue until "the 1 percent goal is in sight".
8 Initially with a remaining maturity of one–two years; in April 2012 extended to three years.
9 Since the program built on the pre-existing "Funds-Supplying Operation against Pooled Collateral", the amount of new assets to be purchased under the Asset Purchase

Program was arguably 5 trillion yen. According to Shirai (2018, p. 30), the newly purchased assets were "decomposed into JGBs (around 1.5 trillion yen), T-Bills (around 2 trillion yen), CPs and corporate bonds (around 0.5 trillion yen each), ETFs (around 0.45 trillion yen), and J-REITs (around 0.05 trillion yen)".

10 The Asset Purchase Program was increased to 40 trillion yen in March 2011, then 50 trillion yen (August 2011), 55 trillion yen (October 2011), 65 trillion yen (February 2012), 70 trillion yen (April 2012), 80 trillion yen (September 2012), 91 trillion yen (October 2012), 101 trillion yen (December 2012) and, finally, in January 2013, to 111 trillion yen (with a target to achieve that amount by the end of 2014).

11 The other arrows are (2) flexible fiscal policy and (3) structural reforms for growth.

12 This was later increased to 80 trillion yen in October 2013.

13 Like the previous BOJ Governor Shirakawa, Fed Chair Ben Bernanke insisted that the Fed's Large Scale Asset Purchases were not QE and the target of open market operations continued to be the overnight, uncollateralized inter-bank lending rate, in the US the Fed Funds Rate.

14 At the October 2013 monetary policy meeting the average maturity of JGBs held by the Bank was also lengthened from about seven years to a range of seven–ten years.

15 Commercial paper and corporate bond purchases initiated in December 2012 and January 2013 as part of the CME continued as well. In October 2013, purchases of risk assets were tripled to 3 trillion yen (ETFs) and 90 billion yen (J-REITs). In December 2015, the BOJ established a new program for purchasing ETFs comprising of stocks issued by companies which were proactively investing in physical and human capital, which increased ETF purchases slightly to around 3.3 trillion yen. Then, in July 2016 the Bank announced a near-doubling of ETF purchases to 6 trillion yen annually.

16 Since some analysts argue that the augmentation of QQE with NIRP and Yield Curve Control has fundamentally changed from QE (balances) back to an interest rate, we restrict our study to the period before 2015.

References

Bernanke, B. S. and Gertler, M. (1995) Inside the black box: The credit channel of monetary policy transmission, *Journal of Economic Perspectives*, 9 (4), 27–48.

Bowman, D., Cai, F., Davies, S. and Kamin, S. (2015) Quantitative easing and bank lending: Evidence from Japan, *Journal of International Money and Finance*, 57 (1), 15–30.

Hosono, K. (2006) The transmission mechanism of monetary policy in Japan: Evidence from banks' balance sheets, *Journal of the Japanese and International Economies*, 20 (3), 380–405.

Kashyap, A. K. and Stein, J. C. (2000) What do a million observations on banks say about the transmission of monetary policy? *American Economic Review*, 90 (3), 407–428.

Keynes, J. M. (1936) *The General Theory of Employment, Interest and Money*. London: Macmillan.

Kopecky, K. J. and VanHoose, D. (2004) A model of the monetary sector with and without binding capital requirements, *Journal of Banking & Finance*, 28 (3), 633–646.

Mishkin, F. S. (1996) The channels of monetary transmission: Lessons for monetary policy, *NBER Working Paper*, No. 5464.

Montgomery, H. and Volz, U. (2019) The effectiveness of unconventional monetary policy in Japan, *Journal of Economic Issues*, 53 (2), 411–416.

Shirai, S. (2018) *Mission Incomplete: Reflating Japan's Economy*, 2nd Edition, Tokyo: Asian Development Bank Institute.

Taylor, J. B. (1995) The monetary transmission mechanism: An empirical framework, *Journal of Economic Perspectives*, 9 (4), 11–26.

4 Japanese banks in the international money markets

Mimoza Shabani, Alexis Stenfors and Jan Toporowski

1 The rise of foreign exchange swaps

Foreign exchange swaps are agreements to buy or sell foreign currency and that are combined with a further re-sell or re-purchase agreement set for a fixed date in the future to reverse the initial purchase or sale. Foreign exchange swaps emerged in an informal fashion at the end of the 1980s. They rapidly proliferated during the 1990s, not least after central banks started using re-purchase or re-sale agreements in securities to regulate liquidity in inter-bank or money markets. Foreign exchange swaps are almost wholly based on swaps between US dollars and other currencies. However, reliable, comprehensive data on the swaps is difficult to find, largely because of their short-term nature. Swaps outstanding at any one time have usually been reversed within a few months, so that the underlying agreements have been settled and no longer count as balance sheet commitments.

The main source for foreign exchange swaps is a triennial survey undertaken by the Bank for International Settlements. This was recently extended in a paper by Borio et al. (2017). As Figure 4.1 from the regular survey shows, the foreign exchange swap market has grown sharply during the last few decades. In 2019, the daily turnover amounted to US$3,202 billion (BIS, 2019).

Most foreign exchange swaps are quoted against US dollars. As can be seen from Figure 4.2, the €/$ swap market is the largest and has clearly benefitted from the consolidation of money markets in the European Monetary Union. Nevertheless, the figure also shows the importance of $/¥ swaps in the international monetary system. The $/¥ foreign exchange swap market is the second largest and, along with the €/$ swaps, shows little sign of having been diminished by the financial crisis that emerged in 2008.

The rise in outstanding $/¥ swaps is the result of a huge expansion in foreign corporate acquisitions and financial investments by Japanese financial institutions. Since these acquisitions are mostly priced in US dollars, but using the liquidity provided by the Bank of Japan through its quantitative easing programme, $/¥ swaps are used to purchase those acquisitions. The scale of these investments is shown in Figure 4.3. The largest share of these investments has been undertaken by long-term investments institutions, that is Japanese pension

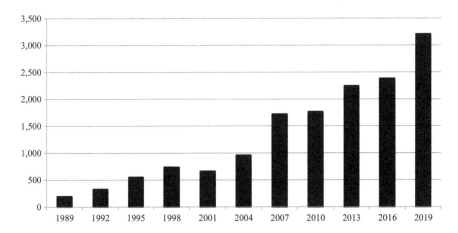

Figure 4.1 The global foreign exchange swap market (daily turnover in April, in US$ billions)

Source: BIS (2005, 2019).

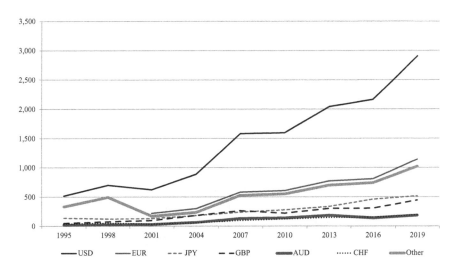

Figure 4.2 Foreign exchange swap market by currency (daily average turnover in April, in US$ billions)

Source: BIS (2005, 2019)

funds and insurance companies, with Japanese depository institutions (banks) holding outward investments on a similar scale.

The reason for the similarity in scale of Japanese banks' foreign investments and the foreign investments of Japanese long-term investments institutions is the latter have been using foreign exchange swaps to 'hedge' their foreign

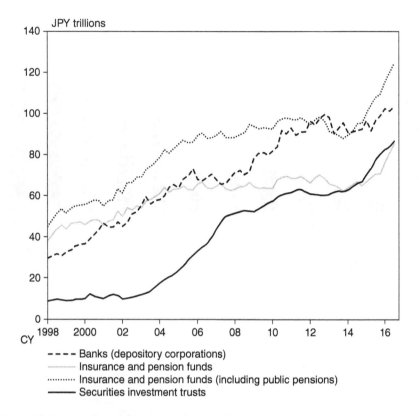

Figure 4.3 Japanese financial institutions' outward investments in foreign securities

Source: The Bank of Japan, Nakaso (2017) https://www.boj.or.jp/en/announcements/press/koen_2017/data/ko170120a2.pdf

investments, that is to place liabilities on their balance sheets in the same currency and to the same value as their foreign currency assets, as a way of eliminating the foreign exchange risk that arises from holding assets in a different currency. The amount of this 'funding' is shown in Figure 4.4, indicating that this is now in excess of $1.2 trillion. The figure also shows that this funding is almost wholly concentrated among the major Japanese banks and institutional investors, that is among those larger institutions that hold long-term foreign currency assets.

2   Japanese bank expansion abroad

During the economic boom that characterised Japan from the early 1950s until the stock market crash in the 1990s,[1] the Japanese banking system developed and thrived both domestically and internationally. In the late 1980s, Japanese banks were considered to be among the strongest in the world. Indeed, in

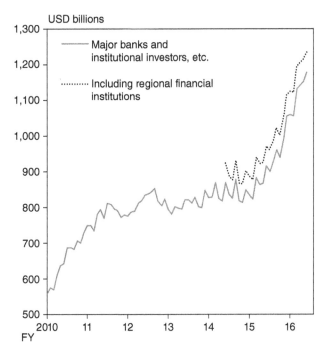

Figure 4.4 Foreign currency funding via foreign exchange swaps by Japanese financial
          institutions

Source: The Bank of Japan, Nakaso (2017) https://www.boj.or.jp/en/announcements/press/koen_2017/data/ko170120a2.pdf

1988, seven Japanese banks were ranked among the world's top ten in terms of assets (Hoshi, 2001). During the 1980s, Japanese banks expanded their overseas operations substantially, especially in the US market. Seth and Quijano (1991) suggest that lending by Japanese banks operating in the US, together with agency lending, rose more than six-fold from 1984 to 1989. By the early 1990s, around 18% of industrial and commercial credit in the US was provided by Japanese banks (Peek and Rosengren, 1999).

   However, in the aftermath of the 1989 stock market crash, the Japanese economy entered a prolonged slump. The economic slowdown and the onset of asset price deflation had a significant negative impact on the health of Japanese banks and other financial institutions. These financial difficulties in the aftermath of the crisis also undermined banks' international position. Japanese banks began to pull back from their international activities and hence significantly reduced their foreign lending. Indeed, external assets fell from over ¥120 trillion in early 1990 to below ¥100 trillion at the start of 1994 (Lam, 2013).

However, while their international lending position started to slow down following the stock market crash, by the mid-1990s Japanese banks began to increase their foreign lending to Asia. They took what seemed like an opportunity given the high rates of economic growth in Asia at the time. However, the region was hit by a financial crisis in 1997. In response to these events, Japanese banks again reduced their overseas lending, which was reflected in a 40% reduction in foreign assets in the two-year period between the mid-1990s, when the expansion to Asia started, to 1997, when the financial crisis occurred (Lam, 2013).

The exposure of the Japanese banks in the Asian market following the financial crisis exacerbated their deteriorating financial position. They not only suffered major losses due to the high number of non-performing loans but also incurred valuation losses on credit provided in the region, lending that was mainly done in foreign currency. This, together with the domestic economic problems following the stock market crash, weakened the soundness of the Japanese banking system – culminating with the spectacular failures of several highly important financial institutions in 1997. By 1998, a total of 19 Japanese banks had been downgraded (Miyajima and Yafeh, 2003). Furthermore, a number of banks, such Daiwa, Yasuda Trust, Mitsui Trust and Nippon Credit Bank announced their plans to shut down their overseas operations completely and thus only operate domestically (Peek and Rosengren, 1999).

Being perceived as less creditworthy than their peers abroad, Japanese banks faced difficulties in raising US dollar funding. The Japanese banking crisis became reflected in the so-called Japan premium in the financial markets (Stenfors, 2019). Since only the Bank of Japan could provide Japanese yen, the Japanese commercial banks had to turn the $/¥ foreign exchange swap markets. This stands in stark contrast to the situation during the financial crisis of 2007–08. This time, Japanese financial institutions were perceived as relatively 'safe' compared to their European and North American peers. The Japanese yen soared, and money market risk premia were lower in Japan than abroad. Indeed, a relatively healthy bank funding position also seemed to be consistent with the credit default swaps (CDS) spreads of the large Japanese banks, which managed to outperform the majority of their foreign competitors.

Paradoxically, some explanations can be traced back to the Japanese banking crisis. After more than a decade of repeated failures, insolvency and financial weakness, Japanese banks not only seemed to have recovered but were also trying to regain their position at an international level. The situation had changed in favour of the Japanese banks, which were once heavily criticised for their structure and took considerable blame for the economic stagnation the country experienced during the late 1990s and early 2000s. Most of the criticism came from commentators in Western developed countries, urging the Japanese authorities to change the regulatory framework and promote a more encouraging approach to financial innovation (Montgomery and Takahashi, 2011).

During the financial crisis of 2007–08, it became apparent that the US banking sector, together with banking systems in other advanced economies, had become too complex in the years preceding the crisis. At the heart of such complexity was financial innovation. By contrast, in the aftermath of the US crisis, Japan seemed to have not been affected by the events happening in the Western economies precisely because financial innovation and complex financial instruments never quite took off in the more traditional approach of the Japanese banking sector. When certain US banks faced significant difficulties, it was the Japanese banks that came to the rescue.

For example, in January 2008, Mizuho Financial Group invested $1.2 billion in purchasing 18% in preferred shares in Merrill Lynch (Montgomery and Takahashi, 2011; Taniguchi and Sato, 2011). In September 2008, Mitsubishi UFJ Financial Group purchased a fifth of Morgan Stanley in a $9 billion deal (Story and Sorkin, 2008). In the same month, Nomura Holding Inc., Japan's largest brokerage firm, announced the purchase of Lehman Brothers' equities and investment banking operations in Europe and the Middle East (Slater, 2008). In 2011, *The Economist* (2011) labelled the strong position of Japanese banks as being 'back from the dead'. The article emphasised that not only the country's three main banks, Mitsubishi UFJ, Sumitomo Mitsui and Mizuho, are amongst the top 30 largest banks in the world by assets, but also how these banks used the crisis in their favour by expanding internationally in the US, Europe and Asia. For instance, in 2013, Mitsubishi UFJ acquired a controlling stake in Thailand's Bank of Ayudhya for ¥560 billion (Lewis, 2015). Mizuho, as well the buying of a stake in Merrill Lynch in 2008 and a 15% stake in the Vietnamese Vietcombank in 2011, acquired $3 billion worth of loans from RBS in 2015 (Inagaki, 2015). During the summer of 2015, it was further reported that Japanese banks, mainly the country's three leading banks, continue their search and eagerness to expand overseas (Lewis, 2015).

Consequently, the international position of Japanese banks in recent years is also reflected in their leading international lending position. Japanese banks' cross-border lending market share rose from 8% in 2007 to 13% in the first quarter of 2013, followed by the US and German banks, accounting for 12% and 11% respectively (BIS, 2013). In 2015 Japanese banks remained at the top with foreign claims amounting to a total of $3.5 trillion, as of March 2015. That is above the UK's total foreign claim amounting to $3.2 trillion (BIS, 2015). Figure 4.5 shows the international claims of Japanese, US and UK banks since 2000. As shown, Japanese banks remain the leader in international lending, increasing significantly since 2015. For the 'Big 3' banks, the ratio of overseas to total loans increased from 15% in 2009 to 26% in 2013. With a loan-to-deposit ratio of around 1.3 overseas, the banks have become perceived to be increasingly vulnerable to currency and liability mismatches (IMF, 2015).

As Lam (2013) notes, policies to revive growth and exit the deflationary era, coupled with the uncertainty with regards to the development of the currency and bond market, encouraged large Japanese banks to take more risk and to diversify abroad. The Bank of Japan's monetary policies gave Japanese banks the liquidity to finance that expansion abroad. But this could only be done by converting that liquidity into the US dollars required for that expansion abroad.

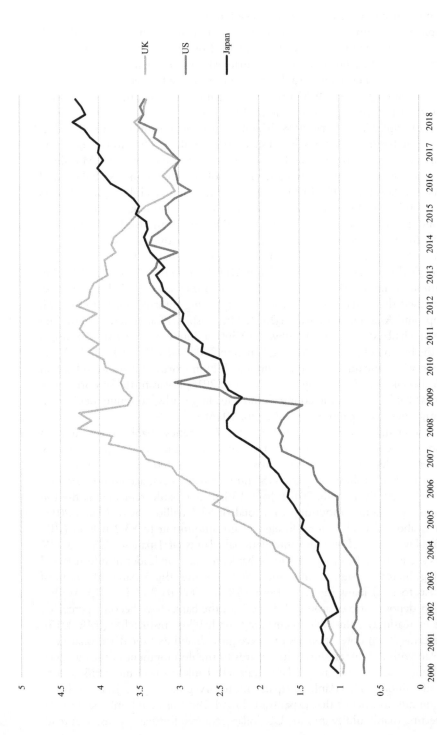

Figure 4.5 International claims of Japan, the UK and the US (US$ trillions)

Source: BIS

3   Funding or derivatives operations?

In this section we discuss the question of whether the large scale operations of Japanese banks and financial institutions in foreign exchange swaps constitute efforts to evade banking regulation, as is widely believed in the 'shadow banking' literature (e.g., Gabor, 2018), or whether the foreign exchange swaps are merely the latest incarnation of a money market that has migrated from the traditional, 'unhedged' inter-bank market (Grahl and Lysandrou, 2006). The difference is fundamental, but largely overlooked in the literature and central banks' discussions. For example, a Handbook of the Bank of England's Centre for Central Banking Studies describes derivatives as follows:

> Derivatives are useful for risk management: they can reduce costs, enhance returns and allow investors to manage risks with greater certainty and precision. . . . An issuer may find it difficult (or even impossible on account of legal or other restrictions) to issue in a particular currency. However, it may be important – e.g., for hedging purposes or for asset/liability management of the company – to have its liability in that currency. It therefore may choose to borrow in another currency . . . and swap the proceeds; this allows the borrower to raise the necessary funds and have the net liability in the chosen currency.
>
> (Gray and Place, 1999)

This view seriously underestimates the role of foreign exchange swaps as money market instruments, that is, in the provision of liquidity to bank balance sheets. This function of foreign exchange swaps arises because the traditional money market is a market for unsecured lending between banks. Since 1988, such unsecured lending has been penalised under the Basel Agreements by a requirement to have capital set aside against the 'risks' inherent in unsecured lending. In the case of foreign exchange swaps, these risks are almost wholly eliminated, reduced to counter-party risk, because each contract in a swap agreement is hedged either by long-term security, or a reverse swap contract. This means that banks do not have to put aside considerably less capital against foreign exchange swaps. While such swaps may seem a complex way of raising short-term liquidity, the minimal scale of risk capital requirements simplifies the procedures for conducting liquidity operations.

The growing use of foreign exchange swaps is also reflected in the liquidity of the market (Stenfors, 2018; Stenfors and Lindo, 2018). For instance, Figure 4.6 shows a comparison between indicative bid-ask spreads for $/¥ 3-month foreign exchange swaps, as well as for 3-month US dollar and yen inter-bank deposit rates. Using this standard proxy for price-based market liquidity, we can see how the foreign exchange swap market became more liquid than the traditional money market already during the late 1990s.

The growing use of foreign exchange swaps has serious implications for the conduct of monetary policy. Since the 1990s, central banks have regarded

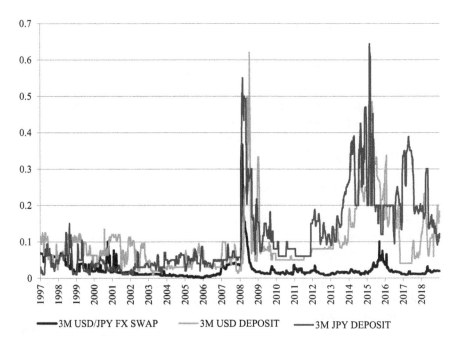

Figure 4.6 Indicative bid-ask spreads 12.08.1997–30.09.2019 (%)

Sources: Bloomberg, Federal Reserve Bank of St. Louis and authors' calculations. Notes: 20-day moving median prices using daily closing bid and ask prices. The daily deposit closing bid and ask prices are averages of the Tokyo, London and New York closing prices.

their control over overnight rates in the inter-bank market as a measure of the effectiveness of the 'monetary transmission mechanism'. However, with foreign exchange swaps displacing the market for unsecured inter-bank borrowing as the key market for bank liquidity, it is obvious the rate of interest in the inter-bank market can no longer be regarded as representative of the cost of short-term funds for banks. Moreover, the advent of 'quantitative easing' in 2001 in Japan, and 2010 in Europe and North America, brought that official money market 'onto the balance sheet of the central banks' in the sense that the official inter-bank market now responds to the initiatives of central banks, rather than to the liquidity needs of banks. The latter are more efficiently met in the foreign exchange swap market. Monetary policy has been reduced to 'manipulating' interest rates in much the same way that LIBOR rates have been acknowledged to have been manipulated by banks setting those rates.

4   Concluding discussion

Japanese banks have been attracted to settle in the international money markets by the need to fund their foreign acquisitions, using foreign exchange swaps to 'hedge' their non-yen assets. This has brought Japanese banks into a complex system of international money markets in which foreign exchange swaps serve as money market instruments rather than as derivatives or hedging devices. In turn, this means that the Bank of Japan no longer has the control over inter-bank liquidity that has traditionally been deemed necessary for the conduct of monetary policy.

This can be illustrated through the policy response to the Japanese banking crisis and to the 2007–08 financial crisis. Domestic liquidity injections during the early days of the 2007–08 financial crisis, or like those of the Bank of Japan during the Japanese banking crisis, were not sufficient to dampen demand by banks since only the Federal Reserve could provide US dollar reserves. Since the demand for dollars was particularly severe for banks outside the US, an international response involving the Federal Reserve was necessary to offer US dollar liquidity. This led to unprecedented co-ordinated international central bank action, led by the Federal Reserve. Temporary reciprocal currency arrangements in the form of foreign exchange swap lines were established with the Federal Reserve to channel dollars to banks in other jurisdictions (Baba and Packer, 2009; McGuire and von Peter, 2012). In December 2007, swap lines were set up with the European Central Bank and the Swiss National Bank. The market reaction was relatively muted. After the collapse of Lehman Brothers and a sharp move in the cross-currency swap and foreign exchange swap markets, the sizes of the central bank swap lines were increased considerably. Other central banks, including Bank of Japan, were added to the list of central banks with which foreign exchange swap lines were established. The dollar liquidity swap lines were designed to improve liquidity conditions in the dollar and foreign financial markets by providing foreign central banks with the capacity to deliver US dollar funding to institutions in their jurisdictions during times of market stress. When the network was created, only two countries with major international financial centres had sufficiently large foreign exchange reserves to serve their banks without the need to draw on foreign exchange swap lines: the United States and Japan (Allen and Moessner, 2010). The response was positive in the sense that markets quickly returned to relative stability from the extreme volatility experienced around the Lehman Brothers bankruptcy. Since, however, the foreign exchange markets have indicated continuing (or even elevated) stress in the international US dollar money market.

Thus, whereas the $/¥ foreign exchange swap market returned to 'normality' as a result of intervention by Japanese authorities following the domestic banking crisis, the establishment of the foreign exchange swap network with the Federal Reserve two decades later (to which the Bank of Japan belongs) now, instead, sets a theoretical cap on cost of borrowing US dollars. Although banks have been reluctant to tap into the foreign exchange swap network, the ability, and determination, to act as a market maker of last resort in the foreign exchange swap market has highlighted the importance of the Federal Reserve with its control over the world's reserve currency (Kaltenbrunner et al., 2010). The new institutional framework formalises an arrangement whereby the

Federal Reserve has an ability to act opportunistically, whereas the Bank of Japan is dependent on its foreign exchange reserve to be able to do so.

The previous considerations suggest that the targeting of the overnight inter-bank rate does not indicate effectiveness of the monetary transmission mechanism, since policy rates of interest in inter-bank markets are marginal to credit and financing decisions made in US dollar foreign exchange swap markets. With liquidity being provided in US dollar foreign exchange swaps, because most debt contracts are in US dollars, the monetary policy of the US Federal Reserve is perhaps even more important for Japanese banks than the monetary policy of the Bank of Japan.

Note

1 Even though Japan's economic high growth era lasted from early 1950 until mid-1970, it continued to grow on average 4% annually until the crisis in the early 1990s.

References

Allen, W. A. and Moessner, R. (2010) Central bank co-operation and international liquidity in the financial crisis of 2008–9, *BIS Working Papers*, No. 310.

Baba, N. and Packer, F. (2009) From turmoil to crisis: Dislocations in the FX swap market before and after the failure of Lehman brothers, *BIS Working Papers*, No. 285.

BIS (2005) Triennial Central Bank Survey: Foreign exchange and derivatives market activity in 2004, March.

BIS (2013) International banking and financial market developments, *BIS Quarterly Review*.

BIS (2015) Statistical release, BIS international banking statistics at end-March 2015, Monetary and Economic Department.

BIS (2019) Triennial Central Bank Survey of foreign exchange and Over-the-Counter (OTC) derivatives markets in 2019, September.

Borio, C., McCauley, R. N. and McGuire, P. (2017) FX swaps and forwards: Missing global debt, *BIS Quarterly Review*, 37–54, September.

The Economist (2011) Japanese banks: Back form the dead, *The Economist*. Available from: www.economist.com/node/18229432

Gabor, D. (2018) Shadow connections: On hierarchies of collateral in shadow banking, in Nesvetailova, A. (ed.) *Shadow Banking Scope, Origin and Theories*. Abingdon, UK: Routledge.

Grahl, J. and Lysandrou, P. (2006) Capital market trading volume: An overview and some preliminary conclusions, *Cambridge Journal of Economics*, 30 (6), 955–979, August.

Gray, S. and Place, J. (1999) *Financial Derivatives CCBS Handbook*, No. 17, London: Bank of England.

Hoshi, T. (2001) What happened to Japanese banks? *Monetary and Economic Studies*, February.

IMF (2015) Navigating monetary policy challenges and managing risks, *Global Financial Stability Report*, April.

Inagaki, K. (2015) Mizuho acquires RBS North America loan assets for $3bn, *The Financial Times*. Available from: www.ft.com/cms/s/0/6993617e-bd6b-11e4-b523-00144feab7de.html#axzz3lWGnIvwE

Kaltenbrunner, A., Lindo, D., Painceira, J. P. and Stenfors, A. (2010) The euro funding gap and its consequences, *Quarterly Journal of Central Banking*, 21 (2), 86–91.

Lam, W. R. (2013) Cross-border Activity of Japanese Banks, *IMF Working Paper*, No. WP/13/235.

Lewis, L. (2015) Japanese mega-banks step up search for foreign targets, *The Financial Times*. Available from: www.ft.com/cms/s/0/fdbbc84c-1260-11e5-bcc2-00144feabdc0.html?siteedition=uk#axzz3duY1Rwe1

McGuire, P. and von Peter, G. (2012) The dollar shortage in global banking and the international policy response, *International Finance*, 15, 155–178.

Miyajima, H. and Yafeh, Y. (2003) Japan's banking crisis: Who has the most to lose? *RIETI Discussion Paper Series*, No. 03-E-010.

Montgomery, H. and Takahashi, Y. (2011) The Japanese big bang: The effects of 'free, fair and global', *The Journal of Social Science*, 72, 49–71.

Peek, J. and Rosengren, E. S. (1999) Japanese banking problems: Implication for lending in the United States, *New England Economic Review*, January–February.

Seth, R. and Quijano, A. (1991) Japanese banks: Customers in the United States, *Federal Reserve Bank of New York Quarterly Review*, 79–82.

Slater, S. (2008) Nomura buys Lehman's Europe investment bank arm, *Reuters*. Available from: http://in.reuters.com/article/2008/09/23/idINIndia-35616020080923

Stenfors, A. (2018) Bid-ask spread determination in the FX swap market: Competition, collusion or a convention? *Journal of International Financial Markets, Institutions and Money*, 58, 78–97.

Stenfors, A. (2019) The covered interest parity puzzle and evolution of the Japan premium, *Journal of Economic Issues*, 53 (2).

Stenfors, A. and Lindo, D. (2018) Libor 1986–2021: The making and unmaking of 'the world's most important price', *Distinktion: Journal of Social Theory*, 19 (2), 170–192.

Story, L. and Sorkin, A. (2008) Morgan agrees to revise terms of Mitsubishi deal, *The New York Times*. Available from: www.nytimes.com/2008/10/13/business/13morgan.html

Taniguchi, T. and Sato, S. (2011) Mizuho may tap BlackRock stake to buy asset managers, *Bloomberg*. Available from: www.bloomberg.com/news/2011-02-14/mizuho-may-leverage-blackrock-stake-to-buy-asia-asset-firms.html

5 The Japanese balance sheet recession 20 years on

Abenomics – economic revival or corporate financialisation?

*Konstantin Bikas, Ewa Karwowski
and Mimoza Shabani*

1 Introduction

The Japanese economy has remained in poor health since the 1990s crisis the country experienced in the aftermath of the stock exchange and real estate market collapse. While the whole economy was hit hard by the crisis, the non-financial corporate (NFC) sector, in particular, witnessed a so-called balance sheet recession (Koo, 2011), which is characterised by high levels of debt and low investment rates. The latest reform package to tackle Japan's malaise was introduced in 2012 by the Japanese Prime Minister Shinzo Abe. Taking as a starting point that Japanese growth during its heyday was primarily driven by corporate investment, this chapter assesses the impact of Abenomics on the balance sheets of Japanese NFCs. Loose monetary policy, an important cornerstone of recent reforms, should tackle this problem, ensuring cheap credit for Japanese corporations. Hence, Abenomics could be the solution to the protracted stagnation in Japan. However, Abenomics has also been identified as an intrinsically neoliberal policy package, for instance, in its efforts to privatise state institutions (such as the Japanese Post Office [Robinson, 2017]). Thus, the suspicion arises that Abenomics might be contributing to corporate financialisation rather than a solution to the Japanese balance sheet recession.

We argue that the balance sheet recession is indeed over in Japan. Corporate liabilities have decreased since their peaks during the mid-1990s. But Abenomics has not achieved as much as hoped in bringing up private investment rates. While we do not find evidence for a US-style financialisation among Japanese corporations because financial assets make up a very small share of NFC's assets, cash holdings have sharply increased. Thus, Japanese firms are 'over-capitalised', i.e. they hold liquid assets beyond their needs. This trend has been reinforced since the introduction of Abenomics and is a symptom of firms' unwillingness to invest, which is at the root of corporate financialisation.

We begin by briefly describing some key facts in Japan's economic history with a focus on NFCs, the measures pursued as part of Abenomics in order to stimulate investment and their theoretical grounding. We then review the balance sheets of Japanese NFCs and show that they are no longer in a 'balance sheet recession' yet continue to hold a large amount of cash. Finally, we discuss whether the policies pursued can bring about corporate financialisation.

2   The lost decade in Japan and Abenomics

First, we will briefly provide some context to Japan's growth trajectory leading up to the 1990s crisis. It is argued that a significant contributing factor to the prolonged stagnation faced by the Japanese economy, often referred to as 'the lost decades', has been the drop in investment by NFCs after the said crisis. Finding a remedy for this problem has been a key focus of the policies pursued under Abenomics.

The early 1990s crisis came after what is commonly referred to as the 'miracle years' of the Japanese economy (1950–1973) when the annual average growth exceeded 9% (Iyoda, 2010). This was followed by more moderate growth rates of around 4% between the mid-1970s until the late 1980s leading to the early 1990s crisis which heralded more than two decades of stagnation (1992–2016) characterised by anaemic growth, hovering at around 1% of GDP (Figure 5.1).

The movements of the GDP indicator distinctly show the booms and busts of the Japanese economy along with the reduced amplitude describing the years of stagnation. Correspondingly, the shaded area shows the contribution of gross fixed capital formation as a proportion of GDP. Starting from the mid-1950s, the 'Jinmu boom'[1] (1956–1957), mainly driven by high private invest-ment (Sadahiro, 1991), set the stage for the 'Iwato[2] boom' (1959–1961), which has largely been attributed to new technologies and the investment demand that they generated. This was followed by the 'Olympic boom' (1962–1964), credited to the constriction projects required for the 1964 games held in Tokyo. The 'Izanagi[3] boom' started in 1965 and is attributed to consumer demand, rise in exports, housing and capital investment and the demand generated by US procurements for the Vietnam War (Nagata, 2016). This was followed by Tan-aka's 'remodeling the archipelago' boom starting in the early 1970s, driven by public investment and excessive money growth, which ended with the first oil crisis in 1973. Finally, the 'Heisei boom' beginning in the late 1980s and lead-ing into the early 1990s crisis is attributed to financial deregulation, which led to aggressive behaviour by financial institutions, the expansion of the monetary base and an overall climate of overconfidence and euphoria (Shiratsuka, 2005). These factors led to a hike in equity and land prices with the capital gains of land and stocks, reaching a staggering 452% of nominal GDP (Okina et al., 2001). A peculiar result of this process was that on the eve of the economic downturn, the aggregate market value of all land in Japan was four times that of the US according to a number of estimates (Cargill et al., 1997).

The beginning of the crisis is often traced to the Plaza Accord in 1985 (Wakatabe, 2015), which ensured the depreciation of the US dollar against the yen and the West German mark, in large to control the US trade deficit. As Japan is classified as an "export-led mercantilist type" economy (Dodig et al., 2015, p. 6), the fact that their exports became less competitive had important

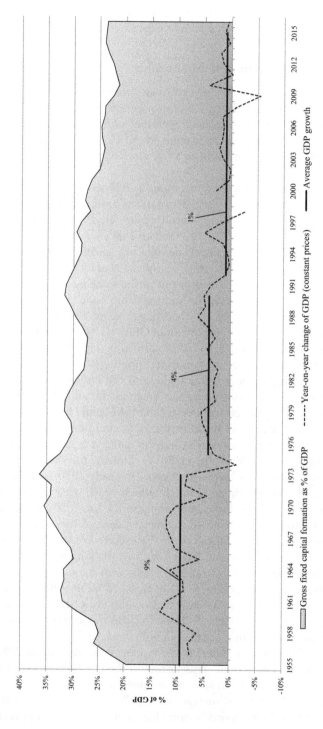

Figure 5.1 GDP growth and proportion of gross fixed capital formation (GFCF) to GDP

Source: Cabinet Office National Accounts.

Notes: Year on year change of GDP: calculations up to 1998 based on constant prices with 1990 as the benchmark year. For calculations from 1999 onward the benchmark year is 2011. GFCF as % of GDP: calculations based on market prices and up to 1998 have 1990 as benchmark year, from 1999 onward the benchmark year is 2011.

implications especially for NFCs and their investment decisions. In the three years after the Plaza Accord, the yen appreciated dramatically from around ¥238 to ¥128 per US dollar (OECD, 2019). The economic impact can be seen in Figure 5.1 as a small slump in GDP growth before the last bubble, which eventually pushed the economy into stagnation. As to the causes of the bubble, it is best explained as an outcome of multiple factors. Some of the most significant being (Okina et al., 2001): the progress of financial deregulation leading to the decline of the main bank system and the liberalisation of deposit interest rates along with the removal of restrictions in firm fundraising regulations. This resulted in banks becoming more aggressive in their search for profit and clients, leading to an increase in the supply of credit, which was used for the purchase of assets in the hope of their appreciation and consequent capital gains. This was coupled with a loose monetary policy by the authorities in their effort to limit the effects of the Plaza Accord and a tax and regulatory framework, which incentivised certain types of investment.

In spring 1989 the Bank of Japan changed its accommodative monetary stance. The discount rate was raised by 3.5% to 6% and new regulations on loans were put in place (Grabowiecki and Dabrowski, 2017), both critical factors contributing to the burst of the bubble. As a result, the stock market depreciated by around 60% within the next two years and continued to decline up to June 1995 (Cargill et al., 1997). This was accompanied by 87% deflation of commercial real estate prices (Koo, 2011).

As stated previously, our focus is on the implications of the crisis and subsequent stagnation on NFCs and their role. The views presented here are in line with those of Koo and the balance sheet recession theory. Fundamental tenets of this theory are that in a balance sheet recession, "the private sector . . . is minimizing debt instead of maximizing profits following the bursting of a nation-wide asset price bubble . . . reduc[ing] aggregate demand and throwing the economy into a very special type of recession" (Koo, 2011, p. 19).

A primary consequence of this debt minimisation and repayment following a crisis is investment expenditure as the private sector, i.e. both financial institutions and non-financial companies, seek to reduce their debts and exposures. This can then lead to a protracted period of trauma, where expenditures and borrowing fail to pick up. A look at the investment expenditure by NFCs along with their net lending or borrowing position (Figure 5.2), re-affirm Koo's position.

Aramaki (2018) separates the stagnation in four periods, 'the initial adjustment period' after the burst of the bubble (1991–1997), 'the financial crisis and its impacts' (1998–2002), 'the long recovery period' (2003–2007) and 'the global financial crisis and after' to argue that it is likely that the reasons for the sustained restraint when it comes to investment by companies might be different for these four periods. According to him, it can be attributed to "the hangover of excessive assets and liabilities" for the first two periods (ibid., p. 249) following the burst of the early 1990s bubble and the financial crisis, in line with Koo's argument. However, given that for the third and fourth periods

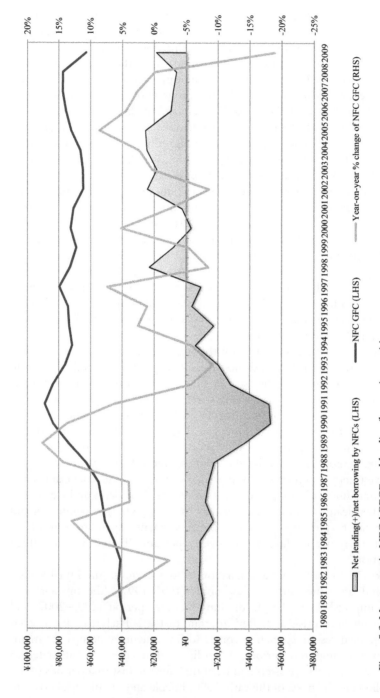

Figure 5.2 Movements in NFCs' GFCF and lending/borrowing position

Source: Cabinet Office, national accounts of 2011.

Notes: The benchmark year is 2000.

of stagnation a large part of the difficulties that followed the bubble and the subsequent financial crisis had been overcome, the reasons for this restraint can perhaps be found in a mixture of two factors. On the one hand, it can be attributed to irrational defensiveness by companies, sort of as a remaining trauma from the events in the early to mid-1990s. On the other, it may be due to the stagnant expectations for the prospects of the domestic economy in relation to the opportunities to be found overseas. Regardless of the reason, the lack of investment in conjunction with its implications on the potential growth rate and wage restraint as part of the defensiveness exhibited by Japanese corporations has induced grave consequences for domestic demand and therefore for economic growth.

3   The aims of Abenomics measures concerning promoting investment

Shinzo Abe was elected for a second time as prime minister in December 2012, after having stepped down in 2007 just a year after assuming office due to "illness, policy setbacks and a slew of scandals" (Nakamoto et al., 2012, para. 5).

The primary aim of Abe, as with many of his predecessors, has been to end decades of stagnation and deflation, returning to sustainable economic growth. The policy package launched, dubbed 'three arrows of Abenomics', was composed of fiscal stimulus, massive monetary expansion and structural reforms in line with a growth strategy, which to a large extent aimed at promoting private investment. The combined aim of the three arrows was to achieve "a vibrant economy that will register over 2% labor productivity in the medium-to long-term, and around 3% nominal gross domestic product (GDP) growth and around 2% real GDP growth, on average, over the next ten years" (Prime Minister of Japan and His Cabinet – Kantei, 2013, p. 2).

The monetary arrow

By far the most pronounced measures have been those taken on the monetary front. In this pursuit, Prime Minister Abe needed a strong ally in the key position of the central bank's governor, which he found when Kuroda assumed his current office in March 2013.

Soon after, in April 2013 the Bank of Japan introduced Quantitative and Qualitative Monetary Easing (QQE): the monetary base became the main operating target instead of the uncollateralised overnight call rate, an inflation target of 2% was introduced and large-scale asset purchases at a rate of ¥60–70 trillion per year was initiated (Bank of Japan, 2013).

Governor Kuroda summarised the main channels through which he expected the stimulus to be transmitted in a speech to the Yomiuri International Economic Society in Tokyo in April 2013. First, he argued the purchase of Japanese government bonds (JGBs), exchange-traded funds (ETFs) and Japanese real estate investment trusts (J-REITs) would create downward pressure on long-term rates and decrease risk premia, stimulating demand for credit. Second, the continuation of asset purchases from investors and private institutions would eventually lead them into switching their portfolios to holding riskier assets and stimulating lending activity. The last transmission channel he mentioned was the impact that the commitment to generate inflation would have on the expectations of markets and economic entities.

In a further pursuit to instigate investment either by increasing the availability of credit, pushing investors to riskier assets (away from government bonds) and changing market expectations, QQE was increased to ¥80 trillion in 2014. A negative interest rate of -0.1% on a portion of financial institutions' deposits held at the Bank of Japan was introduced in 2016 in addition to other measures such as lengthening the maturity of JGB eligible for purchase (2015). Finally, in 2016, the target of monetary policy was changed from monetary base control to maintaining the short-term and long-term interest rates at -0.1% and around 0% respectively. The former rate applied to "policy-rate balances in current accounts held by financial institution at the Bank" and the latter by ensuring through purchases that the 10-year JGB maintain their yield at the said level (Bank of Japan, 2016, pp. 1–2).

The fiscal arrow

On the fiscal front, in January 2013, the Cabinet Office of Japan announced a ¥20.2 trillion financial package (just under $207 billion) of which ¥10.3 trillion was for government expenditure, as part of its 'Emergency Economic Measures for the Revitalization of the Japanese Economy'. Around 27% of the total amount was aimed at disaster prevention and reconstruction following the 2011 Tohoku earthquake and tsunami, 60% predominately for the stimulation of private investment and measures for small and medium-sized enterprises (SMEs), with the remaining amount targeting regional revitalisation and "ensuring a sense of security in daily life" (Cabinet Office, 2013a). This was followed by the 'Economic Measures for the Realization of Virtuous Cycles' package in December of the same year which totalled approximately ¥18.6 trillion (¥5.5 trillion by central government) of which 70% was aimed at measures to "strengthen competitiveness" by targeting the promotion of investments, innovations, infrastructure, energy efficiency and SMEs amongst others (Cabinet Office, 2013b). In December 2014, the 'Immediate Economic Measures for Extending Virtuous Cycles to Local Economies' was announced, totalling ¥3.5 trillion – all government expenditure, mostly aimed at stimulating consumption, job creation and reconstruction (Cabinet Office, 2014). Another package of ¥28.1 trillion was announced in August 2016, titled 'Economic Measures for Realizing Investment for the Future'. The fiscal component accounted for ¥13.5 trillion, primarily aimed at infrastructure developments (38% of total), 39% was aimed mitigating risks due to Brexit with a focus for SMEs and microenterprises and measures supporting the dynamic engagement of the population (such as boosting income and consumption through working-style reform, shortening of pensionable period and other items) accounted for about 12% of the total package (Cabinet Office, 2016).

The growth strategy arrow

In June 2013, the Abe administration set off its third arrow titled 'Japan Revitalization Strategy – Japan is Back', which had three action plans: measures to revitalise the industry, a strategic market creation plan and a strategy for global outreach. It was the beginning of a series of annual announcements, which have since fine-tuned policies and implemented a plethora of measures aimed at structurally reforming the Japanese economy and society. As part of this strategy, it was recognised early on that for the fiscal and monetary arrows not to be temporary, "the vast quantity of funds which lie idle in companies must be directed towards investments that generate future values" (Prime Minister of Japan and His Cabinet – Kantei, 2013, p. 3).

In light of this and in line with Aramaki (2018), part of the reforms in this third arrow has aimed at corporate governance in Japanese firms to induce risk-taking on a management level (Kojima, 2014). Measures have been implemented to introduce external board members in corporations such as the Companies Act of 2015 along with a reduction on the corporate tax rate (Aramaki, 2018, pp. 292–293), in an effort to change the prevailing defensive mindset.

4   The balance sheet recession among Japanese NFCs

As mentioned earlier, the prolonged Japanese recession in the aftermath of the crisis the country experienced in the early 1990s has been labelled as a "balance sheet recession" (Koo, 2011). Even though the Japanese economy has since recovered, albeit at a slow pace, the behaviour of Japanese corporations remains a topic that receives a significant amount of attention, by both academics and policymakers. The key issue is that even though corporate liabilities have decreased, private investment remains an ongoing concern. Indeed, using the Corporate Financial Statements for all industries, excluding finance and insurance, available from the Ministry of Finance, Japanese NFCs appear to have continued the deleveraging process, which started in the mid-1990s. Figure 5.3 shows the leverage ratio, defined here as total liabilities as a share of total assets for all Japanese NFCs, by size.[4]

It is evident that large NFCs have historically had lower levels of debt, with their share of total assets showing a decrease of more than 30% by 2018 compared to the 1970s. A similar trend is observed for all NFC sizes. This suggests that Japanese NFCs have been reluctant to borrow despite interest rates being at a historically low level, as shown in Figure 5.4. Interest rates on borrowing for all NFCs have declined substantially from around 7% in the early 1990s to 1% in the most recent years.

This particular trend, low levels of debt despite falling interest rates, is associated with low investment growth and has been a concern since the 1990s crisis.

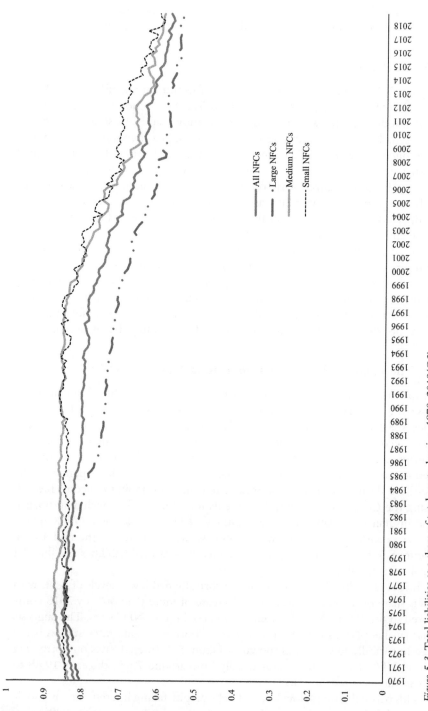

Figure 5.3 Total liabilities as a share of total assets, by size, 1970–2018(Q3)

Source: Ministry of Finance, 'Financial Statements Statistics of Corporations by Industry'

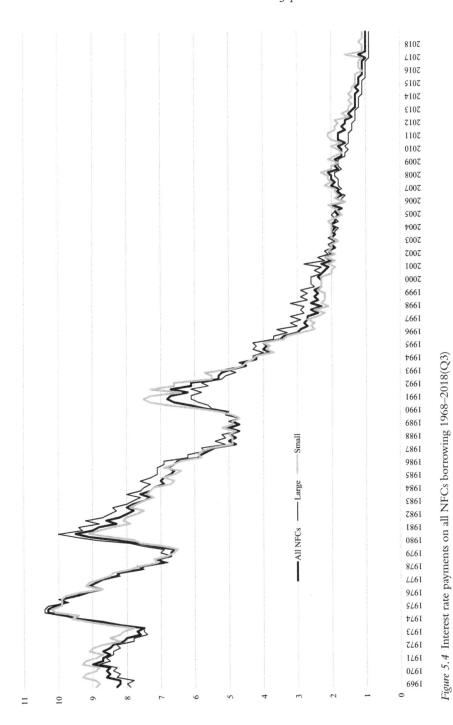

Figure 5.4 Interest rate payments on all NFCs borrowing 1968–2018(Q3)

Source: Ministry of Finance, 'Financial Statements Statistics of Corporations by Industry'

More specifically, the issue concerns private investment, which has largely been the main contributor to the reduction of total investment in Japan since the early 1990s (Kang, 2014). As shown in Figure 5.5, total investment constituted more than 30% of GDP in the early 1990s, reaching its lowest level, 20% of GDP, in 2009, during the global financial crisis. Even though investment has picked up since then, it remains at moderate levels.

Although the reforms under Abenomics were overall deemed "successful" by the IMF in 2017, private investment levels were still an ongoing concern (IMF, 2017). Indeed, the report states that reforms to boost private investment needed to be a continued priority. More particularly, "further corporate governance reforms could help deploy cash reserves and boost investment" (IMF, 2017).

Historically, Japanese corporations have had large cash holdings. The 1990s crisis left corporations with mounting debt levels. Consequently, they began paying back their debt using their cash and deposits throughout the decade following the crisis. However, even after servicing their debt obligations, they continued to retain a large amount of cash on their balance sheet. Kang (2014) notes that by early 2000, Japanese corporation holdings of cash were at the same level as during the 1980s, at a time when investment levels were also high. Similarly, Sher (2014) also points to the high levels of Japanese corporation of cash holdings. The amount of cash assets in 2013 was 50% of GDP and 250% of total investment, which is a significant difference to the cash holdings for 1995, which were 40% of GDP and 130% of total investment (Sher, 2014).

In line with these arguments, the corporate survey data used in this section reveals the high ratio of cash and deposits to total assets, shown in Figure 5.6, associated with all Japanese NFCs. Between the early 1990s and 2008, cash and deposit holdings have declined steadily; however, there seems to be an upward trend since then. Kang (2014) argues that this is mainly due to the increased uncertainty associated with global economic activity following the global financial crisis. Furthermore, the sustained hoarding of cash by Japanese NFCs could be a continued attribute to moderate levels of Japanese private investment, thus acting as a barrier to the success of Abenomics (Sher, 2014).

However, the analysis of NFCs is incomplete when not taking into account the liabilities side of the balance sheet. To provide a better picture of the behaviour of NFCs, we calculate the overcapitalisation ratio, defined here as liquid assets to liquid liabilities, for large NFCs. Toporowski (2008) suggests that overcapitalisation is the process by which NFCs increasingly hold liquid assets, in response to the capital market inflation. That is, in good times, NFCs can raise finance by means of issuing equity and hold the proceeds in liquid assets. On the other hand, when equity market conditions are poor, NFCs can adjust the impact on their equity price by increasing dividends or share buybacks. Therefore, by holding onto liquid assets, NFCs are in effect employing a safe strategy.

Figure 5.7 shows that from 1970 until the early 2000s, the overcapitalisation ratio has remained relatively constant. In situations when NFCs hold high levels of debt and out of precaution also increase their holding of liquid assets,

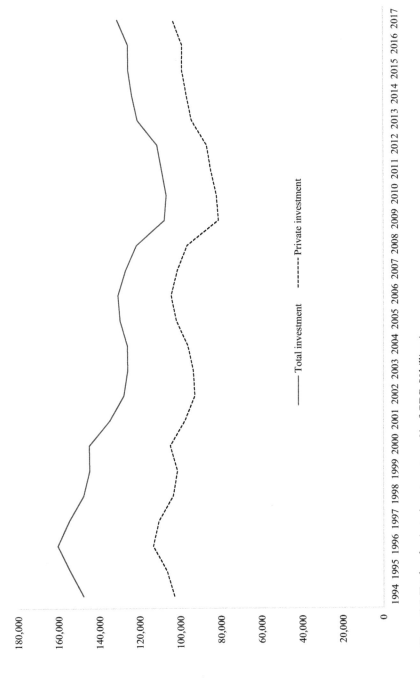

Figure 5.5 Total and private investment as a % of GDP (¥ billions)

Source: Cabinet Office, National Accounts

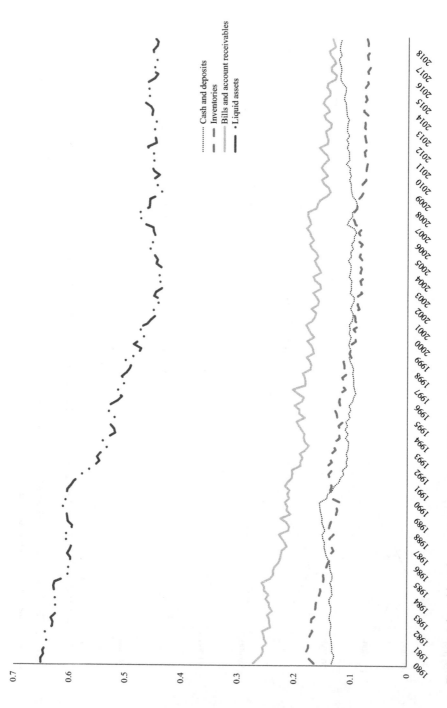

Figure 5.6 Selected liquid assets to total assets, all NFC sizes, 1980–2018(Q3)

Source: Ministry of Finance, 'Financial Statements Statistics of Corporations by Industry'

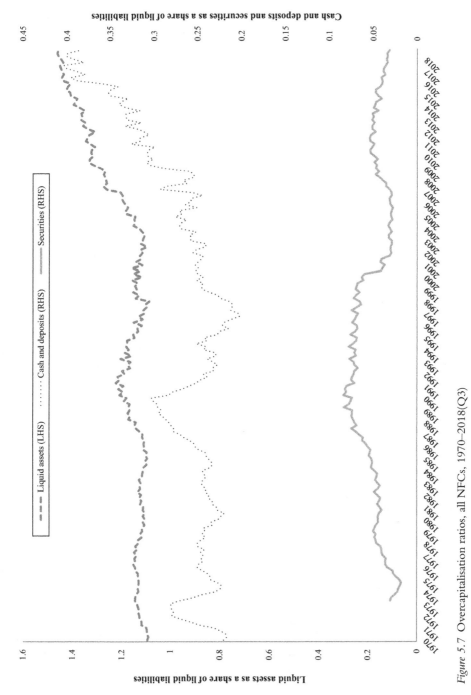

Figure 5.7 Overcapitalisation ratios, all NFCs, 1970–2018(Q3)

Source: Ministry of Finance, 'Financial Statements Statistics of Corporations by Industry'

the overcapitalisation ratio should not change much. However, for the case of Japanese NFCs, the ratio has grown steadily since the mid-2000s. Even though they have low levels of debt, they continue to expand their holdings in liquid assets. Cash and deposits as a share of liquid liabilities have fluctuated more than liquid assets. Their ratio was in the range of 0.20 in the period between the early 1970s and early 1990s. It seems that Japanese NFCs reduced their holdings of cash and deposits to liquid liabilities ratio during the crisis and the subsequent stagnation. However, after 2009, this ratio has significantly increased. According to Ivanova and Raei (2014 cited in Kang, 2014), this corporate behaviour is also evident in many other advanced economies, such as the US and Germany. The securities to liquid liabilities ratio of Japanese NFCs, on the other hand, has fallen since the early 2000s.

5   Are Japanese NFCs financialised?

Japan in recent years has gone through a privatisation wave, with the Japanese Post Office privatised in 2015, Kansai and Osaka International Airport in 2016 and more recently Fukuoka Airport in 2019. These, together with some of the Abenomics reforms (especially the 'third arrow'), are often described as neoliberal reforms. With these developments in place, Robinson (2017) argues that Japan is undergoing financialisation.

There are many symptoms of NFCs' behaviour predicted by financialisation theory. In such, the shareholder value concept (Lazonick and O'Sullivan, 2000; Stockhammer, 2004) highlights the increased pressures of NFCs to improve their financial performance as reflected in high share prices. Faced with this type of pressure, NFCs are prone to leverage their balance sheet to maintain and improve shareholder value. In effect, this should be captured in the debt-to-equity ratios, but Figure 5.8 shows no such evidence among Japanese NFCs. In contrast, the ratio of debt to equity has steadily declined since the mid-1980s, recovering slightly in the mid-1990s, continuing to fall again thereafter.

Furthermore, financialisation theory argues that NFCs, in an attempt to boost shareholder value, increase dividend payments and share buybacks. Indeed, in recent years, Japanese corporations have announced substantial share buybacks amounting to over ¥6 trillion (Lewis, 2019; Tomisawa and John, 2019). Two potential factors could explain this surge in share buybacks. First, the introduction of Japan's Stewardship Code and Corporate Governance Code, in 2014 and 2015, respectively, aimed to increase shareholder value. Second, Japanese corporations have expanded their overseas operations since the mid-1990s, partly due to being more profitable relative to those realised by domestic production (Aramaki, 2018). A potential implication of the internationalisation of Japanese NFCs would likely place them under pressure to maintain high shareholder value in the face of host country competition.

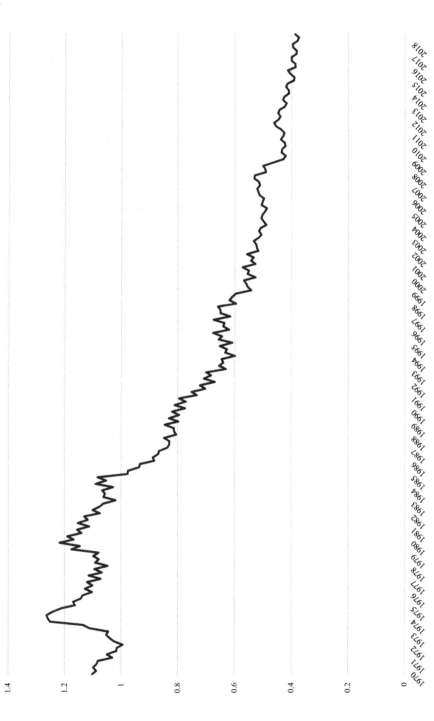

Figure 5.8 Debt to equity ratio, large NFCs, 1970–2018(Q3)

Source: Ministry of Finance, 'Financial Statements Statistics of Corporations by Industry'.

Notes: Equity represents total assets minus liquid liabilities

The international expansion of Japanese NFCs is reflected in outward foreign direct investment (FDI), as shown in Figure 5.9. As can be seen, total world outward FDI has increased substantially since mid-2004, with a decline during 2008–2010 and then picking up thereafter. As of 2017, the outward FDI flow accounted for nearly 35% of GDP. Japanese FDI to Asia and the US seems to have fallen, while increasing to Europe, since 2015.

Another aspect of financialisation is related to the process of moving from normal production activities to financial investment (Krippner, 2005), as a quicker, more profitable way for corporations. Figure 5.10 shows the net interest received by all Japanese NFCs and other non-operating revenue, defined here as other profits as a share of total profits. It can be seen that the net interest income ratio was negative starting in 1984, but turned positive and has remained so since 2012. In 2015 the net interest income received was around 15% of total profits, declining slightly after that. Other profits accounted, on average, for around 35% of total profits during the early 2000s, decreasing from 45% during their peak in the mid-1990s. More recently, they have accounted for approximately 20% of total profits.

If financial operations would be more important for income generation, then the share of financial assets in total assets can be expected to increase. Looking at securities and other financial investment[5] by Japanese NFCs, there is a clear downward trend in the ratio of securities to total assets since the early 2000s, as shown in Figure 5.11. This figure also reinforces the earlier findings that Japanese NFCs have increased their hoarding of cash and deposits since 2009.

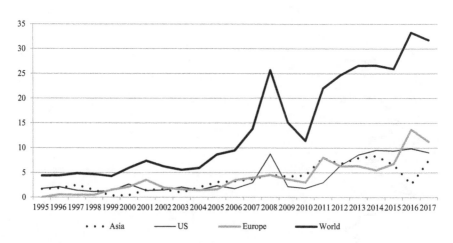

Figure 5.9 Outward FDI stock, by selected country/region (% of GDP)

Source: JETRO, Cabinet Office, National Accounts

Figure 5.10 Net interest received and other profits as a % of total profits, all NFCs, 1984–2018(Q3)

Source: Ministry of Finance, 'Financial Statements Statistics of Corporations by Industry'.

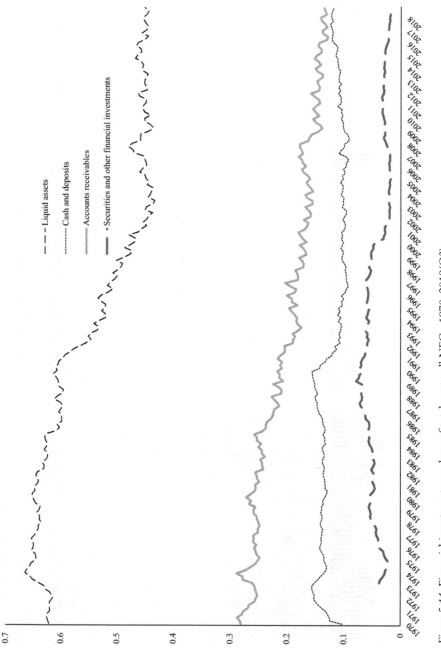

Figure 5.11 Financial investment as a share of total assets, all NFCs, 1970–2018(Q3)

Source: Ministry of Finance, 'Financial Statements Statistics of Corporations by Industry'

6 Conclusion

This chapter has analysed the behaviour of Japanese NFCs, with a focus on recent years, particularly since the Abenomics reforms were introduced. Japan has been associated with low levels of investment following the crisis the country experienced during the 1990s.

There is still no sign of any significant improvement in the level of investment, which remains at moderate levels. On the other hand, the balance sheet recession of Japanese corporations is indeed over. Furthermore, while liabilities of NFCs have steadily decreased since the 1990s crisis, they continue to hoard large amounts of cash.

Aramaki (2018) suggests that Japanese corporations in the aftermath of the 1990s crises converged towards defensive behaviour by avoiding risk-taking. Their search for safety has led them to hold liquid assets beyond their needs, thus leading to them being overcapitalised. The findings already discussed suggest that Abenomics reforms have not been successful in inducing private investment to increase, despite measures taken, especially in the monetary front. Monetary policy measures adopted by the Bank of Japan since Abe took office in 2012 have been associated with higher levels of cash hoarding by Japanese corporations. Indeed, as of end-2018 cash and deposit holdings of Japanese NFCs have increased by more than 31% since the first quarter of 2014.

Nevertheless, it is worth noting here that foreign investment has been growing relative to domestic investment (Aramaki, 2018). This, on the other hand, indicates that Japanese corporations have yet to recover their confidence in their domestic market. Furthermore, whilst it has been argued that Japan's economy has become financialised (Robinson, 2017), we find little evidence that Japanese NFCs are financialised as the share of financial investments remain low. While there has been a trend toward the shareholder value concept, by increasing share buybacks, we argue that this is a process instigated by internationalisation rather financialisation.

Notes

1 Named after the country's first emperor.
2 A reference to an episode in Japanese mythology.
3 A deity in Japanese mythology.
4 The database classifies NFCs by their size of capital: large NFCs consist of ¥1 billion or over, medium are ¥100 million to ¥1 billion and small are ¥10 to ¥100 million. All NFCs consist of all industries, excluding finance and insurance.
5 This includes securities, stock, bonds and debentures and other securities.

References

Aramaki, K. (2018) *Japan's Long Stagnation, Deflation, and Abenomics: Mechanisms and Lessons.* Singapore: McMillan.

Bank of Japan (2013) *Introduction of the 'Quantitative and Qualitative Monetary Easing',* 4 April. Available from: www.boj.or.jp/en/announcements/release_2013/k130404a.pdf [Accessed 28 October 2019].

Bank of Japan (2016) *New Framework for Strengthening Monetary Easing: 'Quantitative and Qualitative Monetary Easing with Yield Curve Control'*, 21 September. Available from: www.boj.or.jp/en/announcements/release_2016/k160921a.pdf [Accessed 28 October 2019].

Cabinet Office (2013a) *Emergency Economic Measures for the Revitalization of the Japanese Economy*, Government of Japan, 11 January. Available from: https://www5.cao.go.jp/keizai1/2013/130111_emergency_economic_measures.pdf [Accessed 28 October 2019].

Cabinet Office (2013b) *Economic Measures for Realization of Virtuous Cycles*, Government of Japan, 5 December. Available from: https://www5.cao.go.jp/keizai1/2013/20131205_economic_measures_all.pdf [Accessed 28 October 2019].

Cabinet Office (2014) *Immediate Economic Measures for Extending Virtuous Cycles to Local Economies*, Government of Japan, 27 December. Available from: https://www5.cao.go.jp/keizai1/keizaitaisaku/2014/141227_economic_measures_all.pdf [Accessed 28 October 2019].

Cabinet Office (2016) *Economic Measures for Realizing Investment for the Future*, Government of Japan, 2 August. Available from: https://www5.cao.go.jp/keizai1/keizaitaisaku/2016/20160802_economic_measures.pdf [Accessed 28 October 2019].

Cargill, T. F., Hutchison, M. M. and Ito, T. (1997) *The Political Economy of Japanese Monetary Policy*. Cambridge, MA: MIT Press.

Dodig, N., Hein, E. and Detzer, D. (2015) Financialisation and the financial and economic crises: Theoretical framework and empirical analysis for 15 countries, *FESSUD Studies in Financial Systems Working Paper Series*, No. 110, University of Leeds.

Grabowiecki, J. and Dabrowski, M. (2017) Abenomics and its impact on the economy of Japan, *Optimum. Studia Ekonomiczne*, 5 (89), 23–35.

Iyoda, M. (2010) *Postwar Japanese Economy: Lessons of Economic Growth and the Bubble Economy*. New York: Springer.

Kang, J. S. (2014) Balance sheet repair and corporate investment in Japan, *IMF Working Paper*, No. 14-141.

Kojima, A. (2014) Foreign investors who became the largest stockholders, and corporate governance reform in Japan', *Discuss Japan, Japan Foreign Policy Forum*, No. 23, 29 October. Available from: www.japanpolicyforum.jp/economy/pt20141029221609.html [Accessed 28 October 2019].

Koo, C. R. (2011) The world in balance sheet recession: Causes, cure and politics, *Real-World Economics Review*, 58, 19–37.

Krippner, G. R. (2005) The financialization of the American economy, *Socio-Economic Review*, 3 (2), 173–208.

Kuroda, H. (2013) Quantitative and qualitative monetary easing, *Speech at a Meeting Held by the Yomiuri International Economic Society in Tokyo*, Bank of Japan, 12 April. Available from: www.boj.or.jp/en/announcements/press/koen_2013/data/ko130412a1.pdf[Accessed 28 October 2019].

Lazonick, W. and O'Sullivan, M. (2000) Maximizing shareholder value: A new ideology for corporate governance, *Economy and Society*, 29 (1), 13–35.

Lewis, L. (2019) Japan's buyback boom has the smell of activism, *The Financial Times*, 19 February. Available from: www.ft.com/content/ae9f218e-3456-11e9-bb0c-42459962a812 [Accessed 28 October 2019].

Nagata, T. (2016) The Japanese economy: Current status and outlook, in Japan Institute for Labour Policy and Training, International Affairs Department (eds.) *Labor Situation in Japan and Its Analysis: General Overview 2015/2016*, pp. 2–13. Tokyo, The Japan Institute for Labour Policy and Training.

Nakamoto, M., Dickie, M. and Soble, J. (2012) LDP crushes rivals in Japanese poll, *Financial Times*, 16 December. Available from: www.ft.com/content/41186cb6-4735-11e2-8f03-00144feab49a [Accessed 18 April 2019].

OECD (2019) *Dataset: Monthly Monetary and Financial Statistics (MEI)*. Available from: https://stats.oecd.org/index.aspx?queryid=169# [Accessed 18 April 2019].

Okina, K., Shirakawa, M. and Shiratsuka, S. (2001) The asset price bubble and monetary policy: Japan's experience in the late 1980s and the lessons', *Monetary and Economic Studies (Special Edition)*, 19 (2), 395–450.

Prime Minister of Japan and His Cabinet – Kantei (2013) *Japan Revitalization Strategy – Japan Is Back*, Prime Minister's Office of Japan, 14 June. Available from: www.kantei.go.jp/jp/singi/keizaisaisei/pdf/en_saikou_jpn_hon.pdf [Accessed 31 October 2019].

Robinson, G. (2017) Pragmatic financialisation: The role of the Japanese Post Office, *New Political Economy*, 22 (1), 61–75.

Sadahiro, A. (1991) The Japanese economy during the era of high economic growth retrospect and evaluation, *Government of Japan: Economic Planning Agency Working Paper*, No. 4.

Sher, G. (2014) Cashing in for growth: Corporate cash holdings as an opportunity for investment in Japan, *IMF Working Paper*, No. 14-221.

Shiratsuka, S. (2005) The asset price bubble in Japan in the 1980s: lessons for financial and macroeconomic stability, *BIS Papers*, No. 21

Stockhammer, E. (2004) Financialization and the slowdown of accumulation, *Cambridge Journal of Economics*, 28 (5), 719–741.

Tomisawa, A. and John, A. (2019) Cash-hoarding Japanese firms please investors as share buybacks hits record, *Reuters*, 17 February. Available from: https://uk.reuters.com/article/japan-stocks-buybacks/cash-hoarding-japanese-firms-please-investors-as-share-buybacks-hit-record-idUKL3N20941K [Accessed 28 October 2019].

Toporowski, J. (2008) Excess capital and liquidity management, *Levy Economics Institute Working Paper*, No. 549.

Wakatabe, M. (2015) *Japan's Great Stagnation and Abenomics: Lessons for the World*. New York: Macmillan.

6 An analysis of the impact of the Bank of Japan's monetary policy on Japanese government bonds' low nominal yields

Tanweer Akram and Huiqing Li

1 Introduction

The nominal yields of long-term Japanese government bonds (JGBs) have been exceptionally low for several decades. This persistence, particularly amid the rising and elevated ratios of government debt, is contrary to the conventional view, which is that higher debt ratios lead to higher government bond yields as investors become concerned about the sustainability of government debt and begin to worry about the increased prospect of debt default. However, the low nominal yields of JGBs are consistent with Keynes's view that the central bank's actions have a decisive influence on long-term government bonds' yields as the Bank of Japan (BOJ) has kept its policy rates low and has undertaken accommodative monetary policy.

The conventional view has guided the mainstream empirical analysis of the dynamics of JGB yields. Analysts acknowledge that JGB yields have stayed persistently low despite a high government debt ratio. Nevertheless, an examination of their arguments and conclusions shows that mainstream analysts firmly believe JGB yields will eventually rise sharply unless authorities can stabilize and reduce the government debt ratio, and that there is a realistic risk of debt default.

In contradistinction to the conventional view, this chapter explains the persistence of low JGB yields from a Keynesian view. It argues that this provides the appropriate framework for understanding the dynamics of JGB yields. The approach taken here is descriptive. The perspective adopted here is based on econometric evidence presented in studies carried out by Akram and Das (2014) and Akram and Li (2018), which show that the Keynesian framework is much more consistent with the observed dynamics of JGBs.

The chapter is arranged as follows. Section 2 describes the evolution of JGBs' nominal yields and puts it in the context of key macroeconomic developments in the Japanese economy. Section 3 explains the conventional view of the drivers of long-term interest rates. Section 4 presents the Keynesian framework as an alternative to the conventional view. Section 5 examines the theoretical and policy implications of the findings. Section 6 concludes with a summary.

2 The evolution of JGB nominal yields and the Japanese economy

A review of the evolution of JGB nominal yields since 1990 reveals that nominal yields on JGBs fell sharply in the mid-1990s. The sharp decline in yields occurred as asset bubbles in the Japanese equities market and the real estate markets came to an end (Akram, 2014 and 2016; Garside, 2012). JGB yields have remained low since then (Figure 6.1). The data in all the figures below are from Macrobond (various years). The yields on JGBs turned very low after the turn of the 21st century. They declined again in the aftermath of the recessions during the global financial crisis and after the Tohoku earthquake. They also declined in response to the launch of the BOJ's quantitative and qualitative monetary easing (QQE) program, which was followed by the adoption of negative interest rates and, subsequently, yield curve control. In fact, nominal yields on JGBs crossed into negative territory in early 2016 as the BOJ's policy shifted to QQE with yield curve control.

Along with the decline in the nominal JGB yields, the standard deviation of JGB yields has fallen noticeably since the mid-1990s (Figure 6.2). This means that the day-to-day volatility of JGB yields has declined as well.

Government debt ratios in Japan have been elevated (Figure 6.3), rising sharply between 1990 to 2018, as measured as net debt and gross debt ratios. This increase occurred because the country had been running fiscal deficits consistently since the mid-1990s (Figure 6.4). Fiscal deficits widened sharply in the late 1990s and stayed wide until 2005. For a few years before the global financial crisis, fiscal deficits did narrow, but with the onset of the financial crisis, they widened again. In recent years, fiscal deficits have again narrowed because of the moderate improvement in economic growth. The rise in government debt ratios is due to various factors, including slower economic growth, fiscal stimulus, increased transfers and the ageing of the population.

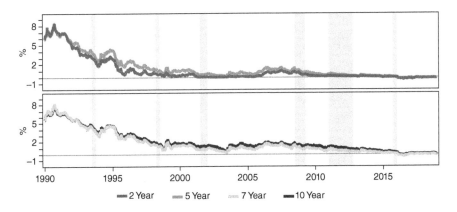

Figure 6.1 The evolution of Japanese government bond (JGB) nominal yields, 1990–2018

Source: Macrobond

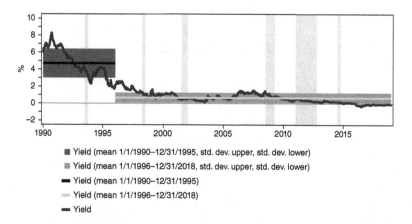

■ Yield (mean 1/1/1990–12/31/1995, std. dev. upper, std. dev. lower)
■ Yield (mean 1/1/1996–12/31/2018, std. dev. upper, std. dev. lower)
━ Yield (mean 1/1/1990–12/31/1995)
━ Yield (mean 1/1/1996–12/31/2018)
━ Yield

Figure 6.2 The compression of the standard deviation of JGB nominal yields, 1990–2018
Source: Macrobond

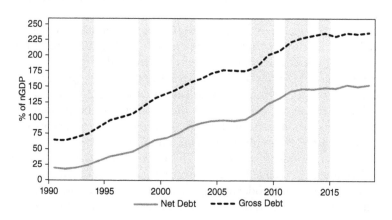

Figure 6.3 The evolution of government debt ratios, 1990–2018
Source: Macrobond

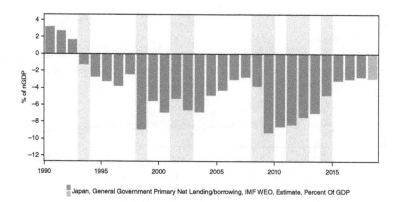

Japan, General Government Primary Net Lending/borrowing, IMF WEO, Estimate, Percent Of GDP

Figure 6.4 The evolution of fiscal balance ratios, 1990–2018
Source: Macrobond

The short-term interest rate in Japan has moved in lockstep with the policy rate (Figures 6.5A and 6.5B). The BOJ began reducing its policy rate in mid-1991 and continued to cut the rate until later in 1995; the short-term interest rate followed suit. The BOJ kept its policy rate low and unchanged from late 1995 to early 2000. The short-term interest rate remained low and range-bound during this period as well.

The BOJ pursued near-zero interest rate policy (ZIRP) from September 2001 until July 2006; the short-term interest rate was close to zero during

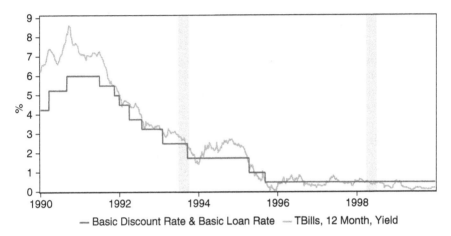

Figure 6.5A The co-evolution of policy rates and short-term interest rates, 1990–1999

Source: Macrobond

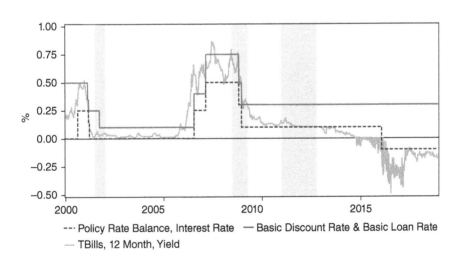

Figure 6.5B The co-evolution of policy rates and short-term interest rates, 2000–2018

Source: Macrobond

this period. As the BOJ raised its policy rate slightly, the short-term interest rate increased modestly. The onset of the global financial crisis, however, caused the BOJ to reduce its policy rate. The short-term interest rate declined with the reduction of the policy rate. The BOJ again resorted to near-zero interest rate policy between December 2008 and December 2015, with the short-term interest rate range bound near zero. However, it began to decline after that in anticipation of accommodative monetary policy action. With the introduction of negative interest rate policy in January 2016, the short-term interest rate fell further, and has been negative ever since.

Japan's economy has been characterized by low inflation and deflationary dynamics since the mid-1990s (Figure 6.6). Core inflation – as measured by (1) consumer price index (CPI) excluding fresh food and (2) CPI excluding food and energy – has been consistently low or in outright deflation with a few exceptions. Since the mid-1990s, the few episodes of increases in these core CPI inflation measures is due to either an increase in the sales tax rate in April 1997 from 3% to 5% and again in April 2014 from 5% to 8%, or an increase in energy prices from 2007 to 2008.

The deflationary dynamics from which the Japanese economy has suffered are also well reflected in the deflators for real GDP and the various expenditure components of aggregate demand. The decline in these deflators (Figure 6.7) shows the persistence of low inflation and deflationary pressures throughout the economy.

The stagnation of the Japanese economy is evident in the evolution of its nominal GDP (nGDP) (Figure 6.8). The nGDP was essentially flat from the

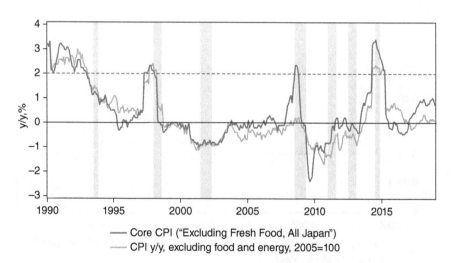

Figure 6.6 Inflationary pressures in Japan as measured by core consumer price indexes (CPI), 1990–2018

Source: Macrobond

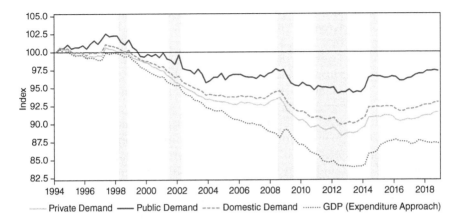

Figure 6.7 The evolution of deflators for GDP and its various components, 1990–2018

Source: Macrobond

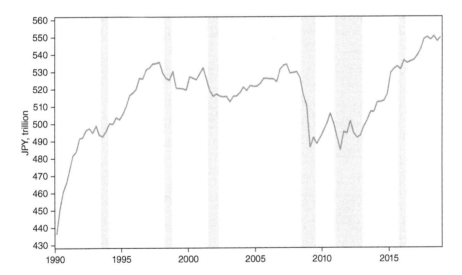

Figure 6.8 The evolution of nominal GDP, 1990–2018

Source: Macrobond

late 1990s to the mid-2000s. It fell during the global financial crisis from 2007 to 2008 and remained flat for a few years afterwards. However, since the advent of Abenomics, nGDP has gradually risen due to the combination of real GDP growth and moderate inflation, even though inflation is still well below the BOJ's target.

The level and growth in Japan's industrial production provides a useful overview of the country's business cycle conditions (Figure 6.9). Since the mid-1990s, the increase in industrial production in Japan has been fairly soft. Industrial production peaked in 2007, and then fell sharply during the global financial crisis. It again fell sharply during the recession caused by the Tohoku earthquake and tsunami. Since then, the growth of industrial production has been tepid. While industrial production has gradually risen since 2017, it is yet to surpass its peak in 2007.

The exchange rate of the Japanese yen has had substantial swings between 1990 and 2018 (Figure 6.10). The yen appreciated strongly from the early 1990s to mid-1990s – from a peak of about ¥160/$ to about ¥80/$. But it depreciated to around ¥140/$ by the late 1990s. Between late 1990 to early 2012, it generally appreciated. Its appreciation peaked at around ¥76/$ in January 2012. The protracted appreciation of the Japanese yen hurt the country's exports, and it reduced Japan's export competitiveness. By late 2012, the appreciation of the yen was reversed. From 2016 to the end of 2018, the yen has traded between ¥100/$ to ¥110/$.

The weakness of wage growth has underscored the persistence of deflation and low inflation in Japan (Figure 6.11). Wages, along with labor productivity and markups, are a key driver of prices. Thus, the weakness of wage growth has resulted in restrained inflation pressure and low inflation expectations. Indeed,

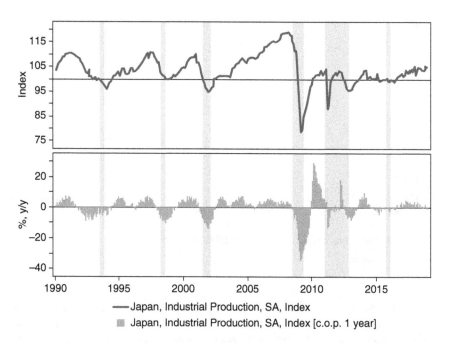

Figure 6.9 The evolution of industrial production, 1990–2018

Source: Macrobond

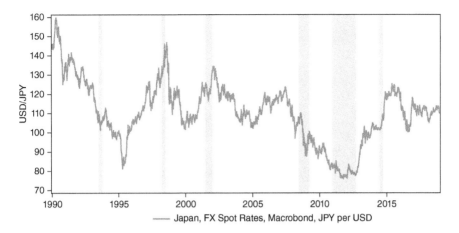

Figure 6.10 The exchange rate of the Japanese yen, 1990–2018

Source: Macrobond

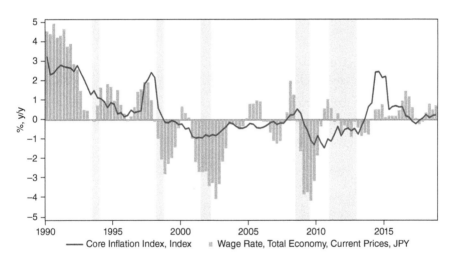

Figure 6.11 Employees' wage rate and inflationary pressure in Japan, 1990–2018

Source: Macrobond

for many years – since the late 1990s – the Japanese economy has been char-acterized by declining wages, resulting in deflation and low inflation for the country.

The BOJ's balance sheet has evolved with the central bank's policy response (Figure 6.12). In the late 1990s, the central bank's balance sheet expanded modestly. This gradual expansion continued amid a zero interest rate policy until 2006, after which the BOJ's balance sheet declined and then remained

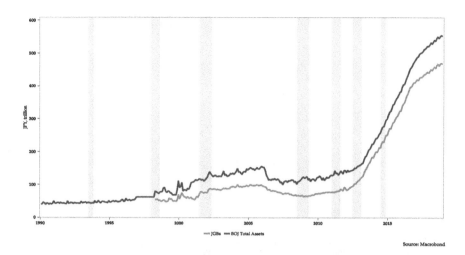

Figure 6.12 The balance sheet of the Bank of Japan, 1990–2018

Source: Macrobond

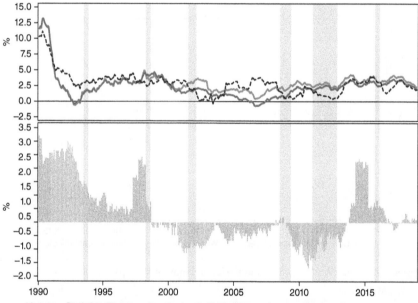

-- Monetary Statistics, Monetary Aggregates, L, Total, Average Amounts Outstanding, SA, JPY [c.o.p. 1 year]

— Monetary Statistics, Monetary Aggregates, M3, All Types of Money, Average Amounts Outstanding, SA, JPY [c.o.p. 1 year]

— Monetary Statistics, Monetary Aggregates, M2, Total, Average Amounts Outstanding, SA, JPY [c.o.p. 1 year]

▦ Consumer Price Index, Total, Excluding Food (Excluding Alcoholic Beverages) & Energy, All Japan, Index [c.o.p. 1 year]

Figure 6.13 Monetary aggregates and core inflation, 1990–2018

Source: Macrobond

flat until the advent of Abenomics and QQE programs. With the launch of QQE, the BOJ's balance sheet expanded stupendously from just ¥175 trillion in April 2013 to nearly ¥550 trillion as of December 2018. This tremendous expansion of the central bank's balance sheet is mainly due to large-scale purchases of JGBs as well as other securities, including exchange-traded funds (ETFs) and Japanese real estate investment trusts (J-REITs).

Since the mid-1990s, various monetary aggregates in Japan – measured in terms of M2, M3 and L – have expanded, though less so than in the early 1990s (Figure 6.13). Nevertheless, the Japanese economy has experienced either low inflation or outright deflation as reflected in the evolution of the two measures of core CPI.

Japan's macroeconomic conditions described here since the mid-1990s have fostered conditions that caused the BOJ to keep its policy rate low and undertake a highly accommodative monetary policy. The BOJ's accommodative monetary policy is responsible for the persistence of low yields of long-term JGBs. As will be shown in the sections that follow, this is exactly in accordance with Keynes's view on the effect of a low policy rate and low short-term interest rate on the long-term interest rate of government bonds.

3 The conventional view

Conventional wisdom holds that elevated government debt ratios lead to higher government bond yields. This is based on the loanable funds theory of interest rates, which says that the interest rate is the price of funds and that the supply of loanable funds (or saving) is discouraged (encouraged) by low (high) interest rate. Increased government net borrowing leads to higher demand for funds. Given a supply schedule, higher demand for funds raises the equilibrium interest rate.

Conventional wisdom also is in accordance with the standard IS-LM model. In the IS-LM model, higher government borrowing shifts the IS curve to the right. When all other factors are held constant, it raises the equilibrium interest rate on government bonds. More sophisticated neoclassical models using the Ramsey model or the overlapping generations model with rational expectations also lead to similar results in which higher government spending and borrowing can crowd out private investment and lead to a higher equilibrium interest rate on government bonds. Similar results are obtained even in New Keynesian dynamic stochastic general equilibrium (DSGE) models with rigidities in nominal prices or wages, or other distortions, although these models often do provide some scope for activist fiscal policy, at least in the short term. Some New Keynesian models that retain nominal rigidities, asymmetric information, market imperfections, hysteresis, coordination failures in the long run, leave scope for activist policies. However, in most New Keynesian models, the classical results prevail in the long run because it is based on the view that the economy eventually gravitates to full employment.

Reinhart and Rogoff (2009) embrace the conventional wisdom concerning the effect of the higher fiscal deficit ratio and elevated government debt ratio on government bond yields. Their claim is that the historical evidence supports the view that high fiscal deficits and elevated government debt ratios have led to higher interest rates on government bonds, increased probability of debt default and financial crisis, slowed economic growth and so forth. Although Reinhart and Rogoff's (2009) interpretation and analysis of the historical data has been questioned and disputed (Nersisyan and Wray, 2010; Herndon et al., 2014), it remains the conventional wisdom.

Most of the existing literature on JGBs, Japanese government debt sustainability, and related issues have been motivated by conventional wisdom. This is illustrated here with reference to the works of various mainstream analysts. These analysts have consistently proclaimed that (1) JGB yields will eventually rise unless the authorities can stabilize and reduce the government debt ratio; and (2) there is a realistic prospect of debt default in the foreseeable future. So far, such fears have proved to be unfounded. Indeed, portfolio managers betting on such views would have consistently lost money.

Tokuoka (2010) insists that the market's capacity to absorb JGBs is likely to diminish. As a result, he conjectures that JGB yields are destined to rise, particularly amid a rapidly ageing population. He believes that a fiscal consolidation is necessary to keep JGB yields low and retain stability in the financial markets. He acknowledges that despite elevated debt ratios, JGB yields have remained low, but he attributes this to the large pool of household savings, the presence of large and stable institutional investors, and a strong home bias.

Lam and Tokuoka (2013) contend that elevated and rising debt ratios are bound to cause JGB yields to rise. They claim that JGB yields have stayed low and stable, due to steady inflows from household and corporate sectors, high domestic ownership of JGBs, and safe-haven flows in light of the European debt crisis.

Atasoy et al. (2014) regard the low and stable yields of JGBs as a puzzle. While they admit that the BOJ's actions have kept JGB yields low, they also attribute it to high domestic bond ownership of households, corporations, and pension and insurance funds.

Horioka et al. (2014) claim that unless the Japanese authorities substantially reduce the government debt ratio, JGB nominal yields are likely to spike.

Doi et al. (2011) assert that Japanese government debt is not sustainable. They argue that unless the government revenue-to-GDP ratio rises substantially, Japan faces a material risk of a sharp increase in JGB yields. They believe that eventually debt default could occur.

Hansen and İmrohoroğlu (2013) argue that without a substantial fiscal adjustment, Japan faces the challenge of fiscal sustainability. They believe that that expected decline in domestic saving (especially household saving) caused by an ageing population will make it necessary for Japan to reduce its government debt ratio. Otherwise, they claim, JGB yields would rise sharply.

In several papers, Hoshi and Ito (2012, 2013, 2014) have maintained that Japan's fiscal situation is unstable. They argue that without a consumption tax hike beyond the 10% rate, a fiscal crisis is almost a certainty. They assert that low JGB yields are justifiable only if investors believe that a fiscal consolidation will occur. But if such expectation of fiscal consolidation changes, a fiscal crisis is inevitable even before the government debt hits the ceiling of the private sector demand for financial assets.

The fear that bond yields will rise if government debt ratios increase is confined not just to analysts who have examined the Japanese case but is fairly widespread in the mainstream of the economics profession.

The findings of three important cross-country panel data time series studies on government bonds yields and countries' fiscal positions are sufficient for illustrating the preponderance of this view:

- Baldacci and Kumar (2010) undertook a study of sovereign bond yields. They claim that higher deficit and government debt ratios lead to a significant increase in the long-term interest rate. Although they acknowledge that empirical findings are often unclear, their view is that large fiscal deficits and government debt ratios are likely to exert upward pressures on government bond yields in many advanced economies, such as Japan, over the medium term.
- Gruber and Kamin (2012) conclude that higher fiscal deficits and government debt ratios exert upward pressure on long-term government bond yields, based on their study of government's fiscal positions and government bond yields in the OECD countries.
- Poghosyan (2014) suggests that in the long term, the potential growth rate of the government debt ratio has a positive impact on government bond yields. However, his empirical findings reveal that the effect of an increase in the government debt ratio on government bond yields is fairly small.

What these analysts do not seem to realize is that for a country such as Japan – with its own currency, central bank and the ability to tax and spend – interest rates on long-term JGBs are largely determined by the central bank's actions on the policy rate and other instruments of monetary policy, rather than other variables, not only in the short run but also in the long run. The perspective from John Maynard Keynes shows how this is possible.

4 The Keynesian framework

4.1 The Keynesian framework to understanding bond yields

In contrast to the conventional view, Keynes (1930) argues in his *Treatise on Money* that the short-term interest rate is the key driver of the long-term interest rate on government bonds. In the Keynesian framework, the central bank's policy rate has a direct and decisive effect on the short-term interest rate on Treasury bills, which influences the long-term interest rate on government bonds.

In Keynes's perspective, the influence of the short-term interest rate is much more than what would be expected under the conventional view based on rational expectations, perfect foresight and full information. The conventional view is that the long-term interest rate depends not just on the current short-term interest rate, but also on expected short-term interest rates in the future and perhaps an appropriate term premium for different tenures of bonds. Under the conventional view, there is no reason to believe that the current short-term interest rate would have the decisive role in determining the long-term interest rate. Rather it would, at best, be just one factor among many others. The New Keynesian view is quite similar to the conventional view; it also implicitly assumes that investors have well-defined mathematical expectations about short-term interest rates in the future.

Keynes's discussion of the relationship between the short-term interest rate and the long-term interest rate is found in Volume II of his *Treatise*. Kregel (2011) provides a detailed exposition of Keynes's analysis. Keynes's view differs markedly from the conventional view, including the New Keynesian view, of how investors form their expectations about the future.

Keynes (1930) starts with the observation that "[t]he main direct influence of the Banking System is over the short-term rate of interest" (p. 352). He asks, "How can we be sure that the long-term rate of interest will respond to the wishes of a Currency Authority which will be exerting its direct influence, as it must, mainly on the short-term rate?" He further noted that

> [f]or whilst it is reasonable that long-term rates should bear a definite relation to the prospective short-term rates, quarter by quarter over the years to come, the contribution of the current three-monthly period to this aggregate expectation should be insignificant in amount – so one might suppose.

He asserts: "[E]xperience shows that, as a rule, the influence of the short-term rate of interest on the long-term rate is much greater than anyone . . . would have expected."

Keynes (1930, p. 353) cites the statistical work of W. W. Riefler (1930) on the relationship between the long-term interest rate and the short-term interest rate in the United States as evidence supporting his assertion. He also relies on some stylized facts about the relationship between the long-term interest rate and the short-term interest rate in the United Kingdom as additional empirical support of his contention.

Keynes offers several theoretical justifications for the influence of the short-term interest rate on the long-term interest rate.

First, Keynes notes that

> if the running yield on bonds is greater than the rate payable on short-term loans, a profit is obtainable by borrowing short in order to carry long-term securities, so long as the latter do not actually fall in value during

the currency of the loan. Thus, the pressure of transactions of this kind will initiate an upward trend, and this, for a time at least, will confirm the investor in a 'bullish' feeling towards the bond market. Moreover, firms . . . will tend to borrow on the security of these bonds when the cost of such borrowing is less than the running yield on the bonds; whilst they will sell the bond outright when the contrary is the case.

Second, Keynes (1930, pp. 357–358) argues that it's the need to generate income from holding financial assets that leads to a strong correlation between the short-term interest rate and the long-term interest rate. This stems from two factors: (1) institutional features of financial intermediaries, such as insurance companies, pensions and trusts; and (2) the psychology of investors. He writes:

> financial institutions . . . vary from time to time the proportionate division of their assets between long-term and short-term securities respectively. Where short-term yields are high, the safety and liquidity of short-term securities appear extremely attractive. But when short-term yields are very low, not only does this attraction disappear, but another motive enters in, namely, a fear lest the institution may be unable to maintain its established level of income, any serious falling off in which would be injurious to its reputation. A point comes, therefore, when they hasten to move into long-dated securities; the movement itself send up the price of the latter; and this movement seems to confirm the wisdom of those who were recommending the policy of the change-over. Thus . . . this price will tend to rise a little, and the initial small price will tend to become a bigger one through its increasing the general anxiety amongst those who cannot afford to see their income from running yields suffice a serious fall, lest they miss the bus.

Third, Keynes (1930, pp. 359–361) believes that investors are much more sensitive to near-term conditions because of ontological uncertainty about the unknown future and that current conditions shape investors' outlook about the future. He argues that investors tend to be "over-sensitive . . . to the near future, about which we may think we know a little" which "even the best-informed . . . know almost nothing about the more remote future." Hence, the value of financial assets, including bonds, "will be found to be sensitive . . . to short-period fluctuations in its known or anticipated profits," compared to that "which a rational observer from an outside might consider." He believes that

> market valuation shows a strong bias towards the assumption that whatever conditions and results have been characteristics of the present and the recent past, and even more those which are expected to be characteristic of the near future, will be lasting and permanent.

According to Keynes, this occurs because "the ignorance of even the best-informed investor about the more remote future is much greater than his knowledge." As a result, investors are "forced to seek a clue mainly here to trends further ahead." He notes that "the vast majority" of investors are subject to "the prey of hopes and fears aroused by transient events." He also notes that the value of a security is often determined "by the small fringe which is the subject of actual dealing" who tend to hold securities for a short-term. Such investors are very much "influenced by cost of borrowing, and still more by their expectations on the basis of past experience of the trend of mob psychology." Hence, "it will be to the advantage of the better informed professional to act in the same way – a short period ahead" rather than

> take long views or to pace even as much reliance as they reasonably might on the dubieties of the long period; – the apparent certainties of the short period, however deceptive we may suspect them to be, are much more attractive.
>
> (1930, p. 361)

In essence, for Keynes "there is no reason to doubt the ability of a Central Bank to make its short-term rate of interest effective in the market" (1930, p. 362).

In the *General Theory*, Keynes (2007 [1936]) extends and elaborates on his alternative theory of interest rates. He firmly rejected the loanable funds theory. For the purpose this chapter, it is worth noting that he states:

> The monetary authority often tends in practice to concentrate upon short-term debts and to leave the price of long-term debts to be influenced by belated and imperfect reactions from the price of short-term debts; – though here again there is no reason why they need do so. Where these qualifications operate, the directness of the relation between the rate of interest and the quantity of money is correspondingly modified.
>
> (Keynes, 2007 [1936], p. 206)

He shrewdly opines:

> If the monetary authority were prepared to deal both ways on specified terms in debts of all maturities, and even more so if it were prepared to deal in debts of varying degrees of risk, the relationship between the complex of rates of interest and the quantity of money would be direct. The complex of rates of interest would simply be an expression of the terms on which the banking system is prepared to acquire or part with debts; and the quantity of money would be the amount which can find a home in the possession of individuals who – after taking account of all relevant circumstances – prefer the control of liquid cash to parting with it in exchange for a debt on the terms indicated by the market rate of interest. Perhaps a

complex offer by the central bank to buy and sell at stated prices gilt-edged bonds of all maturities, in place of the single bank rate for short-term bills, is the most important practical improvement which can be made in the technique of monetary management.

(Keynes, 2007 [1936], p. 206)

Keynes's view on the relationship of the short-term interest rate and the long-term interest rate is based on his analysis of investors' expectations, the importance of business confidence and the state of confidence. He underscores the precariousness of the basis of knowledge about economic and financial convention, the "animal spirits" (Akerlof and Shiller, 2009). Keynes states that "a large proportion of our positive activities depend on spontaneous optimism rather than on a mathematical expectation" (Keynes, 2007 [1936], p. 161) and that "human decision affecting the future . . . cannot depend strictly on mathematical expectation, since the basis for making such calculations does not exist" (p. 163). Given this, investors are forced to take cues about their outlook from current conditions. It is precisely because of these reasons that the short-term interest rate is the key driver of the long-term interest rate.

4.2 Modelling government bond yields based on an interpretation of the Keynesian framework

In recent years, several studies used an interpretation of the Keynesian framework as the basis for modelling the dynamics of government bond yields. An intuitive explanation – rather than a mathematical version – of a model based on an interpretation of the Keynesian framework is provided here. Formal models of government bond yields derived from an interpretation of the Keynesian framework are presented in Akram and Das (2014) and Akram and Li (2017). A simple two-period version of these models appears in Akram and Das (2019).

The long-term interest rate depends on the current short-term interest rate and an appropriate forward rate. What drives the forward rate? The Hicksian view is that the forward rate is driven solely by the pure (mathematical) expectation of future short-term interest rates (Hicks, 2001 [1939], pp. 141–170). The Kaleckian view is that the forward rate is driven not just by the pure expectations of future short-term interest rates but also a margin of safety (Kalecki, 2010 [1954], pp. 73–88).

Typically in most models in financial economics the forward rate is based on excepted short-term interest rates in the future and the term premium, which is defined as some added compensation required to induce investors to hold long-term government bonds. If the central bank follows the Taylor rule the expected future short-term interest rates and the term premium would mainly depend on the expected inflation and the expected growth rate. (It will be assumed here that the central bank operates under a Taylor rule.) Whereas in a world characterized by rational expectations, the expected rate of inflation and the expected growth rate would respectively amount to the mathematical expectations of the possible growth rates and the possible rates of inflation in various states of the world; in a world characterized by ontological uncertainty (Davidson, 2015), the probability of unknown events is incalculable. Under a Keynesian perspective, investors are "over-sensitive . . . to the near future . . . because . . . we know almost nothing about the more remote future" (Keynes, 1930, p. 359). Hence, investors are forced to take cues about the expected rate of inflation and the expected growth rate from the current conditions. The current inflation rate provides the best guess for the expected inflation rate. Similarly, the current growth rate provides the best cue for the expected growth rate. If the Keynesian framework is correct, the forward rate would depend on the current inflation rate and the current growth rate rather than the future inflation and the future growth rate. This implies that the long-term interest rate is based on the current short-term interest rate, current inflation and current growth rate. This also implies that the change in the long-term interest rate is based on the change in the short-term interest rate, the change in current inflation and the change in the growth rate.

If the current government finance variable is thought to affect long-term interest rates – perhaps through influencing the forward rate – then this variable could be incorporated as well. The long-term interest rate would depend on the short-term interest rate, the current inflation, the current growth rate and the government finance variable. Similarly, the change in the long-term interest rate would depend on the changes in these variables. The short-term interest rate is the sum of the policy rate set by the central bank and a spread. Likewise, the change in the short-term interest rate is the sum of the change in the policy rate and the change in the same spread.

The empirical studies, conducted by Akram and Das (2014, 2015, 2017, 2019) and Akram and Li (2016, 2017, 2018, 2019), find that the short-term interest rate is the most important driver of the long-term interest rate on government bonds in Japan, the Eurozone, India and the United States, after controlling for a wide range of macroeconomic variables, such as core inflation, industrial production and fiscal variables (fiscal balance or fiscal debt ratios). Indeed, these studies find that the short-term interest rate is the key driver of the long-term interest rate. Moreover, changes in the short-term interest rate explain most of the changes in the long-term interest rate after controlling for other factors. Quite often the effects of fiscal variables on government bond yields are quite small and sometimes even opposite to that expected under the conventional view. The Keynesian framework provides a simple but compelling explanation of the dynamics of government bond yields.

Akram and Das (2014) examine the relationship between the long-term interest rate on JGBs and the short-term interest rates, as well as other factors, such as inflation and economic growth, from 1994 to the end of 2012. They deploy the two-step feasible and efficient generalized method of moments (GMM) technique. They rely on the second and third period lags of the independent variables as instrument variables. They apply the Hansen J test of the over-identifying restrictions to check for the validity and relevance of the instruments. They find that the BOJ has the ability to keep JGB nominal yields low by ensuring that the short-term interest rate is low.

Akram and Li (2018) also rely on a Keynesian perspective to explain why JGB nominal yields have been low for more than two decades. In examining the period from 1990 to 2017, they deployed several vector error correction (VEC) models to estimate long-term government bond yields. They show that the low short-term interest rate, influenced by the BOJ's accommodative monetary policy, is mainly responsible for keeping long-term JGB nominal yields exceptionally low for a protracted period. Gregory and Hansen's cointegration test is used for detecting structural breaks. After incorporating structural breaks, they find that there is a positive relationship between the short-term interest rate and the long-term interest rate. However, there is a negative relationship between the net government debt ratio and the long-term interest rate. This means that higher government debt and deficit ratios do not exert upward pressure on JGB nominal yields.

These empirical studies show that the Keynesian framework can readily explain the dynamics of JGBs in terms of fundamental macro and financial variables.

5   Policy implications

The findings that are based on a Keynesian framework, as shown by Akram and Das (2014) and Akram and Li (2018), are relevant for ongoing policy debates in Japan and other advanced countries about government bond yields, fiscal sustainability, fiscal policy, monetary policy and financial stability.

The BOJ has a decisive effect on JGB nominal yields through the monetary policy rate that determines short-term interest rates. A lower (higher) short-term interest rate is associated with a lower (higher) long-term interest rate. Hence, by keeping the short-term interest rate low (high) by setting the policy rate low (high), the BOJ keeps the long-term interest rate on JGBs low (high). Furthermore, the BOJ directly influences the long-term interest rate on JGBs and other financial assets through a range of actions, including (1) its purchase of long-duration government bonds and other financial assets from dealers and financial institutions; (2) yield curve control; and (3) policy pronouncements.

The BOJ can effectively control JGB nominal yields and the shape of the yield curve in spite of elevated ratios of government debt and government primary/fiscal deficits. Contrary to conventional wisdom, the elevated government debt and chronic government deficit ratios have not led to higher government bond yields. Furthermore, the BOJ's policy of low interest rates and the expansion of its balance sheet do not appear to be inherently inflationary.

The BOJ's low, near zero and negative interest policies and monetary accommodation in forms of quantitative and qualitative easing, yield curve control and other innovations may well be warranted. Keynes (1930, p. 370) argues that amid economic stagnation regarding monetary policy, "bolder measures are sometimes advisable" regarding monetary policy actions, noting that contrary to widely held beliefs, unconventional monetary policy – such as purchasing long-dated gilt-edged securities – is "quite free from serious dangers." The BOJ's actions have not led to financial instability or the debauching of the currency as many have feared, but it is also correct to say that the BOJ has been unable to attain its target of 2.0% inflation on a sustained basis. Indeed, the target of sustained 2.0% inflation appears to be elusive.

Japan's experience suggests that there is no reason to doubt the ability of the government of Japan to service its debt. Lerner (1943, 1947) holds that a government with monetary sovereignty is not constrained by the principles of "sound finance" that apply to households, businesses and local/state governments. A sovereign government that issues debt payable in its own liabilities is fundamentally different from agents that issue debt that is *not* repayable in the term of their own liabilities, as Wray (2003 [1998], 2012), Fullwiler (2016), and others have pointed out. Japan's considerable experience in keeping the long-term interest rate on JGBs low over a protracted period despite elevated government debt ratios supports Sims's (2013) conjectures about government debt in a fiat money regime, as reflected in his propositions:

- "[N]ominal sovereign debt promises only future payments of government paper, which is always available."
- "[A] central bank can 'print money'. . . . It will not be subject to the usual sort of run. . . . Its liabilities are denominated in government paper, which it can produce at will."

Detailed understanding of fiscal and monetary operations, as analyzed in Bindseil (2004), Fullwiler (2016, 2017 [2008]) and Lavoie (2014), reveal that a variety of conventional wisdom concerning money, monetary operations, government debt and debt sustainability is often erroneous. The conventional view regarding the fears of the consequences of expansionary fiscal policy and low interest rates in response to economic stagnation and low inflation has failed to materialize in Japan. Low JGB yields can be explained within a Keynesian framework.

Going forward, the focus of the debate should shift to the effectiveness, the efficiency and the appropriateness of fiscal and monetary policies and the goals of fiscal policy rather than the perils of an expansionary and activist fiscal and monetary policy stance. This is not to claim that fiscal deficit ratios, government debt ratios or the size of the balance sheet of central banks do not matter. These variables do matter. Indeed, experience suggests that they matter quite substantially. Under certain circumstances, expansionary monetary and fiscal policy can have extremely harmful consequences, including high inflation, hyperinflation, substantial exchange rate depreciation, loss of business and consumer confidence, distortion of incentives, deterioration of the standard of living and effects on the distribution of income and wealth.

Japan faces many economic and social challenges (Akram, 2019), such as slow economic growth, tepid labor productivity growth, declining population, modest real income growth, demographic changes, a lack of openness to immigration and so forth. Addressing these and other issues of growth, stability and environmental sustainability should be the priority for policymakers rather than worrying about the risk of government debt default.

6 Conclusion

In Japan, the low short-term interest rate – induced by the BOJ – has been largely responsible for keeping long-term JGB nominal yields subdued despite chronically large primary/fiscal deficits ratios and elevated government debt ratios. Moreover, since early 2016 the BOJ's has directly targeted the 10-year interest rate on JGBs. Given the influence of the policy rate on the short-term interest rate, the effect on the short-term interest rate on the long-term interest rate, the direct targeting of the long-term interest rate, the regime of yield curve control and other measures undertaken by the BOJ, it can be asserted that the BOJ's actions are the primary driver of the long-term interest rate on JGBs. The BOJ should be able to keep JGB nominal yields low as necessary in the foreseeable future through a combination of a low policy rate, direct targeting of the long-term interest rate and other accommodative monetary policy actions. Despite the elevated government debt ratio, the probability of default on government debt for Japan is extremely remote because the BOJ has the operational ability to always service the government's debt. The fear that JGB yields will dramatically spike even if the BOJ keeps its policy rate low, targets the long-term interest rate and pursues an accommodative monetary policy is misplaced. It is contrary to a Keynesian understanding of the dynamics of government bond yields in a country with a sovereign currency.

Japan faces challenges for the 21st century. The Japanese authorities should focus on issues that are critical to the country's ongoing demographic transformation, economic prospects, and peace and security. The Japanese authorities will have to invest in human capital and capabilities and in the nation's infrastructure. Policies need to foster economic and social institutions that can enable Japan to prosper amid peace and security so that it can contribute meaningfully to national and global well-being and the enrichment of the human civilization. The point of fiscal and monetary policies in Japan will be to achieve worthwhile ends, such as high economic growth at close to full employment, sustained inflation around its target rate, financial stability and shared prosperity.

Acknowledgments: The authors thank the editors for their valuable suggestions, participants at various workshops for their incisive comments and Ms. Mary Rafferty for her copy editing.

Disclaimer: The authors' institutional affiliations are provided solely for identification purposes. Views expressed are solely those of the authors. This paper is for informational purposes only and should not be construed as an offer to buy or sell any investment product or service.

Funding: This research did not receive any specific grant from funding agencies in the public, commercial or not-for-profit sectors.

References

Akerlof, G. A. and Shiller, R. J. (2009) *Animal Spirits: How Human Psychology Drives the Economy, and Why It Matters for Global Capitalism.* Princeton: Princeton University Press.

Akram, T. (2014) The economics of Japan's stagnation, *Business Economics*, 49 (3), 156–175.

Akram, T. (2016) Japan's liquidity trap, *Levy Economics Institute Working Paper*, No. 862.

Akram, T. (2019) The Japanese economy: Stagnation, recovery, and challenges, *Journal of Economics Issues*, 53 (2), 403–410.

Akram, T. and Das, A. (2014) Understanding the low yields of the long-term Japanese sovereign debt, *Journal of Economic Issues*, 48 (2), 331–340.

Akram, T. and Das, A. (2015) A Keynesian explanation of Indian government bond yields, *Journal of Post Keynesian Economics*, 38 (4), 565–587.

Akram, T. and Das, A. (2017) The dynamics of government bond yields in the Eurozone, *Annals of Financial Economics*, 12 (3), 1750011.

Akram, T. and Das, A. (2019) The long-run determinants of Indian government bond yields, *Asian Development Review*, 36 (1), 68–205.

Akram, T. and Li, H. (2016) The empirics of long-term US interest rates, *Levy Economics Institute Working Paper*, No. 863.

Akram, T. and Li, H. (2017) What keeps long-term US interest rates so low? *Economic Modelling*, 60, 380–390.

Akram, T. and Li, H. (2018) The dynamics of Japan government bonds' nominal yields, *Levy Economics Institute Working Paper*, No. 906.

Akram, T. and Li, H. (2019) An inquiry concerning long-term US interest rates using monthly data, *Applied Economics*. https://doi.org/10.1080/00036846.2019.1693696

Atasoy, B. S., Ertuğrul, H. M. and Ozun, A. (2014) The puzzle of low government bond yields in Japan, *The Japanese Political Economy*, 40 (2), 24–47.

Baldacci, E. and Kumar, M. (2010) Fiscal deficits, public debt, and sovereign bond yields, *IMF Working Paper*, No. 10-184.

Bindseil, U. (2004) *Monetary Policy Implementation: Theory, Past, and Present.* Oxford: Oxford University Press.

Davidson, P. (2015) *Post Keynesian Theory and Policy: A Realistic Analysis of the Market Oriented Capitalist Economy.* Cheltenham and Northampton: Edward Elgar.

Doi, T., Hoshi, T. and Okimoto, T. (2011) Japanese government debt and sustainability of fiscal policy, *Journal of the Japanese and International Economies*, 25 (4), 414–433.

Fullwiler, S. T. (2016) The debt ratio and sustainable macroeconomic policy, *World Economic Review*, 7, 12–42.

Fullwiler, S. T. (2017 [2008]) Modern central bank operations: The general principles, in Rochon, L.-P. and Rossi, S. (eds.) *Advances in Endogenous Money Analysis.* Northampton: Edward Elgar.

Garside, W. R. (2012) *Japan's Great Stagnation Forging Ahead, Falling Behind.* Cheltenham: Edward Elgar.

Gruber, J. W. and Kamin, S. B. (2012) Fiscal positions and government bond yields in OECD countries, *Journal of Money, Credit, and Banking*, 44 (8), 1563–1587.

Hansen, G. and İmrohoroğlu, S. (2013) Fiscal reform and government debt in Japan: A neoclassical perspective, *Review of Economic Dynamics*, 21, 201–224.

Herndon, T., Ash, M. and Pollin, R. (2014) Does high public debt consistently stifle economic growth? A critique of Reinhart and Rogoff, *Cambridge Journal of Economics*, 38 (2), 257–279.

Hicks, J. R. (2001 [1939]) *Value and Capital: An Enquiry into Some Fundamental Principles of Economic Theory.* Oxford: Clarendon Press.

Horioka, C. Y., Nomoto, T. and Terada-Hagiwara, A. (2014) Why has Japan's massive government debt not wreaked havoc (yet)? *The Japanese Political Economy*, 40 (2), 3–23.

Hoshi, T. and Ito, T. (2012) Defying gravity: How long will Japanese government bond prices remain high? *National Bureau of Economic Research Working Paper*, No. 18287.

Hoshi, T. and Ito, T. (2013) Is the sky the limit? Can Japanese government bonds continue to defy gravity? *Asian Economic Policy Review*, 8 (2), 218–247.

Hoshi, T. and Ito, T. (2014) Defying gravity: Can Japanese sovereign debt continue to increase without a crisis? *Economic Policy*, 29 (77), 5–44.

Kalecki, M. (2010 [1954]) *Theory of Economic Dynamics: An Essay on Cyclical and Long-Run Changes in Capitalist Economy*, paperback edition. London, UK and New York, NY: Routledge.

Keynes, J. M. (1930) *A Treatise on Money: The Applied Theory of Money*. London: Macmillan.

Keynes, J. M. (2007 [1936]) *The General Theory of Employment, Interest, and Money*. New York: Macmillan.

Kregel, J. (2011) Was Keynes' monetary policy *à outrance* in the treatise, a forerunner of ZIRP and QE? Did he change his mind in the general theory? *Levy Economics Institute, Policy Note*, No. 11–14.

Lam, R. W. and Tokuoka, K. (2013) Assessing the risks to the Japanese government bond (JGB) market, *Journal of International Commerce, Economics and Policy*, 4 (1).

Lavoie, M. (2014) *Post-Keynesian Economics: New Foundations*. Cheltenham: Edward Elgar.

Lerner, A. P. (1943) Functional finance and the federal debt, *Social Research*, 10 (1), 38–51.

Lerner, A. P. (1947) Money as a creature of the state, *American Economic Review*, 37 (2), 312–317.

Macrobond (various years) *Macrobond Subscription Services*. Available from: https://www.macrobond.com [Accessed 20 April 2018].

Nersisyan, Y. and Wray, L. R. (2010) Does excessive sovereign debt really hurt growth? A critique of this time is different, by Reinhart and Rogoff, *Levy Economics Institute Working Paper*, No. 603.

Poghosyan, T. (2014) Long-run and short-run determinants of sovereign bond yields in advanced economies, *Economic Systems*, 38 (1), 100–114.

Reinhart, C. M. and Rogoff, K. S. (2009) *This Time Is Different: Eight Centuries of Financial Folly*. Princeton: Princeton University Press.

Riefler, W. W. (1930) *Money Rates and Money Markets in the United States*. New York: Harper & Brothers.

Tokuoka, K. (2010) The outlook for financing Japan's public debt, *IMF Working Paper*, No. 10–19.

Wray, L. R. (2003 [1998]) *Understanding Modern Money: The Key to Full Employment and Price Stability*. Cheltenham: Edward Elgar.

Wray, L. R. (2012) *Modern Money Theory: A Primer on Macroeconomics for Sovereign Monetary Systems*. New York: Macmillan.

7 Unconventional monetary policy announcements and Japanese bank stocks

Ayhan Nadiri

1 Introduction

Most central banks in developed countries responded to the global financial crisis, which turned out to be the most severe economic downturn since the Great Depression, in a harmonised manner by adjusting key policy interest rates to, or very close to, zero (Gambacorta et al., 2014). Following the zero interest rate policy (ZIRP), to provide an additional stimulus to the economy, the world's largest central banks like the Federal Reserve (Fed), the European Central Bank (ECB) and the Bank of England (BoE) introduced non-traditional monetary policy measures. These so-called unconventional monetary policy measures, such as quantitative easing and forward guidance, have generated a new set of challenges and given rise to a growing body of theoretical research (Ehrmann and Fratzscher, 2004; Bernanke et al., 2004; Swanson and Williams, 2014). Since, several major central banks have faced the challenge to "overcome the zero lower bound" (Nakaso, 2017).[1]

Japan was in an exceptional situation in comparison to the central banks mentioned earlier. The Bank of Japan (BOJ) was the first central bank ever to adopt the zero interest rate policy and unconventional monetary policy measures (Kuroda, 2014). Looking back towards the early 1990s, economic activity in Japan was sluggish, and both business and consumer sentiment was weak. Together with the collapse of the financial bubble, Japan's economy started to experience economic stagnation and deflation – what came to be coined as the "Lost Decade" (Saxonhouse and Stern, 2002). The BOJ took a string of actions to overcome that Lost Decade, including unconventional monetary policy measures. The slow recovery of the Japanese economy has naturally raised questions about the effectiveness of these measures and their accompanying announcements.

In the existing literature, various studies have investigated the impacts and effectiveness of unconventional monetary policy measures on both the macroeconomic and microeconomic level.

For instance, Borio et al. (2015) examined the impact of monetary policy announcements on banks' profitability between 1995 and 2015. The authors used a dataset encompassing 109 large international banks headquartered in

14 advanced economies. They then measured the link between monetary policy announcements and bank profitability through a non-linear approach, and found that between 2009 and 2010 (the first two post-crisis years) implemented unconventional policy announcements had a positive impact on bank profitability. However, during the following four years (2011–2014), a negative impact was detected. Further, Guerini et al. (2018) investigated the effectiveness of unconventional monetary policy announcements in reaching targeted inflation rates. The authors focused on unconventional monetary policy announcements implemented by the ECB and the Fed between 2008 and 2016. They conclude that while unconventional monetary policy announcements are useful and effective, they need to be better coordinated with fiscal, micro and macro prudential policies to provide more comprehensive results that might positively affect the real economy beyond the financial system. Further, Panizza and Wyplosz (2016) examine the decreasing effectiveness hypothesis on advanced economies (the euro area, Japan, the UK and the US) that implemented large-scale asset purchases (LSAP). Based on a subsample analysis, the authors obtain ambiguous results. For some empirical specifications, they find decreasing effectiveness, for others not. Tillman and Meinusch (2014), on the other hand, explore the impacts of the implemented quantitative easing (QE) programmes by the Fed based on a Qual VAR model. The authors conclude that QE shocks have a large impact on real and nominal interest rates, as well as financial conditions, but smaller impact on real activity. Overall, these studies investigate the impacts and effectiveness of the implemented unconventional monetary policy announcements on bank profitability, inflation, interest rates and the economy as a whole.

Several studies focus specifically on the link between monetary policy and stock markets. Stock markets are accepted as an important indicator for measuring the performance of an economy and also act as a barometer for measuring the effectiveness of government actions on investor actions (Somani, 2015). From the governmental perspective, it is important to manage the expectations of the investors and financial market participants for being able to control and contribute to the economic performance of countries that host these stock markets (Boubakari and Jin, 2010). As outlined by numerous studies (e.g. Bomfin, 2003; Ehrmann and Fratzscher, 2004; Bernanke and Kuttner, 2005; Bredin et al., 2010; Chulia et al., 2010; Rangel, 2011; Rosa, 2011; Maio, 2014; Meinusch, 2016), stock markets tend to react to monetary policy announcements.

Lately, and particularly since the outbreak of the global financial crisis, several central banks in advanced developed countries have shifted towards unconventional monetary policy measures. Two key empirical studies, by Ricci (2014) and Fiordelisi et al. (2014), show that unconventional monetary policy announcements have a statistically significant impact on those markets where these policies are adopted.

Japan stands out by being a pioneer with regards to unconventional monetary policy. However, the impact and effectiveness of the measures dating back to the late 1990s and early 2000s remain a matter of debate. It is generally argued that the policy actions had less satisfactory results than initially expected by the policymakers. Since, the country has continued to face deflationary pressures and muted economic growth.

Nonetheless, new bold steps were taken by Prime Minister Abe in 2013. After decades of deflation and stagnation, Japan's economy had struggled to compete in foreign markets. With the eruption of the 2008 financial crisis, prices of Japanese exports had sharply increased, primarily due to the safe-haven status of the Japanese yen. Inflation targeting was introduced, and a string of unconventional monetary policy measures have since been adopted. Moreover, the Bank of Japan substantially increased its purchase in exchange-traded funds (ETFs) to boost stock market prices.

Therefore, the aim of this chapter is to shed light on the reaction by the stock market to unconventional monetary policy announcements by the BOJ. More specifically, it covers the period 1999 to 2016 in order to determine whether a shift has taken place since the launch of Abenomics and the more aggressive easing policy.

The main findings can be summarised as follows. Between 1999–2012, very few (and mainly regional) bank stocks showed statistically significant reactions to unconventional monetary policy announcements. This includes announcements during and in the immediate aftermath of the global financial crisis. However, between 2012 and 2016, they started to have an immediate impact on Japanese bank stock returns. Thus, from the perspective of the stock market, the monetary transmission mechanism differs sharply between the pre-Abenomics and the post-Abenomics periods.

The rest of the chapter proceeds as follows. Section 2 provides a review of the related literature and past empirical studies. Section 3 describes the data selection and methodology. In Section 4, the results of the event study are presented and discussed and Section 5 offers some concluding remarks.

2   Monetary policy announcements and stock returns

2.1   *Conventional monetary policy announcements*

The effects of the monetary policy announcements on stock returns have been examined extensively by academics since the early 1960s (Brunnermeier and Koby, 2016). From the perspective of both monetary policymakers and financial market participants, the relationship between monetary policy announcements and stock returns is an important indicator. In the last 25 years, stock markets, as an essential part of financial markets alongside with the commodity markets, money markets, interbank markets and foreign exchange markets, have shown significant growth and development. Today, most people are either directly or indirectly involved in the stock markets. Each day, market participants, such as individual retail investors, bankers, insurance company representatives and mutual fund managers invest in the stock markets. From the perspective of a financial market participant, the predictability of monetary policy announcements plays a vital role in their future investment strategy. From the perspective of a policymaker, monetary policy measures are formulated based on a variety of economic and financial sources. Indeed, according to Hördahl and Packer (2007),

> asset prices play various related roles in the monetary policy/financial stability frameworks. These roles include acting as sources of information concerning market expectations and markets' risk attitudes, acting as leading indicators of output, inflation and financial distress, and acting as indicators of the shocks that hit the economy.

Together with the increasing complexity of the global economic structure, the role of stock markets within the financial system has become more crucial, especially after the devastating wave of the recent global financial crisis (Doh and Connolly, 2013). Moreover, numerous studies show that the performance of a stock market mirrors the economic performance of the country hosting it (Ricci, 2014). In other words, stock markets act as economic barometers (Yin and Yang, 2013). Along these lines, Petros (2012), Ariccia et al. (2018) and Boubakari and Jin (2010) demonstrate that countries with well-performing stock markets tend to have better-performing economies in terms of GDP growth than those with poorly performing stock markets.

Central banks are, through various tools, able to indirectly affect the level and volatility of stock markets (Rosa, 2011). Among these tools, the most important one is monetary policy actions (Levy, 2012). There is a growing empirical literature that examines the impact of monetary policy announcements on stock returns. For instance, Basistha and Kurov (2008) investigate the effect of the Fed's monetary policy announcements. They use firm-level data to examine the reaction of stock returns to certain monetary shocks (unexpected changes in the federal funds rate). They find that during a recession and tight credit market conditions, stock returns show stronger responses to unexpected changes in the federal funds rate. Also, they report that financially constrained firms react more than relatively unconstrained firms to monetary shocks. Overall, these results are consistent with the credit channel of the monetary policy transmission mechanism.

Furthermore, Rangel (2011) investigates the impact of the macroeconomic announcements on stock market volatility. The author examines the US stock market (S&P 500) volatility between 1992 and 2008. The study concludes that while inflation shocks have persistent effects on stock returns, monetary policy announcements and employment shocks show only short-lived results.

Rosa (2011) also examines the reaction to statements and decisions by the Fed and focuses on US stock returns using a high-frequency event-study methodology. By using such a dataset, the author strives to identify the impact of the policy shocks more fully and precisely. Also, the use of tick data and narrow event windows allows the author to better control for the endogeneity reverse causality and omitted variables problems. Rosa concludes that unexpected policy announcements have a more pronounced impact on stock returns than expected policy announcements.

Maio (2014), by contrast, investigates the impact of monetary policy announcements on stock returns of companies with different characteristics (e.g. size and book-to-market ratio). The study shows that changes in the federal funds rate have a more significant impact on the stock returns of small firms. Thus, the author concludes that the effect of the monetary policy announcements on stock returns shows variations depending on the characteristics of the firms.

Bomfin (2003) also examines the relationship between monetary policy announcements and the reaction in the US stock market. As opposed to previous studies, however, which tend to focus on the impact on the level of stock returns, the author also investigates the potential effect of unexpected policy announcements on the volatility of the stock returns. The results of the study show that unexpected changes in the target federal funds rate increase the volatility of stock market reactions.

Bernanke and Kuttner (2005) also examine the relationship between monetary policy announcements and stock market volatility. In line with the Bomfin (2003), the authors document that stock markets show relatively strong and consistent reactions to unexpected monetary policy announcements.

The impact of the Fed's monetary policy decisions on US stock markets and volatility is also investigated by Rosa (2011). The author incorporates the Fed's communication method and the surprise components of the monetary policy statements. The study concludes that the central banks' communication strategy about its future policy actions is an essential tool for the effectiveness of the implemented monetary policy measure from the perspective of the stock markets.

Some researchers also report that the effects of the monetary policy announcements on stock markets are likely to be different for different currency areas (see, for instance, Poole and Rasche, 2000; Kuttner, 2001; Bomfin, 2003; Pennathur et al., 2014). In parallel, Chen (2007) and Chiarella et al. (2013) show that stocks in different industries and sectors (e.g. technology, transportation, cyclical consumer goods, finance) show different reactions to monetary policy announcements.

To sum up, monetary policy announcements seem to have an impact on stock market returns and volatility. However, the scale of the impact depends on the content and delivery of the announcement, and may also vary across countries and sectors of the stock market.

2.2   *Unconventional monetary policy announcements*

Following the global financial crisis, the majority of the world's major central banks implemented a series of extraordinary and non-traditional monetary policy measures. The unconventional monetary policy measures were intended to stabilise the financial markets and alleviate the impact of the crisis on economic activity. The sharp downturn impact of the crisis triggered central banks to cut interest rates to the effective lower bound of 0%. Hitting the zero lower bound, central banks started to implement unconventional monetary policies, such as LSAP and forward guidance. However, the new policy tools came with a significant degree of uncertainty regarding their effectiveness, especially whether the standard transmission channels of monetary policy through financial asset markets would work as smoothly as they had done in the past (Glick and Leduc, 2013). Since then, several studies have examined the impact of such *unconventional* monetary policy announcements on stock markets and financial markets in general.

Glick and Leduc (2012) investigate the impact of LSAP announcements on the US stock market. They report that the average daily stock prices rose following the announcement day of the policy. Rogers et al. (2014) and Wright (2012) study the impact of LSAP announcements on intraday returns in the US stock markets. Similarly to Glick and Leduc (2012), they report that LSAP announcements by the Fed significantly boost stock returns. Furthermore, Swanson (2015) examines the impact of the Fed's unconventional monetary policy announcements on asset prices between 2009 and 2015. The author finds that forward guidance has a relatively limited effect on long-term Treasury yields and virtually no impact on corporate bond yields. However, LSAPs have a significant effect on such bond yields, but little impact on short-term Treasuries. Both policy types have significant effects on medium-term Treasury yields, stock prices and exchange rates.

2.3 *Monetary policy announcements and bank stock returns*

Banks are not only important participants in the financial market. They also play a central role in the monetary transmission mechanism. This should, in theory, make banks sensitive to monetary policy announcements and, being key providers of capital to investors, particularly to unconventional measures (Nakajima, 2011). As outlined by, for instance, Born and Moser (1990), Madura and Schnusenberg (2000), Hordahl and Frank, (2007) and Yin et al. (2010), bank share prices are important indicators for investors, supervisors and central banks, which aim to maintain financial stability. Bank stock returns summarise and reflect publicly available information about the bank, including the potential risk, with a single number.

Along the lines of the efficient market hypothesis, that single number also includes a forward-looking element containing both positive and negative expectations of potential future earnings (Ricci, 2014). Moreover, as the financial service industry has become increasingly complex, the traditional supervisory process has become more challenging (Flannery, 2012). Following this logic, forward-looking information sources have become more crucial than ever. Importantly, during financial crises, banks tend to become the main subjects of many monetary policy announcements (Ricci, 2014; Fiordelisi et al., 2014).

Several studies focus directly on the impact on bank share prices. For instance, using an event study methodology, Born and Moser (1990) investigate the reaction of US bank stock returns to changes in the Fed's discount rate. They find that bank stock returns react positively (negatively) to a decreasing (increasing) discount rate. Using a similar methodology, Madura and Schnusenberg (2000) examine the reaction of bank stock returns to changes in both the discount rate and the federal funds rate. They report that there is an inverse relationship between the direction of the changes in the Fed's monetary policy tools and bank stock returns. Like Madura and Schnusenberg (2000) and Born and Moser (1990), Yin et al. (2010) conduct similar studies using an event study methodology. However, they find that bank stock returns do not respond to expected policy interventions. Instead, the stock market reacts to *unexpected* central bank actions, and the reactions display significant differences depending on the type of policy change. Similarly, Yin and Yang (2013) also investigate the impact of the monetary policy announcements on bank stock returns. However, as opposed to the studies mentioned earlier, the authors also examine how banks of different sizes and with different capital ratios and funding sources react to the implemented monetary policy actions. They use data from 1988 to 2007 on all publicly listed US banks and report that banks with different characteristics show different reactions to monetary shocks. For instance, they observe that a change in the federal funds rate has a significantly greater impact on the stock returns of larger, rather than smaller, banks.

However, all these studies that were discussed earlier solely investigate the impacts of *conventional* monetary policy announcements on bank stock returns. Ricci (2014) and Fiordelisi et al. (2014), by contrast, examine the effects of *unconventional* monetary policy announcements on bank stock returns extensively and in detail. Ricci (2014) focuses on ECB monetary policy announcements and the stock prices of large European banks between 2007 and 2013. By running a short-horizon event study, the author compares the effectiveness of conventional and unconventional policy measures on bank stock prices. The results indicate that unconventional monetary policy announcements have a more pronounced impact on the chosen bank stock returns in comparison with traditional decisions (such as interest rates). The unconventional monetary policy announcements in the study include monetary easing decisions (e.g. quantitative easing and credit easing) and liquidity provisions (e.g. swap agreements and extension of accepted collaterals). The strongest (negative) reaction is detected around the announcement of ending/reduction of monetary easing programmes.

Fiordelisi et al. (2014) also examine the impact of both conventional and unconventional monetary policy announcements on bank stock returns using a short-horizon event study method. The main distinction between the studies by Ricci and Fiordelisi et al. is as follows. While Ricci's investigation only examines the reaction within the Eurozone, Fiordelisi et al. examine five monetary areas: the Eurozone, Japan, Switzerland, the UK and the US) between 2007 and 2012. The authors examine stock price reactions of global systematically important financial institutions (G-SIFIs), as defined by the Financial Stability Forum on 4 November 2011. In line with Ricci's study, they find that bank stock returns are more sensitive to unconventional than to conventional monetary policy announcements. The authors also observe that stock prices of G-SIFISs show strong positive, and statistically significant, reactions to expansionary monetary easing programmes. Interest rate cuts, by contrast, are not associated with statistically significant stock price reactions.

This chapter focuses specifically on the Bank of Japan and the Japanese stock market. As mentioned previously, the BOJ is a front-runner in terms of the implementation of unconventional monetary policy measures. Indeed, following the BOJ, other major central banks, such as the Fed and the ECB, have also implemented similar actions. Some researchers report that the effectiveness of unconventional policy actions displays variations depending on the underlying financial and economic conditions (Gagnon et al., 2011; Hancock and Passmore, 2011; Kozicki et al., 2011). Therefore, regarding the existing literature, it can be concluded that both conventional and unconventional monetary policy interventions have an impact on bank stock returns. However, the consequences may vary according to the size, capital ratio and funding sources of the selected banks. Moreover, central bank interventions also show variations. Consequently, by examining the impact of the BOJ's unconventional monetary policy announcements on Japanese bank stock returns, and by comparing with the findings with the studies mentioned, this chapter seeks to shed light on whether unconventional monetary policy announcements have similar effects as in other countries – with an emphasis on bank stocks.

3 Methodology

To examine the impact of the Bank of Japan's unconventional monetary policy announcements on Japanese bank stock returns, this study employs a short-horizon event study method to capture abnormal returns in the stock market for the pre-specified announcement period (following Brown and Warner, 1980, 1985). In the economics and finance literature, the event study methodology is one of the most frequently used statistical methods to assess the impact of specific events on certain dependent variables (Corrado, 2011). As outlined in the previous section, many researchers have employed a short-horizon event study approach to examine the relationship between the stock market and monetary policy announcements (e.g. Thorbecke, 1997; Bernanke and Kuttner, 2005; Kurov, 2012; Gospodinov and Jamali, 2012; Ricci, 2014; Fiordelisi et al., 2014; Smith, 2014). As an initial task to conduct a successful event study, the events (BOJ's unconventional monetary policy announcements) and the event windows must be identified and carefully selected.

3.1 BOJ unconventional monetary policy announcements and event windows

The BOJ works to maintain financial stability and steady growth in the Japanese economy by conducting and implementing monetary policy. As the monetary authority, the BOJ is responsible for regulating the size of Japan's money supply, controlling the international value of the Japanese yen and regulating the availability and cost of credit for the Japanese market (BOJ, 2019). Looking back at the early 1990s, economic activity in Japan was sluggish, and both business and consumer sentiment was weak. Together with the collapse of the financial bubble, Japan's economy started to experience economic stagnation and deflation – the "Lost Decade" (Saxonhouse and Stem, 2002). The Lost Decade has been a widely debated topic among economists and policymakers and is generally accepted as unique to Japan until the global financial crisis.

Having experienced and faced the consequences of a severe burst of a bubble and deflation, the BOJ has developed a variety of new policy measures, i.e. unconventional monetary policy measures (Ito and Mishkin, 2004). As a pioneer of such, the BOJ introduced a zero interest rate policy in February 1999. The move was unprecedented across the world and was followed up by quantitative easing (QE) in March 2001 and quantitative and qualitative monetary easing (QQE) in April 2013. The zero interest rate policy was an important milestone in monetary policy. By implementing it, the BOJ was aiming to fight deflationary pressures and boost the economy. As the BOJ expected, the policy was effective in lowering deflationary pressures, and the Japan economy showed signs of gradual recovery (Fujiwara et al., 2016). Hence, the zero interest rate policy was abandoned in August 2000. However, towards the end of 2000, with a sharp downturn in the global economy, the Japanese economic recovery came to a standstill (Bernanke, 2017). This prompted the BOJ to note that the economy had failed to achieve sustainable growth and, perhaps, even had started to weaken.

On 19 March 2001, the BOJ introduced a new and unprecedented monetary policy measure: QE (McCallum, 2003). Under the QE programme, the BOJ conducted large-scale asset purchases, which were aimed to stimulate the economy by increasing the money supply and reducing long-term interest rates (Eggertsson and Woodford, 2003). Between 2001 and 2006, the vast majority of the BOJ's large-scale asset purchases consisted of Japanese government bonds. However, two years after the implementation of the first QE programme, the BOJ increased its monetary base by approximately 60% and prevented the Japanese economy from falling into a deflationary spiral (Andolfatto and Li, 2013). After the global financial crisis, in April 2013, the BOJ implemented a more aggressive policy measure intending to achieve price stability of 2%: QQE (Hirakata, 2018). QQE is made up of two main components: strong commitment policy aiming to work on inflation expectations, and large-scale Japanese government bond (JGB) purchases intended to lower long-term interest rates.

This study covers the period 1999–2016 and includes 12 unconventional monetary policy announcements. Ueda (2012) categorises the unconventional monetary policy measures adopted by major central banks into three types: forward guidance of policy rates, large-scale asset purchases and quantitative easing. This has become a relatively widely accepted classification of policies adoptable near the zero lower bound on interest rates. During 1999–2016, the BOJ held more than 100 official central bank monetary policy committee meetings.

Throughout these meetings, various decisions were made, and most of them involved a continuation of the previously implemented unconventional policy measure (Shibamoto and Tachibana, 2017). The selected 12 unconventional monetary policy announcements include crucial changes or the introduction of new policy measures (see Table 7.1). All statements are accommodative from a monetary policy perspective.

Table 7.1 Key unconventional monetary policy announcements by the BOJ, 1999–2016

Date	Unconventional monetary policy announcement	Description/content of the policies
13.4.1999	04/1999 (Bank of Japan, 2019a)	• The BOJ decided, by majority vote, to maintain its zero interest rate policy to assure permeation of the effects of monetary easing
19.3.2001	03/2001 (Bank of Japan, 2019b)	• Change in the operating target for money market operations • CPI guideline for the duration of the new procedures • Increase in the current account balance at the BOJ and reduction in interest rates • Increase in outright purchase of long-term government bonds
28.2.2002	02/2002 (Bank of Japan, 2019c)	• Providing ample liquidity towards the end of a fiscal year • Increasing the outright purchase of long-term government bonds • Easing the restriction on the use of the Lombard-type lending facility • Examining issues to broaden the range of eligible collateral
8.4.2003	04/2003 (Bank of Japan, 2019d)	• The BOJ will conduct money market operations, aiming at the outstanding balance of current accounts held at the Bank at around 17 to 22 trillion yen
18.9.2008	09/2008 (Bank of Japan, 2019e)	• The BOJ will encourage the uncollateralised overnight call rate to remain at around 0.5%
18.12.2009	12/2009 (Bank of Japan, 2019f)	• Clarification of the "Understanding of Medium- to Long-Term Price Stability"
30.8.2010	08/2010 (Bank of Japan, 2019g)	• The BOJ, based on the results of the Monetary Policy Meeting of the Policy Board held today, will start providing additional funds with a six-month term in an amount of approximately 10 trillion yen in the fixed-rate funds-supplying operation against pooled collateral, while maintaining the outstanding amount of funds provided by the existing three-month term operations at 20 trillion yen.

(Continued)

Table 7.1 (Continued)

Date	Unconventional monetary policy announcement	Description/content of the policies
22.1.2013	01/2013 (Bank of Japan, 2019h)	• Specifically, the Bank decided to (1) introduce the "price stability target", and (2) introduce the "open-ended asset purchasing method" (i.e., to purchase assets without setting any termination date) under the Asset Purchase Program. Furthermore, the Bank decided to release the joint statement with the government.
18.2.2014	02/2014 (Bank of Japan, 2019i)	• Statement on Monetary Policy: Extension and Enhancement of the Stimulating Bank Lending Facility and the Growth-Supporting Funding Facility
21.1.2015	01/2015 (Bank of Japan, 2019j)	• Extension of the Stimulating Bank Lending Facility and the Growth-Supporting Funding Facility
29.1.2016	01/2016 (Bank of Japan, 2019k)	• The Policy Board of the Bank of Japan decided to introduce "Quantitative and Qualitative Monetary Easing (QQE) with a Negative Interest Rate" in order to achieve the price stability target of 2% at the earliest possible time. Going forward, the Bank will pursue monetary easing by making full use of possible measures in terms of three dimensions; quantity, quality and interest rate.
21.9.2016	09/2016 (Bank of Japan, 2019l)	• The Policy Board of the Bank of Japan conducted a comprehensive assessment of the developments in economic activity and prices under "Quantitative and Qualitative Monetary Easing (QQE)" and "QQE with a Negative Interest Rate" as well as their policy effects, and compiled "The Bank's View".

Another critical feature for conducting a successful event study is considering the possible negative impact of the confounding effect on the statistical results (Barber and Lyon, 1997). The confounding effect can be explained as the collapse of the impact of the different events with each other (Basdas and Oran, 2014). If the confounding effect occurs, it is almost impossible to identify the impact of a specific event. By using a daily dataset and short-horizon event windows, the risk has been minimised and almost eliminated for this study.[2] In the existing literature, the majority of studies which examine the relationship between monetary policy announcements and stock market reactions have also employed a short-horizon event study methodology, with event windows of a few days before and after the announcement dates (e.g. Bomfin, 2003; Ehrmann and Fratzscher, 2005; Chulia et al., 2010; Rosa, 2011; Ait-Sahalia et al.,

2011, 2012; Ricci, 2014; Fiordelisi et al., 2014). By taking into account the nature of the events that have been tested, and referring to the empirical studies by Ricci (2014) and Fiordelisi et al. (2014), this study focuses on the following two short-term event windows: 5 days (-1; +3) and 3 days (-1; +1).

3.2 Bank selection

There are 215 actively operating banks in Japan (BOJ, 2019). Among these banks, 56 are branches of foreign banks. The remaining 159 banks consist of 5 city banks, 64 regional banks, 40 member banks of the second association of regional banks, 15 trust banks, 22 bank holding companies and 13 other banks.

Table 7.2 List of selected Japanese banks

77 Bank	Gunma Bank	San-in Godo Bank
Aichi Bank	Hachijuni Bank	Senshu Ikeda Holdings
Akita Bank	Hiroshima Bank	Seven Bank
Aomori Bank	Hokkoku Bank	Shiga Bank
Aozora Bank	Hokuhoku Financial Group	Shikoku Bank
AWA Bank	Howa Bank	Shimane Bank
Bank of Iwate	Hyakugo Bank	Shimizu Bank
Bank of Japan	Hyakujushi Bank	Shinkin Central Bank Preferred
Bank of Kochi	IYO Bank	Shinsei Bank
Bank of Kyoto	Jimoto Holdings	Shizuoka Bank
Bank of Nagoya	Juroku Bank	Sumitomo Mitsui Financial Group
Bank of Okinawa	Keiyo Bank	Sumitomo Mitsui Trust Holdings
Bank of Saga	Kita-Nippon Bank	Suruga Bank
Bank of the Ryukyus	Kiyo Bank	Taiko Bank
Chiba Bank	Mebuki Financial Group	The Bank of Toyama
Chiba Kogyo Bank	Michinoku Bank	Tochigi Bank
Chikuho Bank	Minami-Nippon Bank	Toho Bank
Chugoku Bank	Mitsubishi UFJ Financial Group	Tohoku Bank
Chukyo Bank	Miyazaki Bank	Tokyo Kiraboshi Financial Group
Daishi Hokuetsu Financial Group	Miyazaki Taiyo Bank	Tomato Bank
Daito Bank	Mizuho Financial Group	Tomony Holdings
Ehime Bank	Musashino Bank	Tottori Bank
Eighteenth Bank	Nagano Bank	Towa Bank
Fidea Holdings	Nanto Bank	Tsukuba Bank
Fintech Global	North Pacific Bank	Yamagata Bank
Fukui Bank	Ogaki Kyoritsu Bank	Yamaguchi Financial Group
Fukuoka Chuo Bank	Oita Bank	
Fukushima Bank	Resona Holdings	

Source: Datastream

Consistent with the primary purpose of this study, the selected banks need to meet the following requirements: (1) they should be local Japanese banks, and (2) they should be listed on a stock exchange and daily stock price data should be available. Between 1999 and 2016, a large number of Japanese banks went bankrupt, were nationalised or merged with another financial institution (Boswell, 2013). While selecting the Japanese banks, the banks that were merged with or acquired by another financial institution were eliminated.[3] Out of the listed 90 banks, 82 meet the needed criteria of the study. The daily stock returns (from 27 February 1999 to 31 December 2016) were collected from Datastream.

3.3   Calculating and testing the abnormal return

To measure the reaction of the Japanese bank stock returns to the selected unconventional monetary policy announcements, abnormal returns (ARs) have been estimated. Abnormal returns are an important measure to assess the impact of an event. The main idea of this measure is to separate the effect of that specific event from other general market movements. The abnormal return is calculated by taking the differences between the realised return and the expected (benchmark) return given the absence of the event (Kothari, 2006):

$$AR_{i,t} = R_{i,t} - E(R_{i,t}) \tag{1}$$

Where $AR_{i,t}$ is the abnormal return of stock i at the time t; $R_{i,t}$ is the realised return of stock i at the time t; and $E(R_{i,t})$ is the expected return of stock i at the time t.

The expected return represents the return that is uncorrelated to the event of interest. Regarding the calculation method of the benchmark (expected) return, this study uses the constant market (so-called market-adjusted) method. The constant market method assumes that all stocks, on average, generate the same rate of return (Bruner, 1999; Weber et al., 2008). Therefore, in the constant market method, the expected return is the market index (return) in the same time period. Hence:

$$E(R_{i,t}) = R_{m,t} \tag{2}$$

Where $R_{m,t}$ is the return of the stock market m at time t. In this study, the Tokyo Stock Price Index (TOPIX) is used to estimate the benchmark return.

Once the ARs calculated, the next step is the grouping of those excess returns for further analysis. One of the most commonly used methods for grouping the abnormal returns is to calculate cumulative abnormal returns (CARs) (Barber and Lyon, 1997). CARs refer to the summation of ARs over the event window. As mentioned before, in this study, the following short-horizon event widows are used: 5 days (-1; +3) and 3 days (-1; +1). For each of these event windows, CARs are obtained as follows (Fiordelisi et al., 2014):

$$CAR = \sum_{t=t_1}^{t_2} AR_{i,t} \tag{3}$$

Where t_1 and t_2 represent the start and the end dates of the selected event windows, respectively.

After the calculation of the CARs, as a final step to have reliable and convincing results about whether the tested events had a significant impact or not on the Japanese bank stock returns, a parametric test of t-statistics is applied. From the CAR, we can test whether the chosen unconventional monetary policy announcements of the BOJ influence bank stock returns by testing the null (H0) CAR=0. The null hypothesis (H0: CAR=0) is rejected if the test statistic exceeds a critical value. To test H0, the test statistics for CAR is determined as follows (Boehmer et al., 1991):

$$t - test = \frac{CAR}{S(AR_{t,i}) \star \sqrt{T}} \tag{4}$$

Where CAR is the summation of abnormal returns of a specific stock over the event window (t_1, t_2); $S(AR_{t,i})$ is the estimate of standard deviation of the average abnormal returns in the estimation period; T is the number of days in the considered event window (t_1, t_2). The t-statistics for this study are set at 10%, 5% and 1% levels of significance.

4 Empirical results

Tables 7.3–7.5 summarise the results of the CARs conducted on the 82 banks and 12 unconventional monetary policy announcements by the BOJ between 1999 and 2016. All statements refer to a more accommodative policy and should, therefore, help to boost share prices.

A detailed analysis of each bank is beyond the scope of this study. However, the main results can be summarised as follows.

Table 7.3 displays the results for the unconventional monetary policy announcements between 1999 and 2003: 04/1999, 03/2001, 02/2002 and 04/2003. During these years, very few of the tested Japanese banks show a statistically significant reaction to the implemented unconventional monetary policy announcements. For 04/1999, which included maintaining the zero interest rate policy by the majority of the votes from the committee, only 1 of the 82 banks shows statistically significant reactions. For the 03/2001 announcement, which includes an increase in the current account balance at the Bank of Japan, a reduction in interest rates and an increase in the outright purchase of long-term government bonds, only 9 of 82 banks show statistically significant results. For 02/2002, which entailed an increase in the outright purchase of long-term government bonds (like 03/2001) and an easing in the restriction on the use of the Lombard-type lending facility, none of the sampled 82 banks display any statistically significant reactions. For 04/2003 (similar to 04/1999 and 03/2001), very few bank stocks show a response to the unconventional monetary policy announcement. The majority of the detected reactions are obtained from the (-1, +1) event window, and the majority of the detected significant ones are strongly significant (1% level). Notably, the

Table 7.3 Bank stock return reactions to unconventional announcements by the BOJ, 1999–2003

Announcement	04/1999	04/1999	03/2001	03/2001	02/2002	02/2002	04/2003	04/2003
Event window	(-1, +1)	(-1, +3)	(-1, +1)	(-1, +3)	(-1, +1)	(-1, +3)	(-1, +1)	(-1, +3)
77 Bank	0.030	0.001	-0.040	0.008	0.036	-0.023	-0.015	0.008
Aichi Bank	-0.028	-0.006	0.013	0.049	-0.013	-0.040	0.010	0.018
Akita Bank	0.028	-0.194	-0.022	-0.078	-0.021	-0.065★	0.014	0.038
Aomori Bank	-0.001	-0.017	0.018	-0.030	0.007	-0.029	0.009	0.033
Aozora Bank	NA	NA	NA	NA	NA	NA	NA	NA
AWA Bank	0.009	0.012	0.046	0.072	0.050	0.102	0.071	0.030
Bank of Iwate	0.072★	0.080	0.014	0.036	0.055	0.188	0.009	0.049
Bank of Japan	0.004	0.051	0.051	0.219	0.046	0.062	0.011	0.010
Bank of Kochi	NA	NA	NA	NA	-0.015	-0.023	-0.008	0.004
Bank of Kyoto	-0.004	-0.027	0.038	0.017	-0.021	-0.016	0.002	0.007
Bank of Nagoya	-0.011	-0.009	0.010	0.105★	-0.019	-0.074	-0.005	0.011
Bank of Okinawa	-0.004	0.008	0.037	-0.039	-0.022	-0.064	-0.004	0.006
Bank of Saga	-0.017	-0.015	-0.000	0.000	-0.023	-0.055	-0.003	0.009
Bank of the Ryukyus	0.008	0.017	-0.015	-0.071	-0.048	-0.087	0.011	0.072
Chiba Bank	0.012	0.028	0.041	-0.023	-0.081★	-0.033	0.013	0.021
Chiba Kogyo Bank	-0.028	-0.039	-0.011	0.048	-0.001	-0.018	0.014	0.025
Chikuho Bank	-0.001	-0.006	-0.013	-0.063★	-0.050	-0.084	-0.007	0.006
Chugoku Bank	-0.008	-0.008	-0.009	-0.025	-0.010	-0.024	0.013	0.025
Chukyo Bank	0.007	0.045	-0.049	-0.013	0.041	0.013	0.017	-0.007
Daishi Hokuetsu Financial Group	0.000	0.001	0.008	-0.002	-0.019	-0.062	0.009	0.014
Daito Bank	-0.000	-0.000	0.024	0.030	-0.052	-0.093	-0.010	0.006
Ehime Bank	0.005	0.006	-0.006	-0.018	-0.013	-0.071	-0.028	-0.015
Eighteenth Bank	0.001	0.012	-0.009	-0.035	-0.018	0.022	-0.000	-0.024
Fidea Holdings	NA	NA	NA	NA	NA	NA	NA	NA
Fintech Global	NA	NA	NA	NA	NA	NA	NA	NA
Fukui Bank	0.013	0.014	-0.013	-0.058	-0.046	-0.069	-0.021	0.012
Fukuoka Chuo Bank	-0.000	-0.005	0.005	-0.063★	-0.007	0.016	0.010	0.034
Fukushima Bank	-0.008	-0.050	0.096★	-0.001	-0.032	0.063	0.365	0.072★

Gunma Bank	0.029	0.011	−0.007	−0.063	−0.051	−0.099	−0.041	−0.026
Hachijuni Bank	0.015	0.022	−0.009	−0.028	−0.094*	−0.022	0.012	0.028
Hiroshima Bank	0.002	0.008	−0.025	−0.011	−0.025	−0.018	0.039	0.019
Hokkoku Bank	0.029	0.017	−0.013	−0.064	0.007	0.016	−0.000	0.010
Hokuhoku Financial Group	0.012	0.081	−0.001	−0.021	0.034	0.007	−0.023	−0.049
Howa Bank	−0.001	−0.028	−0.013	−0.064	−0.046	−0.090	−0.012	−0.042
Hyakugo Bank	0.034	0.042	0.091*	0.018	−0.048	−0.024	−0.008	−0.003
Hyakujushi Bank	−0.027	−0.028	−0.022	−0.055	0.018	−0.031	−0.000	0.054
IYO Bank	−0.026	−0.045	−0.014	−0.047	−0.007	−0.013	−0.001	−0.006
Jimoto Holdings	NA	NA	NA	NA	NA	NA	NA	NA
Juroku Bank	−0.024	−0.033	−0.016	−0.080	−0.040	−0.089	−0.004	0.008
Keiyo Bank	−0.054	−0.054	−0.009	−0.013	−0.019	−0.069	−0.004	0.000
Kita–Nippon Bank	−0.027	0.020	−0.074*	−0.137**	−0.036	−0.082*	−0.022	−0.009
Kiyo Bank	NA	NA	NA	NA	NA	NA	NA	NA
Mebuki Financial Group	−0.023	−0.018	0.029	0.015	−0.039	−0.051	−0.024	0.009
Michinoku Bank	−0.010	−0.005	0.029	−0.019	0.001	−0.045	−0.007	0.000
Minami–Nippon Bank	−0.000	−0.000	−0.013	−0.065	−0.046	−0.090	0.025	0.022
Mitsubishi UFJ Financial Group	NA	NA	NA	NA	NA	NA	NA	−0.016
Miyazaki Bank	0.001	0.001	−0.013	−0.063	−0.048	−0.092	−0.007	0.016
Miyazaki Taiyo Bank	0.002	0.011	−0.024	−0.050	−0.008	−0.002	−0.015	0.006
Mizuho Financial Group	NA	NA	−0.051	−0.042	−0.021	−0.025	−0.001	0.004
Musashino Bank	−0.024	−0.028	−0.027	−0.047	0.000	−0.048	−0.001	0.006
Nagano Bank	−0.020	0.040	−0.008	−0.059	0.001	−0.012	−0.007	0.000
Nanto Bank	0.011	0.012	−0.008	−0.061	−0.041	−0.093*	−0.019	−0.001
North Pacific Bank	NA	NA	NA	NA	NA	NA	NA	NA
Ogaki Kyoritsu Bank	−0.000	−0.009	−0.018	−0.076	−0.005	−0.004	−0.005	−0.043
Oita Bank	−0.017	−0.007	−0.011	−0.025	−0.020	−0.073*	−0.017	0.012
Resona Holdings	−0.009	−0.018	0.042	0.028	0.310***	0.016	0.010	0.000
San–in Godo Bank	0.002	0.008	−0.017	0.055	−0.034	−0.085*	0.022	0.007
Senshu Ikeda Holdings	NA	NA	−0.021	−0.012	−0.018	−0.041	0.009	−0.001
Seven Bank	NA	NA	0.026	0.036	−0.038	0.005	−0.012	−0.040

(*Continued*)

Table 7.3 (Continued)

Announcement	04/1999	04/1999	03/2001	03/2001	02/2002	02/2002	04/2003	04/2003
Shiga Bank	-0.051	-0.049	0.018	-0.025	-0.039	-0.077	-0.002	0.014
Shikoku Bank	-0.009	-0.009	-0.001	-0.027	-0.013	-0.052	0.000	-0.013
Shimane Bank	-0.021	-0.029	-0.004	-0.043	0.014	-0.000	-0.006	0.002
Shimizu Bank	-0.017	-0.001	-0.004	-0.072	-0.022	-0.004	-0.005	0.000
Shinkin Central Bank Preferred	-0.001	-0.002	-0.009	-0.011	0.015	-0.003	0.002	-0.000
Shinsei Bank	0.001	0.000	-0.023	-0.045	0.033	0.058	0.009	0.007
Shizuoka Bank	0.025	0.005	-0.004	-0.072	-0.022	-0.004	-0.005	0.000
Sumitomo Mitsui Financial Group	-0.028	-0.048	0.018	-0.014	0.009	0.012	-0.001	0.002
Sumitomo Mitsui Trust Holdings	-0.026	-0.047	0.029	-0.023	0.011	0.022	-0.007	-0.005
Suruga Bank	-0.015	-0.029	-0.029	-0.025	-0.002	-0.003	-0.002	0.059
Taiko Bank	-0.018	-0.031	-0.013	-0.063★	-0.007	0.008	-0.015	-0.066
The Bank of Toyama	-0.000	0.084	0.089	-0.050	-0.059	-0.126★★★	-0.007	0.011
Tochigi Bank	-0.008	0.016	0.017	0.033	-0.048	-0.022	-0.007	0.009
Toho Bank	-0.002	-0.006	0.027	0.042	-0.034	-0.026	0.009	0.000
Tohoku Bank	0.008	-0.001	0.017	0.045	-0.022	-0.023	-0.001	0.008
Tokyo Kiraboshi Financial Group	0.001	0.001	0.019	-0.026	0.008	-0.034	-0.004	0.001
Tomato Bank	0.006	0.007	0.100★	0.023	0.048	0.022	-0.008	-0.009
Tomony Holdings	0.000	0.001	-0.028	-0.057	-0.006	0.005	-0.000	0.000
Tottori Bank	-0.017	-0.026	-0.038	-0.029	-0.002	-0.005	-0.001	-0.021
Towa Bank	-0.033	-0.039	-0.006	-0.068★	0.014	-0.037	-0.000	0.000
Tsukuba Bank	-0.021	-0.011	-0.004	-0.055	0.029	-0.033	0.006	0.017
Yamagata Bank	-0.008	-0.003	-0.061	0.011	-0.004	0.024	0.000	-0.002
Yamaguchi Financial Group	0.003	-0.006	0.011	0.024	-0.011	0.076★	-0.018	0.029

Note: ★/★★/★★★ statistically significant at p < 0.10/0.05/0.01 level. Standard errors have been omitted for space reasons (available from the author on request).

Table 7.4 Bank stock return reactions to unconventional announcements by the BOJ, 2008–2010

Announcement	09/2008	09/2008	12/2009	12/2009	08/2010	08/2010
Event window	(-1, +1)	(-1, +3)	(-1, +1)	(-1, +3)	(-1, +1)	(-1, +3)
77 Bank	0.009	-0.051*	-0.037	-0.026	-0.010	-0.002
Aichi Bank	0.113**	0.095	-0.008	-0.047	0.014	0.008
Akita Bank	0.028	-0.036	-0.009	-0.022	0.034	0.059*
Aomori Bank	0.088***	0.046	-0.015	-0.024	0.018	0.009
Aozora Bank	0.008	-0.025	-0.056	-0.069	-0.000	-0.045
AWA Bank	0.012	-0.014	0.003	-0.015	0.033*	0.037
Bank of Iwate	0.027	-0.034	-0.020	-0.029	-0.075	-0.015
Bank of Japan	-0.072	-0.089	-0.010	-0.024	-0.011	-0.029
Bank of Kochi	-0.052	-0.022	-0.018	-0.017	0.008	0.004
Bank of Kyoto	0.040	0.017	-0.020	-0.023	0.001	0.004
Bank of Nagoya	-0.016	0.054	-0.006	-0.010	0.029	0.031
Bank of Okinawa	0.003	-0.040	-0.025	-0.040	0.027	0.024
Bank of Saga	0.000	0.001	-0.008	-0.005	0.017	0.008
Bank of the Ryukyus	0.088	0.083	-0.011	-0.022	-0.005	0.015
Chiba Bank	0.050	0.064	0.012	-0.028	-0.001	0.003
Chiba Kogyo Bank	0.001	-0.023	0.007	0.027	-0.002	-0.003
Chikuho Bank	0.000	-0.017	-0.024	-0.002	0.042	-0.007
Chugoku Bank	0.020	-0.004	-0.002	-0.040	-0.014	0.003
Chukyo Bank	0.010	-0.020	0.004	-0.008	0.031	0.009
Daishi Hokuetsu Financial Group	-0.001	-0.018	-0.008	-0.008	0.028	0.030
Daito Bank	-0.011	-0.028	0.026	-0.021	-0.034	-0.047
Ehime Bank	0.058	0.034	-0.003	0.024	0.000	-0.006
Eighteenth Bank	0.023	0.028	-0.008	-0.012	0.017	0.008
Fidea Holdings	0.009	-0.002	-0.028	-0.012	0.005	0.018
Fintech Global	0.015	0.012	0.026	-0.011	-0.030	0.010
Fukui Bank	0.004	-0.031	0.026	0.014	0.077*	0.003

(*Continued*)

Table 7.4 (Continued)

Announcement	09/2008	09/2008	12/2009	12/2009	08/2010	08/2010
Fukuoka Chuo Bank	-0.031	-0.048	0.007	-0.005	0.008	-0.010
Fukushima Bank	-0.079	-0.110***	-0.029	-0.042	-0.011	-0.009
Gunma Bank	0.008	0.012	-0.038	-0.018	-0.012	0.000
Hachijuni Bank	-0.002	0.000	0.031	0.012	-0.005	-0.011
Hiroshima Bank	0.000	0.018	0.023	0.084*	0.009	0.008
Hokkoku Bank	0.037	0.064	-0.022	-0.030	0.001	0.001
Hokuhoku Financial Group	0.021	0.018	-0.016	-0.027	0.000	-0.006
Howa Bank	-0.031	-0.040	0.027	0.059	-0.019	-0.037
Hyakugo Bank	0.065	0.062	0.039	0.018	0.023	0.010
Hyakujushi Bank	0.042	0.008	-0.016	-0.023	0.008	0.009
IYO Bank	0.017	0.003	-0.011	-0.028	-0.008	-0.008
Jimoto Holdings	NA	NA	NA	NA	-0.003	-0.000
Juroku Bank	-0.075	-0.098	0.010	-0.002	0.001	0.008
Keiyo Bank	-0.038	0.009	-0.024	-0.039	0.034	0.002
Kita–Nippon Bank	0.018	-0.008	0.007	-0.013	-0.013	0.005
Kiyo Bank	NA	NA	NA	NA	0.011	-0.037
Mebuki Financial Group	0.056	0.008	-0.023	-0.042	0.027	0.031
Michinoku Bank	-0.009	-0.028	0.022	0.027	0.026	-0.006
Minami–Nippon Bank	-0.029	-0.038	0.026	0.017	0.003	-0.009
Mitsubishi UFJ Financial Group	0.062	0.087	0.014	0.003	-0.016	-0.036
Miyazaki Bank	-0.016	-0.046	0.080	0.067	0.037	-0.009
Miyazaki Taiyo Bank	-0.006	-0.015	0.029	0.064	0.002	-0.010
Mizuho Financial Group	0.014	0.042	-0.043	-0.028	0.025	0.037
Musashino Bank	0.010	0.006	-0.010	0.005	-0.001	-0.016
Nagano Bank	-0.027	-0.034	0.111**	0.076	0.033	-0.004
Nanto Bank	0.047	0.032	-0.005	-0.016	0.003	0.012
North Pacific Bank	NA	NA	NA	NA	0.026	0.002
Ogaki Kyoritsu Bank	0.056*	0.021	0.014	0.001	0.020	0.0009
Oita Bank	0.079	0.063	0.004	-0.025	0.016	0.019

Resona Holdings	0.239***	0.324***	-0.015	0.029	-0.079	-0.135*
San-in Godo Bank	-0.042	-0.029	-0.012	-0.030	-0.008	0.009
Senshu Ikeda Holdings	NA	NA	NA	NA	NA	NA
Seven Bank	NA	NA	-0.029	-0.041	-0.012	-0.010
Shiga Bank	-0.044	-0.085	-0.014	-0.027	0.016	0.022
Shikoku Bank	0.028	0.011	-0.027	-0.043	-0.016	-0.001
Shimane Bank	0.011	0.009	-0.062	-0.153*	0-.044	-0.039
Shimizu Bank	0.011	0.001	0.005	-0.010	0.006	0.018
Shinkin Central Bank Preferred	-0.050	0.006	0.004	0.001	0.008	-0.008
Shinsei Bank	0.019	0.033	-0.029	-0.032	0.006	0.000
Shizuoka Bank	0.064*	0.035	-0.028	-0.023	0.014	0.036
Sumitomo Mitsui Financial Group	0.025	0.059	-0.010	-0.027	-0.003	-0.045
Sumitomo Mitsui Trust Holdings	-0.045	-0.018	0.023	0.023	-0.002	0.004
Suruga Bank	-0.024	0.013	-0.018	-0.026	0.000	0.023
Taiko Bank	-0.015	-0.000	-0.006	0.024	0.014	-0.028
The Bank of Toyama	-0.003	-0.014	0.026	-0.075	-0.051	-0.046
Tochigi Bank	0.026	0.016	-0.009	-0.025	0.014	0.002
Toho Bank	0.018	0.011	-0.034	-0.023	-0.008	0.001
Tohoku Bank	-0.067	-0.088*	0.017	-0.007	0.015	0.093*
Tokyo Kiraboshi Financial Group	-0.004	-0.002	-0.019	-0.033	0.071*	0.010
Tomato Bank	0.013	0.043	-0.002	-0.012	0.015	0.028
Tomony Holdings	-0.023	0.006	0.018	0.048	0.025	0.034
Tottori Bank	0.013	0.008	-0.028	-0.013	-0.015	0.002
Towa Bank	-0.018	-0.045	0.024	-0.004	-0.033	-0.008
Tsukuba Bank	-0.019	-0.051	0.031	-0.001	0.034	0.017
Yamagata Bank	-0.023	-0.059*	0.016	0.025	-0.023	-0.008
Yamaguchi Financial Group	-0.063	-0.013	0.017	-0.003	0.028	0.022

Note: */**/*** statistically significant at p < 0.10/0.05/0.01 level. Standard errors have been omitted for space reasons (available from the author on request).

Table 7.5 Bank stock return reactions to unconventional announcements by the BOJ, 2013–2016

Announcement	01/2013	01/2013	02/2014	02/2014	01/2015	01/2015	01/2016	01/2016	09/2016	09/2016
Event window	(−1, +1)	(−1, +3)	(−1, +1)	(−1, +3)	(−1, +1)	(−1, +3)	(−1, +1)	(−1, +3)	(−1, +1)	(−1, +3)
77 Bank	0.023*	0.026	0.032*	0.038	−0.022**	0.001	−0.191***	−0.240***	0.038*	0.003
Aichi Bank	0.111*	−0.030	0.073**	0.034	0.017*	−0.014	−0.092***	−0.091**	0.067*	0.020
Akita Bank	0.085*	−0.020	0.054**	0.031	−0.038*	−0.024	−0.075*	−0.075**	−0.082	−0.027
Aomori Bank	0.029**	0.012	−0.022*	−0.002	−0.072**	−0.018	−0.066**	−0.042*	0.017*	0.048
Aozora Bank	0.043**	0.066	−0.078**	−0.019	0.086***	0.018	−0.103***	−0.064**	0.035*	−0.014
AWA Bank	0.200*	0.348***	0.128**	0.349**	0.034*	0.094	0.384***	0.172	0.101**	0.040
Bank of Iwate	0.125*	0.082	0.201*	0.076	0.101*	0.104	0.215***	0.086	0.123*	0.059
Bank of Japan	0.055	0.079	0.001	0.034	0.375***	0.031	0.194***	0.039	0.098	0.021
Bank of Kochi	0.128***	0.143**	0.145**	0.072*	0.140***	0.015	0.147***	0.153***	0.176***	0.025
Bank of Kyoto	0.079**	0.001	0.189***	0.075	0.234**	0.063	0.132***	0.017	0.148***	0.052
Bank of Nagoya	0.203***	0.276*	0.789***	0.378***	0.754**	0.135	0.573***	0.136	0.092*	0.025
Bank of Okinawa	0.077*	0.058*	0.113***	0.023	−0.165**	−0.027	−0.122***	−0.117***	0.092**	0.087
Bank of Saga	−0.048**	−0.012	−0.042*	−0.039*	−0.078**	−0.022	−0.103***	−0.101**	0.039	0.033
Bank of the Ryukyus	0.102***	0.074	−0.087*	−0.045	−0.159**	0.071	−0.148**	−0.188***	0.187**	0.050
Chiba Bank	0.095*	0.029	−0.048**	0.021	−0.165***	0.038	−01.24***	−0.170***	0.053*	0.011
Chiba Kogyo Bank	0.088*	0.013	−0.139***	−0.158***	−0.056*	0.025	0.106***	−0.080**	0.092***	0.026
Chikuho Bank	0.049**	0.050	−0.098**	−0.087**	−0.196***	0.071	−0.185***	−0.122**	0.042*	0.022
Chugoku Bank	−0.052*	−0.044**	−0.145**	−0.046	−0.099**	−0.022	−0.062*	−0.057	0.055*	0.034
Chukyo Bank	−0.076**	−0.065*	−0.102***	−0.022	−0.046*	−0.072*	−0.124***	−0.049	0.117***	0.016
Daishi Hokuetsu Financial Group	0.055*	0.023	0.064*	0.038	0.113**	0.019	0.148**	0.138*	0.154***	0.024
Daito Bank	0.032*	0.029*	−0.037*	−0.041*	0.056*	0.015	−0.063*	−0.049*	0.055*	0.025
Ehime Bank	0.135***	0.049*	0.055*	0.046	0.126***	0.043	0.097***	0.055*	0.144***	0.015
Eighteenth Bank	−0.070*	−0.029	0.152***	0.048	0.088*	0.010	−0.141***	−0.116***	0.080**	0.024
Fidea Holdings	−0.048*	−0.025	0.105**	0.055*	−0.130**	−0.038	0.077*	0.063*	0.071*	0.021
Fintech Global	0.121***	0.033	0.066*	0.098*	−0.109**	−0.045*	0.148***	0.154***	0.125***	0.120**
Fukui Bank	0.050*	0.028	−0.189***	−0.023	0.099**	0.043	−0.109**	−0.178***	0.149***	0.087*

Fukuoka Chuo Bank	0.092*	0.044	0.071**	0.066	0.123***	0.024	0.102**	0.062*	0.124*	0.334**
Fukushima Bank	-0.123**	-0.076*	0.145***	0.054	0.083	0.051	0.048*	-0.021	0.187***	0.062*
Gunma Bank	-0.172***	-0.074*	0.133**	-0.012	0.092*	0.012	0.187***	0.096*	0.081*	0.032
Hachijuni Bank	0.098*	0.023	0.057*	0.047	0.103**	0.120	-0.106**	-0.101**	0.059*	0.048
Hiroshima Bank	0.110**	0.029	0.101**	0.056*	0.056*	0.028	0.146***	0.133***	0.178***	0.029
Hokkoku Bank	-0.142***	-0.076*	-0.189***	-0.034	0.178***	0.058	0.111**	0.128***	0.170*	0.046
Hokuhoku Financial Group	0.131***	0.099**	0.143***	0.057	0.141***	0.106**	0.178***	0.182***	0.171***	0.149
Howa Bank	0.083*	0.031	0.086*	0.028	-0.055*	-0.016	0.116**	0.072*	0.120**	0.032
Hyakugo Bank	0.059*	0.012	0.156***	0.086*	0.032	0.022	0.109***	0.043	0.075*	0.013
Hyakujushi Bank	-0.045*	-0.026	-0.066*	-0.024	0.102**	0.019	0.171***	0.121***	0.121***	0.064
IYO Bank	0.136***	0.009	0.133***	0.037	0.043	0.028	0.106***	0.080*	0.124***	0.055
Jimoto Holdings	0.129***	0.025	0.062*	0.033	0.135***	-0.011	-0.103**	0.029	0.139***	0.044
Juroku Bank	0.156***	0.027	0.123**	0.028	0.139***	0.030	0.091*	0.103**	0.089*	0.076
Keiyo Bank	-0.042*	-0.025	0.176***	0.032	0.130***	0.041	0.145**	0.019	0.144**	0.018
Kita-Nippon Bank	0.132***	0.065	-0.056*	-0.044	-0.052	0.022	0.199***	0.179***	-0.067*	-0.000
Kiyo Bank	0.155***	0.153***	0.167***	0.059	0.132**	0.065*	0.129**	0.031	0.174*	0.072
Mebuki Financial Group	0.015	0.090*	0.133***	0.023	0.085*	-0.029	0.145***	0.155***	0.090*	0.029
Michinoku Bank	0.141**	0.032	0.109**	0.037	0.169***	0.035	0.184***	0.119***	0.178***	0.076
Minami-Nippon Bank	0.058*	0.044	-0.054*	0.021	0.115**	0.033	-0.056*	-0.068	0.040*	0.010
Mitsubishi UFJ Financial Group	0.120*	0.023	0.122**	-0.018	0.099**	0.007	-0.115**	-0.129***	0.146***	0.044
Miyazaki Bank	-0.052*	-0.021	0.013	0.004	0.028	0.084*	-0.123**	-0.068*	0.134**	0.032
Miyazaki Taiyo Bank	0.076*	0.059*	0.049*	0.047	-0.153***	-0.066	-0.183*	0.029	0.178***	0.055
Mizuho Financial Group	0.134***	0.048	0.139***	0.037	0.022	0.022	-0.135***	-0.068*	0.103***	0.017
Musashino Bank	-0.075*	-0.043*	0.178**	0.028	0.085*	-0.048	0.112***	0.052	0.119***	0.023
Nagano Bank	0.050	0.012	0.137***	0.011	0.032	0.029	0.045*	0.042	0.129***	0.035*
Nanto Bank	0.126***	0.031	0.156***	0.034	0.149***	0.048	0.158**	0.178**	0.045*	0.024
North Pacific Bank	0.093*	0.128***	0.085*	-0.025	0.132***	0.010	0.107**	0.138***	0.038*	0.004
Ogaki Kyoritsu Bank	0.134***	0.045	0.109**	0.038	0.185***	0.078*	0.142***	0.150***	0.045*	0.022
Oita Bank	0.075*	0.029	-0.065*	-0.039	0.133**	0.031	0.098*	0.138**	0.125**	0.032
Resona Holdings	0.122***	0.037	0.156***	0.032	0.128**	0.139**	0.142***	0.076*	0.035*	0.005
San-in Godo Bank	0.056*	0.023	0.167***	0.055*	-0.080*	-0.034	0.141***	0.032	0.042*	0.036
Senshu Ikeda Holdings	0.194***	0.028	-0.108**	0.053	0.144**	0.041	0.109**	0.126***	0.049*	0.009

(Continued)

Table 7.5 (Continued)

Announcement	01/2013	01/2013	02/2014	02/2014	01/2015	01/2015	01/2016	01/2016	09/2016	09/2016
Seven Bank	0.091*	0.012	0.062*	-0.027	0.077*	0.064	0.163***	0.146***	0.188*	0.030
Shiga Bank	-0.078*	-0.045	0.048*	0.042	0.023*	0.124**	0.093*	0.052	0.044**	0.083*
Shikoku Bank	0.128**	0.024	0.167***	0.036	0.171***	-0.016	0.104***	0.092*	0.165**	0.045
Shimane Bank	0.149***	0.124***	0.198***	-0.013	-0.084*	-0.058	-0.097**	-0.033	-0.038	-0.022
Shimizu Bank	0.012	0.071	0.025	0.074	0.034	0.040	0.198***	0.143***	0.128***	0.038
Shinkin Central Bank Preferred	0.053*	0.049	0.102**	0.032	0.065*	0.109**	0.106**	0.112**	0.166**	0.049
Shinsei Bank	0.147***	0.023	-0.143***	-0.047	0.142***	0.035	0.137***	0.187***	0.047*	0.018
Shizuoka Bank	0.186***	0.044	0.099**	0.044	0.156**	0.005	0.132**	0.100**	0.040*	0.018
Sumitomo Mitsui Financial Group	0.086*	0.050	-0.074*	-0.042	0.169**	0.024	-0.159***	-0.168***	0.112**	0.024
Sumitomo Mitsui Trust Holdings	-0.049*	-0.034	0.134**	0.032	-0.084**	0.051	0.134***	0.113**	0.045	0.066
Suruga Bank	0.106**	0.011	0.068*	-0.028	0.120**	0.023	-0.074*	-0.054*	-0.062*	-0.033
Taiko Bank	0.048*	0.037	0.020*	0.064	0.048*	0.028	0.167***	0.125**	0.155***	0.038
The Bank of Toyama	0.051*	0.023	0.099***	0.043	0.010	0.145**	0.073*	0.030	0.065*	0.067*
Tochigi Bank	0.042*	-0.007	-0.052*	-0.037	0.150**	0.001	0.101***	0.098**	0.200**	0.083
Toho Bank	0.180***	0.044	0.178***	0.019	0.049*	0.026	0.193**	0.152**	0.150**	0.029
Tohoku Bank	-0.052*	-0.019	-0.032*	-0.007	0.181***	0.061	-0.149***	-0.115**	0.133**	0.038
Tokyo Kiraboshi Financial Group	0.154***	0.046	0.177***	0.028	0.049	0.052	0.140***	0.166***	0.178***	0.062
Tomato Bank	0.198***	0.035	0.134***	0.061*	0.100**	0.097**	0.073*	0.074*	0.129***	0.003
Tomony Holdings	0.069*	0.071*	0.089*	0.018	-0.045*	-0.039	0.061*	0.157***	0.131***	0.088*
Tottori Bank	-0.059*	-0.054*	0.168***	0.034	0.123***	0.026	0.118***	0.019	0.198***	0.102
Towa Bank	0.064*	0.016	0.032*	-0.009	0.137***	0.044	-0.097*	0.075*	0.099*	0.031
Tsukuba Bank	0.028	0.024	0.033	0.065	0.102**	0.132***	0.142***	0.155***	0.129***	0.167***
Yamagata Bank	0.059*	0.112**	-0.039*	-0.035	-0.045*	-0.073*	0.061*	-0.191***	-0.145***	-0.040
Yamaguchi Financial Group	0.023	0.002	0.098*	0.006	0.043	0.036	0.194***	0.044*	0.085*	0.038

Note: */**/*** statistically significant at $p < 0.10/0.05/0.01$ level. Standard errors have been omitted for space reasons (available from the author on request).

bank stocks that show statistically significant reactions to the unconventional monetary policy announcements 04/1999, 03/2001 and 04/2003 are mainly regional banks.[4]

Table 7.4 shows the results for the unconventional monetary policy announcements between 2008 and 2010 (09/2008, 12/2009 and 08/2010), i.e. during and in the aftermath of the global financial crisis. For the 09/2008 announcement, in which the BOJ stated they would encourage the uncollat-eralised overnight call rate to remain at around 0.5%, again, very few (only 8) bank stocks show statistically significant reactions. For 12/2009, which includes the clarification of the "Understanding of Medium- to Long-Term Price Stability", similar to previous policy announcements, out of the 82 sampled banks only 3 stand out with immediate reactions. For the 08/2010 announcement, 6 bank stocks are statistically significant (at the 1% confidence level). During this meeting, the BOJ stated that they would provide extra funds with a six-month term of approximately 10 trillion yen in the fixed-rate funds-supplying operation against pooled collateral while maintaining the outstanding amount of funds provided by the existing three-month term operations at 20 trillion. Similar to the unconventional monetary announcements during 1999–2003, the majority of the banks with statistically significant reactions during 2008–2010 are regional banks.

Table 7.5 displays the results for the unconventional monetary policy announcements between 2013 and 2016 (01/2013, 02/2014, 01/2015, 01/2016 and 09/2016), i.e. since the launch of Abenomics. As can be seen from Table 7.5, in contrast to Table 7.3 and Table 7.4, the majority of the bank stocks show statistically significant reactions to the implemented unconventional monetary policy announcements. More than 90% of the detected responses are at the (-1, +1) event windows for 01/2013, 02/2014, 01/2015, 01/2016 and 09/2016. For the 01/2013 announcement, 79 of the sampled 82 banks are statistically significant. During this central bank meeting, the BOJ decided to introduce the price stability target and introduce the "open-ended asset purchasing method" (i.e. to purchase assets without setting any termination date) under the Asset Purchase Program. The 02/2014 announcement included a statement about the "Extension and Enhancement of the Stimulating Bank Lending Facility and the Growth-Supporting Funding Facility". Here, 77 bank stocks show reactions (22 statistically significant at the 1% confidence level, 27 at 5% and 28 at 10%).

Similarly, market participants also react strongly to the 01/2015 announcement. However, 01/2016 is the event that shows the most widespread reaction among all bank stocks. It included the decision of the Policy Board of the BOJ to introduce "Quantitative and Qualitative Monetary Easing (QQE) with a Negative Interest Rate" to achieve the price stability target of 2% at the earliest possible time. At this meeting, it was also stated that the central bank, going forward, would pursue monetary easing by "making full use of possible measures in terms of three dimensions; quantity, quality, and interest rate" (Bank of Japan, 2016). The last announcement in this study (09/2016) is also crucial – with 78 bank stocks reacting to it.

5 Conclusion

This chapter has investigated the impacts of the BOJ's unconventional monetary policy announcements on Japanese bank stock returns between 1999 and
2016. Amongst more than 100 announcements, 12 key policy actions were
selected and then tested on 82 Japanese banks. A short-horizon market structure model was used to measure CARs for various event windows. The results
show that the unconventional monetary policy announcements by the BOJ
during 1999–2012 appear to have had a limited immediate impact on Japanese bank stocks. This contradicts the findings by Ricci (2014) and Fiordelisi
et al. (2014), who find that unconventional monetary policy announcements
have a statistically significant impact on bank stock returns. However, since
the launch of Abenomics in 2013, Japanese bank stocks have reacted very
strongly to new interventions of the BOJ. This started with the implementation of the 2% inflation target (announcement 01/2013) and was followed
up by measures such as large-scale asset purchases, a negative interest rate and
yield curve control. The results suggest that there is a clear difference between
how the monetary policy transmission mechanism has functioned before and
after Abenomics (Grabowiecki and Mariusz, 2017). Alternatively, the sheer
scale of the unconventional monetary policy measures since 2013 might be a
crucial factor.

Notes

1 Previously, many academics and economists viewed this zero lower bound as a problem,
   but it was not widely perceived as an actual serious policy challenge (Kocherlakota, 2017;
   Altavilla, 2019).
2 While selecting the 12 unconventional monetary policy announcements, this study
   involved checking if there were any other important announcements or events on or near
   the chosen dates.
3 The reason for that is when a bank is merged with or acquired by another bank, it affects
   its stock returns (Shah et al., 2012).
4 The "NA" signs in the tables mean "no available data" for those specific announcement
   dates on the Tokyo Stock Exchange. Also, it should be noted that both positive and
   negative coefficients have been detected for specific policy announcements by the different banks. While some banks show positive (significant or insignificant) reactions to a
   particular policy announcement, others show negative responses to the same news. One
   of the reasons for those different reactions to the same announcements might be the result
   of the different characteristics of the tested Japanese banks (e.g. size and book-to-market
   ratio) (Maio, 2014).

References

Ait-Sahalia, Y., Andritzky, J., Jobst, A., Nowak, S. and Tamirisa, N. (2012) Market response
   to policy Initiatives during the global financial crisis. *Journal of International Economics*, 87
   (1), 162–177.
Aït-Sahalia, Y., Mykland, P. A. and Zhang, L. (2011) Ultra high frequency volatility estimation with dependent microstructure noise. *Journal of Econometrics*, 160 (1), 160–175.

Altavilla, C. (2019) Is there a zero lower bound? The effects of negative policy rates on banks and firms, *ECB Working Paper Series*, No. 2289.

Andolfatto, D. and Li, L. (2013) Is the Fed monetizing government debt? *Economic Synopses*, Federal Reserve Bank of St. Louis, Missouri (United States).

Ariccia, G., Rabanal, P. and Sandri, D. (2018) Unconventional monetary policies in the euro area, Japan, and the United Kingdom, *Journal of Economic Perspectives*, 32 (4), 147–172.

Bank of Japan. (2016) *What Is Quantitative and Qualitative Monetary Easing (QQE) with Yield Curve Control?*, 20 November 2016, Available from: https://www.boj.or.jp/en/announcements/education/oshiete/seisaku/b27.htm/ [Accessed 19 September 2019].

Bank of Japan (2019a) *Statement on Monetary Policy*, 13 April 1999. Available from: www.boj.or.jp/en/mopo/mpmdeci/state_1999/index.htm/ [Accessed 10 October 2019].

Bank of Japan (2019b) *Statement on Monetary Policy*, 19 March 2001. Available from: www.boj.or.jp/en/mopo/mpmdeci/state_2001/index.htm/ [Accessed 10 October 2019].

Bank of Japan (2019c) *Statement on Monetary Policy*, 28 February 2002. Available from: www.boj.or.jp/en/mopo/mpmdeci/state_2002/index.htm/ [Accessed 10 October 2019].

Bank of Japan (2019d) *Statement on Monetary Policy*, 8 April 2003. Available from: www.boj.or.jp/en/mopo/mpmdeci/state_2003/index.htm/ [Accessed 10 October 2019].

Bank of Japan (2019e) *Statement on Monetary Policy*, 18 September 2008. Available from: www.boj.or.jp/en/mopo/mpmdeci/state_2008/index.htm/ [Accessed 10 October 2019].

Bank of Japan (2019f) *Statement on Monetary Policy*, 18 December 2009. Available from: www.boj.or.jp/en/mopo/mpmdeci/state_2009/index.htm/ [Accessed 10 October 2019].

Bank of Japan (2019g) *Statement on Monetary Policy*, 30 August 2010. Available from: www.boj.or.jp/en/mopo/mpmdeci/state_2010/index.htm/ [Accessed 10 October 2019].

Bank of Japan (2019h) *Statement on Monetary Policy*, 22 January 2013. Available from: www.boj.or.jp/en/mopo/mpmdeci/state_2013/index.htm/ [Accessed 10 October 2019].

Bank of Japan (2019i) *Statement on Monetary Policy*, 18 February 2014. Available from: www.boj.or.jp/en/mopo/mpmdeci/state_2014/index.htm/ [Accessed 10 October 2019].

Bank of Japan (2019j) *Statement on Monetary Policy*, 21 January 2015. Available from: www.boj.or.jp/en/mopo/mpmdeci/state_2015/index.htm/ [Accessed 10 October 2019].

Bank of Japan (2019k) *Statement on Monetary Policy*, 29 January 2016. Available from: www.boj.or.jp/en/mopo/mpmdeci/state_2016/index.htm/ [Accessed 10 October 2019].

Bank of Japan (2019l) *Statement on Monetary Policy*, 21 September 2016. Available from: www.boj.or.jp/en/mopo/mpmdeci/state_2016/index.htm/ [Accessed 10 October 2019].

Barber, B. M. and Lyon, J. D. (1997) Detecting long-run abnormal stock returns: The empirical power and specification of test statistics, *Journal of Financial Economics*, 43 (3), 341–372.

Basdas, U. and Oran, A. (2014) Event studies in Turkey, *Borsa Istanbul Review*, 14 (3), 167–188.

Basistha, A. and Kurov, A. (2008) Macroeconomic cycles and the stock market's reaction to monetary policy, *Journal of Banking & Finance*, 32 (12), 2606–2616.

Bernanke, B. S. (2017) Monetary policy in a new era, *Peterson Institute for International Economics*, 29–42.

Bernanke, B. S. and Kuttner, K. N. (2005) What explains the stock market's reaction to Federal Reserve policy? *The Journal of Finance*, 60 (3), 1221–1257.

Bernanke, B. S., Reinhart, V. R. and Sack, B. P. (2004) Monetary policy alternatives at the zero bound: An empirical assessment, *Finance and Economics Discussion Series*, No. 2004-48, Divisions of Research & Statistics and Monetary Affairs, Federal Reserve Board, Washington, DC.

Boehmer, E., Musumeci, J. and Poulsen, A. (1991) Event-study methodology under conditions of event-induced variance, *Journal of Financial Economics*, 30, 253–272.

BOJ. (2019) *Trends in the Money Market in Japan*, 18 October 2019. Available from: https://www.boj.or.jp/en/paym/market/market1911.htm/ [Accessed 10 November 2019].

Bomfin, A. N. (2003) Pre-announcement effects, news effects, and volatility: Monetary policy and the stock market, *Journal of Banking & Finance*, 2 (7), 133–151.

Borio, C. E., Erdem, M., Filardo, A. J. and Hofmann, B. (2015) The costs of deflations: A historical perspective, *BIS Quarterly Review*, March, 31–54.

Born, J. A. and Moser, J. T. (1990) Bank-equity returns and changes in the discount rate, *Journal of Financial Services Research*, 4 (3), 223–241.

Boswell, R. (2013) Japan completes first offshore methane hydrate production test—Methane successfully produced from deepwater hydrate layers. Center for Natural Gas and Oil, 412, 386-7614.

Boubakari, A. and Jin, D. (2010) The role of stock market development in economic growth: Evidence from some Euronext countries, *International Journal of Financial Research*, 1 (1), 14–20.

Bredin, D., Hyde, S. N. D. and O'Reilly, G. (2010) UK stock returns and the impact of domestic monetary policy shocks, *Journal of Business Finance and Accounting*, 34, 872–888.

Brown, S. J. and Warner, J. B. (1980) Measuring security price performance. *Journal of Financial Economics*, 8(3), 205–258.

Brown, S. J. and Warner, J. B. (1985) Using daily stock returns: The case of event studies. *Journal of Financial Economics*, 14 (1), 3–31.

Bruner, J. (1999) Narratives of aging. *Journal of Aging Studies*, 13 (1), 7–9.

Brunnermeier, M. K. and Koby, Y. (2016) The reversal interest rate: An effective lower bound on monetary policy, *Working Paper*, Princeton University.

Chen, S. S. (2007) Does monetary policy have asymmetric effects on stock returns, *Journal of Money, Credit and Banking*, 39 (2–3), 667–688.

Chiarella, C., Flaschel, P., Groh, G. and Semmler, W. (2013) Disequilibrium, growth and labor market dynamics: Macro perspectives, *Springer Science & Business Media*.

Chulia, H., Martens, M. and van Dijk, D. (2010) Asymmetric effects of federal funds target rate changes on S&P100 stock returns, volatilities and correlations, *Journal of Banking & Finance*, 3 (4), 834–839.

Corrado, C. J. (2011) Event studies: A methodology review. *Accounting & Finance*, 51 (1), 207–234.

Doh, T. and Connolly, M. (2013) Has the effect of monetary policy announcements on asset prices changed? *Economic Review*, Federal Reserve Bank of Kansas City.

Eggertsson, G. B. and Woodford, M. (2003) Optimal monetary policy in a liquidity trap, *National Bureau of Economic Research Working Paper*.

Ehrmann, M. and Fratzscher, M. (2004) Monetary policy transmission to equity markets, *Journal of Money, Credit and Banking*, 3 (6), 719–737.

Ehrmann, M. and Fratzscher, M. (2005) Exchange rates and fundamentals: New evidence from real-time data. *Journal of International Money and Finance*, 24(2), 317–341.

Fiordelisi, F., Galloppo, G. and Ricci, O. (2014) The effect of monetary policy interventions on interbank markets, equity indices and G-SIFIs during financial crisis, *Journal of Financial Stability*, 1 (1), 49–61.

Flannery, M. J. (2012) Corporate finance and financial institutions. *Annual Review of Financial Economics*, 4(1), 233–253.

Fujiwara, I., Hirose, Y. and Shintani, M. (2016) Can news be a major source of aggregate fluctuations? A Bayesian DSGE approach, *Journal of Money, Credit and Banking*, 43 (1), 1–29.

Gagnon, J., Matthew, R., Julia, R. and Brian, S. (2011) The financial market effects of the Federal Reserve's large-scale asset purchases, *International Journal of Central Banking*, 7 (1), 3–43.

Gambacorta, L., Hofmann, B. and Peersman, G. (2014) The effectiveness of unconventional monetary policy at the zero lower bound: A cross-country analysis, *Journal of Money, Credit and Banking*, 46 (4), 615–642.

Glick, R. and Leduc, S. (2012) Central bank announcements of asset purchases and the impact on global financial and commodity markets, *Journal of International Money and Finance*, 31 (8), 2078–2101.

Glick, R. and Leduc, S. (2013) The effects of unconventional and conventional US monetary policy on the dollar, *Federal Reserve Bank of San Francisco Working Paper Series*.

Gospodinov, N. and Jamali, I. (2012) The effects of Federal funds rate surprises on S&P 500 volatility and volatility risk premium, *Journal of Empirical Finance*, 19 (4), 497–510.

Grabowiecki, J. and Mariusz, D. (2017) Abenomics and its impact on the economy of Japan, *Optimum. Studia Ekonomiczne*, 5 (89), 23–35.

Guerini, M., Lamperti, F. and Mazzocchetti, A. (2018) Unconventional monetary policy between the past and future of monetary economics, *LEM Working Paper Series*.

Hancock, D. and Passmore, W. (2011) Did the Federal Reserve's MBS purchase program lower mortgage rates? *Journal of Monetary Economics*, 58 (5), 498–514.

Hirakata, N. (2018) The Labor Share, Capital-Labor Substitution, and Factor Augmenting Technologies, *Bank of Japan*. 18–20.

Hördahl, P. and Packer, F. (2007) Understanding asset prices: An overview, *BIS Working Papers*, No. 34.

Ito, T. and Mishkin, F. S. (2004) Monetary policy in Japan: Problems and solutions.

Kocherlakota, N. R. (2017) The decentralized central bank: A review essay on the power and independence of the Federal Reserve by Peter Conti-Brown, *Journal of Economic Literature*, 2 (55), 621–636.

Kothari, C. R. (2006) *Research Methodology: Methods and Techniques*.

Kozicki, S., Santor, E. and Suchanek, L. (2011) Unconventional monetary policy: The international experience with central bank asset purchases, *Bank of Canada Review*, 13–25.

Kuroda, H. (2014) *Opening Remarks at the 2014 BOJ-IMES Conference Hosted by the Institute for Monetary and Economic Studies*, Bank of Japan. Available from: www.boj.or.jp/en/announcements/press/koen_2014/ko140528a.htm/ [Accessed 8 August 2019].

Kurov, A. (2012) What determines the stock market's reaction to monetary policy statements?. *Review of Financial Economics*, 21(4), 175-187.

Kuttner, K. N. (2001) Monetary policy surprises and interest rates: Evidence from the Fed funds futures market, *Journal of Monetary Economics*, 47 (3), 523–544.

Levy, M. D. (2012) Monetary Policy: Little Economic Impact, High Risks. *Shadow Open Market Committee*.

Madura, J. and Schnusenberg, O. (2000) Effect of Federal Reserve policies on bank equity returns, *The Journal of Financial Research*, 23 (4), 421–447.

Maio, P. (2014) Another look at the stock response to monetary policy actions, *Review of Finance*, 1 (8), 321–371.

McCallum, B. T. (2003) A Japanese monetary policy, 1991–2001, *Federal Reserve Bank of Richmond Economic Quarterly*, 89, 1–31.

Meinusch, A. (2016) The macroeconomic impact of unconventional monetary policy shocks, *Journal of Macroeconomics*, 4 (7), 58–67.

Nakajima, J. (2011) Monetary policy transmission under zero interest rates: An extended time-varying parameter vector autoregression approach, *IMES Discussion Paper Series*, No. 11-E-08, Institute for Monetary and Economic Studies, Bank of Japan.

Nakaso, H. (2017) *Japan's Economy and Monetary Policy*, 8 August. Available from: www.bis. org/review/r170808f.htm [Accessed 10 October 2019].

Panizza, U. and Wyplosz, C. (2016) The folk theorem of decreasing effectiveness of monetary policy: What do the data say? *Jacques Polak Annual Research Conference 'Macroeconomics After the Great Recession'*, 3–4.

Pennathur, A., Smith, D. and Subrahmanyam, V. (2014) The stock market impact of government interventions on financial services industry groups: Evidence from the 2007–2009 crisis, *Journal of Economics and Business*, 71, 22–44.

Petros, J. (2012) The effect of the stock exchange on economic growth: A case of the Zimbabwe stock exchange, *Research in Business and Economics Journal*, 6 (1), 1–17.

Poole, W. and Rasche, R. H. (2000) Perfecting the market's knowledge of monetary policy, *Journal of Financial Services Research*, 18 (2–3), 255–298.

Rangel, J. G. (2011) Macroeconomic news, announcements, and stock market jump intensity dynamics, *Journal of Banking & Finance*, 3 (5), 1263–1276.

Ricci, O. (2014) The impact of monetary policy announcements on the stock price of large European banks during the financial crisis, *Journal of Banking & Finance*, 5 (2), 245–255.

Rogers, J., Scotti, C. and Wright, J. (2014) Evaluating asset-market effects of unconventional monetary policy: A Cross-country comparison, *International Finance Discussion Papers*, No. 1101.

Rosa, C. (2011) Words that shake traders. The stock market's reaction to central bank communication in real time, *Journal of Empirical Finance*, 1 (8), 915–934.

Saxonhouse, R. G. and Stem, M. R. (2002) Japan's lost decade: Origins, consequences, and prospects for recovery, *Research Seminar in International Economics Discussion Paper*, No. 485.

Shibamoto, M. and Tachibana, M. (2017) The effect of unconventional monetary policy on the macro economy: Evidence from Japan's quantitative easing policy period, *RIEB Discussion Paper*.

Smith, A. (2014) House prices, heterogeneous banks and unconventional monetary policy options. *Federal Reserve Bank of Kansas City Working Paper*, 12–14.

Somani, S. (2015) *The Effects of Government Policies on the Stock Market*, 13 April 2015. Available from: https://www.sc.edu/about/offices_and_divisions/research/news_and_pubs/ caravel/archive/2015/2015-caravel-stock-market.php [Accessed 25 September 2019].

Swanson, E. T. (2015) Measuring the effects of unconventional monetary policy on asset prices, *National Bureau of Economic Research Working Paper*, No. 21816.

Swanson, E. T. and Williams, J. (2014) Measuring the effect of the zero lower bound on medium- and longer-term interest rates, *American Economic Review*, 104, 3154–3185.

Thorbecke, W. (1997) Who pays for disinflation, *Levy Economics Institute of Bard College Public Policy Brief*, No. 38.

Tillmann, P. and Meinusch, A. (2014) *The Macroeconomic Impact of Unconventional Monetary Policy Shocks*. In Annual Conference 2014 (Hamburg): Evidence-based Economic Policy (No. 1000331). Verein für Socialpolitik/German Economic Association.

Ueda, K. (2012) Deleveraging and Monetary Policy: Japan since the 1990s and the United States since 2007. *Journal of Economic Perspectives*, 26 (3), 177–202.

Weber, S. Chatel, B. and Girard, B. (2008) Factoring numbers with interfering random waves. *EPL (Europhysics Letters)*, 83 (3), 34008.

Wright, J. H. (2012) What does monetary policy do to long-term interest rates at the zero lower bound? *The Economic Journal*, 122, 564–571.

Yin, H. and Yang, J. (2013) Bank characteristics and stock reactions to federal funds rate target changes, *Applied Financial Economics*, 2 (3), 1755–1764.

Yin, H., Yang, J. and Handorf, W. C. (2010) State dependency of bank stock reaction to federal funds rate target changes, *Journal of Financial Research*, 33 (3), 289–315.

8 Bank of Japan and the ETF market

Masayuki Susai and Ho Yan Karen Wong

1 Introduction

The Bank of Japan (BOJ) has been implementing a monetary easing policy for a number of years. Since the launch of "Abenomics" in 2013,[1] this policy has become even more pronounced. To meet an inflation target of 2%, the BOJ was urged to reduce risk premia to uplift investment. Consequently, a policy combination of monetary easing, fiscal expansion and structural reform was adopted.

Under Abenomics, Japan has reached moderate growth. However, inflation remains below 2%. The BOJ has been keeping the short-term interest rate close to 0% or slightly negative.[2] As such, there is little room for lowering interest rates, which is the primary tool in monetary policy. To reduce risk premia, in addition to controlling interest rates, BOJ, therefore, decided to purchase exchange-traded funds (ETFs). Since, ETF interventions have become one of the important monetary policy instruments under Abenomics.[3] The logic can be summarised as follows. If risk premia decrease in the financial markets, demand for risky assets will increase, and the prices of these rise. As a result, the cost of capital for private companies declines. Hence, we should expect that this policy has a positive impact on inflation through the increase of investment by the private sector.[4]

Higher risk premia are typically associated with falling and/or more volatile stock markets. In other words, the BOJ should try to support the stock market when stock prices fall, and also intervene when the market volatility increases. Thus, to evaluate the effectiveness of the BOJ's ETF purchases, we explore the impact on the change in these risk premia.

The ETF purchasing programme has not come without controversy. Crucially, the Japanese central bank has already become a major shareholder in several listed companies in Japan through the purchase of ETFs, such as Fast Retailing Co., Ltd and Kyocera Corporation (Harada, 2017a). This has triggered discussions surrounding the changing corporate governance caused by the BOJ. Furthermore, significant ETF sales are expected after the programme has been completed. This obviously raises concerns that such sales will result in considerably lower share prices. In sum, with the BOJ's extensive and continuously increasing holdings of ETFs, the risk of a sharp stock market fall after the end of the ETF purchase programme is elevated.

Nonetheless, in line with ongoing ETF purchases, it is likely that specific measures have already been taken within the BOJ. The aim with this chapter is to evaluate the BOJ's monetary policy through ETF interventions – mainly in terms of whether these manage to reduce risk premia in the stock market. More specifically, we investigate if the purchase of ETFs has succeeded in supporting falling stock prices and/or suppressing the rise in stock price volatility.

2   The ETF market

2.1   Background

ETFs are baskets of securities in the form of investment units. They are listed on stock exchanges, and the trading is akin to trading listed stocks in the sense that investors can buy and sell ETFs anytime during the opening trading hours. ETFs were first launched in the United States in 1993. As of 2018, there were 6,478 ETFs listed around the world, and the total assets of these amounted to USD 4.63 trillion (Statista, 2019). The traditional ETFs are named as "index funds", where an ETF tracks the performance of a benchmark index. The ETF holds a portfolio of underlying assets of the corresponding index and aims to track the price and yield performance of the index. ETF benchmarks encompass indices linked to stock markets, sectors, bonds, etc., which act as indicators for specific markets. The trading value of ETFs in Japan increased from JPY 4,415,282 million in 2011 to JPY 39,493,221 million in 2017 (JPX, 2017). As of 10 February 2019, there are 227 ETFs listed on the Japan Exchange Group (JPX).

2.2   Bank of Japan and ETFs

Japan has been struggling with low inflation and low interest rates for many years. A decade ago, Masaaki Shirakawa, the former Governor of the Bank of Japan, indicated that the BOJ was eager to formulate new policy measures to stabilise the market. At the Monetary Policy Meeting on 28 October 2010, it was announced that the BOJ would use ETFs as an alternative to lower the risk premium in the financial market (Bank of Japan, 2010a). ETFs turned out to be an instrument for the BOJ to accomplish its monetary policy goal.

However, this is not the first time a monetary authority has intervened in the financial markets via ETFs. Hong Kong is a classic example of where ETFs have been used by a monetary authority to intervene in stock markets. Like the BOJ, the Hong Kong Government also aimed to stabilise the stock markets using ETFs. The case of Hong Kong happened during the financial crisis in 1998 and was completed successfully.[5]

The process of ETF purchasing is as follows. The BOJ appoints a trust bank as trustee and establishes a money trust. Considering market conditions, the

BOJ gives a standard prescription to the trustee bank, which follows the order from the central bank to purchase ETFs and Japanese real estate investment trusts (J-REITs). The ETFs and J-REITs bought become trust property. The maximum amount of each ETF outstanding is set to be proportionate to the total market value of the particular ETF issued (Bank of Japan, 2013).[6]

The purchase of ETFs has been modified repeatedly since the BOJ started the asset-purchase programme in 2010. We document the relevant modification phases in Table 8.1.

Table 8.1 shows that the ETF purchased by the BOJ soared six-fold from JPY 900 billion in 2011 to JPY 6 trillion in 2018. Thus, the BOJ has not only been conducting the programme for nearly a decade but has also increased the volume of ETF purchases over time.

Table 8.1 Major modification events in the purchase of ETFs

	Event	*Announcement date*	*Source*
1	Purchasing of ETFs which track TOPIX or Nikkei 225.	5 November 2010	Bank of Japan (2010b)
2	Total amount increased to about JPY 0.45 trillion (conditional on obtaining authorisation).	14 March 2011	Bank of Japan (2011a)
3	Total intended intervention amount increased to JPY 1.4 trillion.	4 August 2011	Bank of Japan (2011b)
4	Total intended intervention amount increased to JPY 2.1 trillion (by the end of 2013).	30 October 2012	Bank of Japan (2012)
5	End of 2013 projection: JPY 2.5 trillion, end of 2014 projection: JPY 3.5 trillion.	4 April 2013	Bank of Japan (2013)
6	The pace of annual increase: JPY 3 trillion. Projected amount for the end of 2014: JPY 3.8 trillion.	31 October 2014	Bank of Japan (2014)
7	Supplementary programme incurred an annual purchase of JPY 300 billion. Outstanding ETF amount to increase at an annual pace of about JPY 3 trillion.	18 December 2015	Bank of Japan (2015)
8	The annual purchase amount of JPY 5.7 trillion. JPY 3 trillion to be used for ETFs that track any of the three indices. The remaining JPY 2.7 trillion will be used for ETFs that track the TOPIX.	21 September 2016	Bank of Japan (2016)
9	ETF amount outstanding to increase at an annual pace of about JPY 6 trillion.	30–31 July 2018	Bank of Japan (2018b)

3   Previous studies on BOJ interventions and the ETF market

The objective of the BOJ intervention in the ETF market is to support the stock markets by (1) boosting stock prices and (2) limiting the volatility.

There are a limited number of papers that test the effects of the BOJ intervention. Barbon and Gianinazzi (2018) construct a theoretical model and conduct empirical work based on this model. They find that intervention has a positive and persistent impact on stock prices. Matsuki et al. (2015) examine the impact of the BOJ's quantitative and qualitative easing (QQE) policy. With daily data from 2012 to 2014, and using a multivariate time series method, they find that the BOJ policy can achieve lower interest rates and a higher inflation rate. They also conclude that ETF purchases stimulate the stock market. Positive results on stock prices are also reported by Ide and Minami (2013). The authors found that 44% of returns of ETFs in the afternoon session (when the BOJ intervened the market was positive) are positive, compared to only 24% when the BOJ did not intervene. They also noted the following: a BOJ intervention was not associated with a single trading day when ETF prices declined considerably in the afternoon trading session.

By contrast, Kobayashi (2016) uses an EGARCH model and daily data from 2010 to 2012 and the author does not find any impact on ETF prices and volatility. Kobayashi (2017) uses an AR-GJR model to test the effect of QQE on the stock and REIT markets and, similarly, does not report any impact of the BOJ intervention on the returns of ETFs. However, Kobayashi (2017) and Serita and Hanaeda (2017) find that BOJ intervention reduces volatility in the market. Both use a dummy variable that takes the value of 1 after 2010 when the BOJ started to intervene through purchasing ETFs. Serita and Hanaeda (2017) test the volatility of individual stock prices and use control variables such as depth and company size. They also investigate the deviation of the ETF from its net asset value (NAV) and find that a BOJ intervention may act to reduce the individual stock price volatility. Itzhak et al. (2017a) show that ETFs lower volatility, whereas Ivanov et al. (2018) find that the impact of ETFs on volatility is insignificant. Thus, the impact of ETFs on underlying asset price volatility is ambiguous.

Another related topic is the impact of BOJ interventions on market efficiency, or whether the policy distorts stock prices. Because the BOJ has been purchasing ETFs for many years, the BOJ's shareholding ratio of certain individual stocks is high. For instance, Harada (2017a) uses daily data to analyse the effect on individual stock prices. The author then compares the price change and trading volume of two companies during a day when one company is adopted to the Nikkei 225 index, and another company is excluded from the index. The differences in the price and volume change are significant, prompting the author to conclude that BOJ intervention might have an impact on the price formation process. Harada (2017b) also explores the impact of exclusion from the Nikkei 225 index on the price change. Indeed, when a stock is removed from the composition of the index, the stock price declines considerably.[7] Ide and Minami (2013) find that stock overvaluation is associated with BOJ intervention. Furthermore, Barbon and Gianinazzi (2018) show that purchasing of ETFs tracking Nikkei 225 (a price-weighted stock market index) may generate price distortions relative to ETFs tracking TOPIX (a value-weighted stock market index).

4 Overview of our study

In this chapter, we examine the impact of ETF purchases under the BOJ policy on the return and the volatility. As the previous section demonstrates, the answer as to whether BOJ intervention has the intended impact cannot be answered fully. Hence, we use several methods and proxies to shed more light on this. Our methodology and contribution can be summarised as follows.

Our study covers the period 2010–2018. We divide the whole sample into days when the BOJ intervenes ("intervention days") and days when the BOJ does not intervene in the market ("non-intervention days"). Following the result of a CUSUM (cumulative sum) test to find structural breaks, we separate the period into before 4 August 2016 ("Phase 1 and 2") and after ("Phase 3"). We then compare the mean returns of the afternoon trading session between intervention days and non-intervention days.

Next, we examine the impact of interventions on the stock market indices. The findings imply that the BOJ intervention in the stock market follows two routes. One is a direct route whereby the ETF purchases increase the demand for stocks in the market. Market participants lead another route, by learning how to anticipate a BOJ intervention when the TOPIX or Nikkei 225 experiences a decline in the morning session.

The BOJ does not release its criteria for intervention. However, since the start of the ETF intervention programme, there has been a widespread belief among market participants that if stock prices decline more than 1% in the morning session, an intervention will take place (see, for instance, Koyama 2012; Kobayashi, 2016, 2017). Kobayashi (2016) explored this "1% rule" and found that, between December 2010 and December 2012, only 1 out of 504 trading days is exceptional. Further, Kobayashi (2016) showed that between December 2010 and December 2011, on only one day when TOPIX declined more than 1%, no BOJ intervention took place.[8] If market participants can anticipate a BOJ intervention, they will try to make a profit to buy the stocks before the intervention (and sell after that). Consequently, the buy transaction will have a positive impact on stock prices.

Figure 8.1 shows the change in stock prices and BOJ interventions from 15 December 2010 to 31 December 2018.

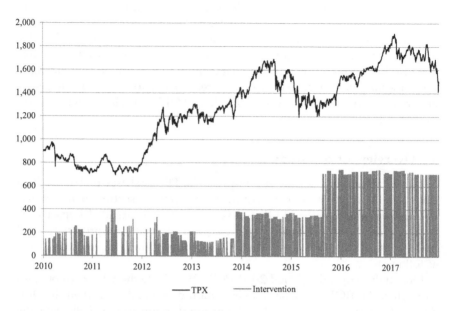

Figure 8.1 TOPIX and intervention volume (in JPY 10 billion), 15.12.2010–07.12.2018
Note: TOPIX afternoon closing price.

As can be seen, stock prices have risen in line with increasing ETF interventions. We can also clearly see three distinct phases with regards to the BOJ intervention volume. Throughout the chapter, we refer to these as follows:

- *Phase 1* (15 December 2010–31 October 2014)
- *Phase 2* (1 November 2014–3 August 2016)
- *Phase 3* (4 August 2016–7 December 2018)

5   Data

The BOJ publishes the intervention volume daily on its website (Bank of Japan, 2019). The first purchase of ETFs by the BOJ took place on 15 December 2010. Our dataset covers the period from 15 December 2010 to 7 December 2018.

The ETFs bought by the BOJ are benchmarked to two stock market indices: TOPIX and Nikkei 225. We address the impact on both stock market indices, as well as their futures contracts. Two ETFs tracking TOPIX and two tracking Nikkei 225 are covered in this study. We abbreviate these as follows:

- *TPX* (TOPIX)
- *NKY* (Nikkei 225)
- *TP1* (TOPIX future)

- *NK1* (Nikkei 225 future)
- *05* (1305 ETF, Daiwa ETF-TOPIX from Daiwa Asset Management Co., Ltd.)
- *06* (1306 ETF, TOPIX ETF from Nomura Asset Management Co., Ltd.)
- *20* (1320 ETF, Nikkei 225 ETF from Daiwa Asset Management Co., Ltd.)
- *21* (1321 ETF, Nikkei 225 ETF from Nomura Asset Management Co., Ltd.)

Importantly, the Japanese market has an official lunch break. Therefore, we include the opening and closing prices in morning and afternoon sessions, as well as the highs and lows during both trading sessions. In addition to prices, we collect trading volume data for the morning and afternoon sessions for TOPIX and Nikkei 225. All data are extracted from Bloomberg.

After checking the stationarity of the price series, we use returns (log difference of opening and closing prices in a trading session). Each trading day contains four price snapshots, which we abbreviate as follows:

- *am_op* (morning open)
- *am_cl* (morning close)
- *pm_op* (afternoon open)
- *pm_cl* (afternoon close)

Hence, three sets of returns are calculated in our study, which we abbreviate as:

- *am* (the return in the morning session ($\log(P_{am\_cl}/P_{am\_op})$)
- *ampm* (the return between the am and pm sessions ($\log(P_{pm\_op}/P_{am\_cl})$))
- *pm* (the return in the afternoon session ($\log(P_{pm\_cl}/P_{am\_op})$)),

where P is the asset price. We calculate the returns for all assets (TOPIX, Nikkei 225, their futures and ETFs) for each session. The return is expressed as r_{ij} where i is the asset index, and j is the session index. For instance, the morning return of 1305 ETF is described as r_{05am}.

Market liquidity is a crucial element for stabilising the market volatility. In our analysis, we use the Amihud liquidity measure and calculate this based on the trading volume (the number of stocks traded in the sessions) in both the morning and the afternoon sessions:

$$Liquidity_{ij} = \frac{|r_{ij}|}{Volume_{ij}} \tag{1}$$

As one of the goals of the BOJ intervention is to limit volatility, we need to measure the volatility to evaluate the impact. To do so, we compare the volatility in the morning and afternoon sessions. In general, returns can be used as the index of volatility. In this chapter, among many volatility measures, we calculate the Garman Klass volatility index. Because we can use high and low prices of each index in each session, we calculate this volatility measure. The Garman Klass volatility index is calculated as follows:

$$\text{Volatility}_{ij} = \sqrt{\frac{N}{2}} \sqrt{\sum n \frac{1}{2}\left(In\left(\frac{high_{ij}}{low_{ij}}\right)\right)^2 - (2\ In(2)-1)\left[\left(In(r_{ij})\right)\right]^2} \qquad (2)$$

where N is the total number of trading days, n is the sample size and $\sqrt{\dfrac{N}{n}}$ is a scaling factor. $high_{ij}$ (low_{ij}) is the highest (lowest) price of asset i in session j.

6   Impact of BOJ interventions on stock prices

6.1   Basic statistics

The basic statistics of all indices, futures and ETFs are shown in Tables 8.2 to 8.4.

As can be seen from Table 8.2, all mean returns in the morning session are negative, and more than half (9 out of 16) of the mean returns in the afternoon session are positive. Thus, the market appears to perform worse in the morning than in the afternoon sessions.

From Table 8.3, we can observe that the Amihud liquidity measure and volatilities of TOPIX and Nikkei 225 are lower in the afternoon session than those in the morning session. Following the definition of the Amihud liquidity measure, this means that the market is deeper – in other words more liquid. Hence, the results indicate that the volatility in the afternoon sessions tends to be lower than in the morning session.[9] This is consistent when checking the Garman Klass volatility measure (see Table 8.4).

6.2   Impact on returns

The number of the days when BOJ intervened the market is 538. This corresponds to 27% of all the trading days in our sample. To investigate the difference between "intervention" days and "non-intervention" days, we separate the corresponding trading days accordingly and study the basic statistics of the samples.

Table 8.5 lists the mean returns of TOPIX, Nikkei 225, TOPIX futures, Nikkei 225 futures, as well as 1305 ETF, 1306 ETF, 1320 ETF and 1321 ETF on intervention days (538 days) and non–intervention days (1,435 days). Thus, we calculate the mean session returns when the BOJ intervened the market, and when it did not (see, for instance, Ide and Minami, 2013). We should

Table 8.2 Summary statistics of returns, 15.12.2010–07.12.2018

	r_{05am}	r_{06am}	r_{20am}	r_{21am}	r_{NK1am}	r_{NKYam}	r_{TP1am}	r_{TPXam}
Mean	-0.00014	-8.33E-05	-4.42E-05	-7.26E-05	-2.42E-05	-1.96E-05	-5.94E-05	-9.27E-05
Std. dev.	0.0057	0.0056	0.0059	0.0057	0.0042	0.0028	0.0040	0.0027
Skewness	-0.1061	-0.0287	-0.4786	-0.2705	-0.9643	-0.5699	-0.9399	-0.7021
Kurtosis	11.7652	9.7731	11.0931	7.4224	12.8983	9.5935	13.1989	11.6275
Observations	1973	1973	1973	1973	1973	1973	1973	1973

	r_{05pm}	r_{06pm}	r_{20pm}	r_{21pm}	r_{NK1pm}	r_{NKYpm}	r_{TP1pm}	r_{TPXpm}
Mean	-0.000217	3.63E-05	-5.21E-05	-6.82E-05	9.16E-05	-8.28E-05	0.0001	-3.35E-05
Std. dev.	0.0053	0.0055	0.0060	0.0058	0.0033	0.0026	0.0030	0.0024
Skewness	-0.7504	0.0630	0.1740	-0.8149	-0.1995	-1.4556	-0.2568	-0.8336
Kurtosis	19.3336	21.6288	29.7777	20.9095	6.6524	23.5450	7.5665	17.0920
Observations	1973	1973	1973	1973	1973	1973	1973	1973

	r_{05ampm}	r_{06ampm}	r_{20ampm}	r_{21ampm}	$r_{NK1ampm}$	$r_{NKYampm}$	$r_{TP1ampm}$	$r_{TPXampm}$
Mean	2.29E-05	-4.35E-05	-8.45E-05	6.14E-05	-0.000115	2.84E-05	-6.58E-05	1.26E-05
Std. dev.	0.0025	0.0029	0.0035	0.0025	0.0059	0.0010	0.0056	0.0008
Skewness	-7.6239	-14.0111	-16.2282	-6.7199	0.6292	-1.3843	0.6677	-2.0931
Kurtosis	141.4943	324.5987	433.6095	115.2242	7.3065	18.8005	8.4095	25.6404
Observations	1973	1973	1973	1973	1973	1973	1973	1973

Table 8.3 Summary statistics of liquidity (Amihud liquidity measure), 15.12.2010–07.12.2018

	$Liquidity_{NKYam}$	$Liquidity_{NKYpm}$	$Liquidity_{NKYwhole}$	$Liquidity_{TPXam}$	$Liquidity_{TPXpm}$	$Liquidity_{TPXwhole}$
Mean	1.88E-12	1.45E-12	2.99E-12	1.82E-12	1.42E-12	2.88E-12
Median	1.43E-12	1.10E-12	2.28E-12	1.40E-12	1.10E-12	2.21E-12
Std. dev.	1.69E-12	1.32E-12	2.69E-12	1.64E-12	1.23E-12	2.54E-12
Skewness	1.892	1.860	1.793	2.028	1.676	1.736
Kurtosis	9.393	8.350	8.389	10.878	7.365	8.089
Observations	1973	1973	1973	1973	1973	1973

Note: "Whole" refers to the morning and afternoon sessions combined.

Table 8.4 Summary statistics of volatility, 15.12.2010–07.12.2018

	$Volatility_{05am}$	$Volatility_{05pm}$	$Volatility_{06am}$	$Volatility_{06pm}$	$Volatility_{NKYam}$	$Volatility_{NKYpm}$	$Volatility_{20am}$	$Volatility_{20pm}$	$Volatility_{21am}$
Mean	2.72E-05	2.75E-05	3.27E-05	2.99E-05	3.22E-05	2.79E-05	3.03E-05	3.45E-05	3.54E-05
Median	1.54E-05	1.10E-05	2.00E-05	1.41E-05	1.69E-05	1.14E-05	1.66E-05	1.34E-05	1.36E-05
Std. dev.	5.16E-05	1.65E-04	5.46E-05	1.22E-04	6.21E-05	9.30E-05	5.41E-05	1.36E-04	1.67E-04
Skewness	10.746	32.985	11.806	28.298	10.066	16.959	8.783	17.738	24.153
Kurtosis	184.963	1256.908	243.344	991.354	161.711	389.398	125.975	403.341	742.457
Observations	1973	1973	1973	1973	1973	1973	1973	1973	1973

	$Volatility_{NKY1am}$	$Volatility_{NKY1pm}$	$Volatility_{TPX1am}$	$Volatility_{TPX1pm}$	$Volatility_{TPXam}$	$Volatility_{21pm}$
Mean	8.28E-05	6.17E-05	8.12E-05	5.04E-05	2.99E-05	2.46E-05
Median	4.10E-05	3.23E-05	4.23E-05	2.44E-05	1.59E-05	1.07E-05
Std. dev.	3.24E-04	1.17E-04	3.10E-04	1.02E-04	6.65E-05	9.33E-05
Skewness	31.375	9.485	29.438	12.576	14.770	23.651
Kurtosis	1196.501	142.882	1073.996	289.305	322.483	718.960
Observations	1973	1973	1973	1973	1973	1973

Table 8.5 Basic statistics of mean returns

Session	Sample	r_{05}	r_{06}	r_{20}	r_{21}	r_{NK1}	r_{NKY}	r_{TP1}	r_{TPX}
am	Non-intervention	9.1.E-04	9.5.E-04	1.1.E-03	1.0.E-03	4.91.E-04	6.5.E-04	4.24.E-04	5.9.E-04
	Intervention	-2.9.E-03*	-2.8.E-03*	-0.003*	-2.9.E-03*	-1.30.E-03*	-2.E-03*	-1.30.E-03*	-1.9.E-03*
	Phase 3	-1.6.E-03*	-1.6.E-03*	-0.0023*	-2.2.E-03*	-8.00.E-04*	-1.E-03*	-7.00.E-04*	-1.3.E-03*
ampm	Non-intervention	1.9.E-05	-6.1.E-06	-6.8.E-05	6.8.E-05	-1.87.E-03	2.7.E-05	-1.75.E-03	1.5.E-05
	Intervention	3.4.E-05	-1.4.E-04	-1.3.E-04	4.4.E-05	4.55.E-03	3.2.E-05	4.43.E-03	5.8.E-06
	Phase 3	1.6.E-04	1.3.E-04	1.3.E-04	-6.5.E-07	3.00.E-03*	4.0.E-05	2.70.E-03*	5.1.E-05
pm	Non-intervention	-3.4.E-04	-8.2.E-05	-1.1.E-04	-1.2.E-04	9.79.E-04	-7.5.E-05	8.60.E-04	-8.2.E-05
	Intervention	1.0.E-04	3.4.E-04	1.0.E-04	5.7.E-05	-2.20.E-03	-1.1.E-04	-1.92.E-03	9.3.E-05
	Phase 3	8.5.E-04*	9.2.E-04*	0.00064*	7.8.E-04*	-1.79.E-03*	3.E-04*	-1.60.E-03	4.4.E-04*

Note: * difference from non-intervention statistically significant at $p < 0.01$ level.

expect that returns in the morning are lower, and returns in the afternoon higher, during intervention days (i.e. for BOJ intervention to have an impact).

Indeed, we can see that morning returns during intervention days are significantly lower than those during non-intervention days. Moreover, all the mean returns during Phase 3 (after 4 August 2016 when the BOJ significantly increased the intervention volume) are statistically higher than those during non-intervention days. Except for futures contracts, all the mean returns in afternoon sessions are positive and higher than those of non-intervention days. From this simple analysis, we can confirm that the returns of afternoon sessions for the intervention sample are higher than those for the non-intervention sample – and this tendency is stronger for Phase 3. These results show that the BOJ intervention may have a positive impact on the stock market, and particularly when the intervention volume is larger.

Now, let us further investigate the impact of BOJ interventions on the afternoon returns. Following studies that use a Generalised Autoregressive Conditional Heteroscedasticity (GARCH) model on ETF price returns, we employ an Exponential Generalised Autoregressive Conditional Heteroskedastic (EGARCH) model to test the impact. Previous studies that examine the impact of intervention using ARCH models have tended to incorporate an intervention dummy into the mean equation. We include the intervention volume directly into the mean equation as follows:

$$r_{ijt} = c + \rho \ \textit{Intervention}_t + \delta_1 \ \textit{Liquidity}_t + \delta_2 \ \textit{Volatility}_t + \varepsilon_t \tag{3}$$

$$log(\sigma_t^2) = \omega + \sum \beta_\tau log(\sigma_{t-\tau}^2) + \sum \alpha_i \left| \frac{\varepsilon_{t-\gamma}}{\sigma_{t-\gamma}} \right| + \sum \gamma k \frac{\varepsilon_{t-k}}{\sigma_{t-k}} \tag{4}$$

where *Intervention* is the volume of intervention (in billion JPY), *Liquidity* is the Amihud liquidity measure and *Volatility* is the Garman Klass volatility measure. *Liquidity* and *Volatility* are treated as control variables.

As can be seen from Table 8.6, the intervention parameters are positive regardless of the control variables. With control variables, the impact of interventions is more muted but still statistically significant. From these results, we can see that the BOJ intervention volume has a positive effect on returns in the afternoon sessions. These findings are contrary to some previous studies. For instance, Ide and Minami (2013) found that less than 45% of ETF returns are positive in the afternoon session when the BOJ intervenes the market.

The question is: what might cause this difference? One of the differences between our analysis and previous studies relate to the sample. Many of the earlier investigations use datasets starting from when the BOJ began to purchase ETFs until a date before the beginning of Phase 3 (i.e. before 4 August 2016). As already mentioned, the BOJ increased the volume of intervention dramatically after this date. Table 8.7 shows that all intervention parameters are positive

Table 8.6 Impact of intervention on afternoon returns

	r_{TPX}		r_{NKY}		r_{05}	
C	0.0002	-1.8.E-04★	2.1.E-04★	-2.1.E-04★	-3.1.E-05	-4.7.E-04★
	(7.48.E-05)	(4.3.E-05)	(6.9.E-05)	(4.4.E-05)	(1.4.E-04)	(9.2.E-05)
Intervention	8.65.E-07★	9.1.E-07★	5.3.E-07★	6.5.E-07★	1.6.E-06★	1.4.E-07★
	(7.41.E-08)	(9.6.E-08)	(1.1.E-07)	1.5.E-07	(1.8.E-07)	(2.2.E-07)
Liquidity	-3.E+08★		-2.5.E+08★		-3.5.E+08★	
	(2.E+07)		(2.1.E+07)		(4.3.E+07)	
Volatility	-2.55★		-5.86★		-1.71★	
	(0.4)		(0.33)		(0.61)	
R^2	0.013	0.004	0.017	0.001	0.008	0.005
AIC	-9.50	-9.47	-9.40	-9.35	-8.00	-7.99

	r_{06}		r_{20}		r_{21}	
C	-1.8.E-04	-2.5.E-04★	-3.0.E-04	-2.7.E-04★	-4.5.E-05	-2.8.E-04★
	(1.2.E-04)	(9.2.E-05)	(2.0.E-04)	(1.0.E-04)	(1.7.E-04)	(1.1.E-04)
Intervention	1.4.E-06★	1.1.E-06★	1.3.E-06★	1.4.E-06★	1.5.E-06★	1.5.E-06★
	(2.1.E-07)	(2.3.E-07)	(3.4.E-07)	(3.5.E-07)	(3.2.E-07)	(3.4.E-07)
Liquidity	-4.8.E+08★		-5.0.E+08★		-2.3.E+08★	
	(3.9.E+07)		(5.0.E+07)		(5.0.E+07)	
Volatility	-8.1★		-4.31★		-4.03★	
	(0.36)		(0.34)		(0.42)	
R^2	0.008	0.002	0.021	0.001	0.016	0.002
AIC	-8.00	-7.94	-7.69	-7.67	-7.74	-7.72

Note: ★ statistically significant at $p < 0.01$ level. Standard errors in parentheses.

Table 8.7 Impact of intervention on afternoon returns (Phase 3 and Phase 1)

	r_{TPX}		r_{NKY}		r_{05}	
	Phase 3	Phase 1	Phase 3	Phase 1	Phase 3	Phase 1
C	1.3.E-04	1.8.E-04	1.0.E-04	3.4.E-04★	2.0.E-04	1.0.E-04
	(1.2.E-04)	(9.8.E-05)	(1.0.E-05)	(9.1.E-05)	(1.4.E-04)	(2.0.E-04)
Intervention	1.3.E-06★	8.8.E-07★★	8.0.E-07★	-3.1.E-08	1.7.E-06★	1.8.E-06
	(1.4.E-07)	(4.4.E-07)	(1.5.E-07)	(3.3.E-07)	(2.1.E-07)	(1.5.E+00)
Liquidity	-2.9.E+08★	-2.3.E+08★	-2.3.E+08★	-3.3.E+08★	-4.3.E+08★	-4.4.E+08
	(4.1.E+07)	(3.1.E+07)	(2.9.E+07)	(3.0.E+07)	(4.8.E+07)	(4.8.E+00)
Volatility	-6.77	-0.55	-8.81★	-4.92★	-10.65★	(0.64)
	(1.26)	(0.63)	(1.18)	(0.53)	(2.42)	(1.3)
R^2	0.0216	0.0270	0.0390	0.0130	0.0110	0.0270
AIC	-10.152	-9.320	-10.129	-9.200	-9.166	-7.570

	r_{06}		r_{20}		r_{21}	
	Phase 3	Phase 1	Phase 3	Phase 1	Phase 3	Phase 1
C	1.0.E-04	1.5.E-04	-6.4.E-04★	-3.6.E-04	-5.0.E-04★★	2.7.E+04
	(1.6.E-04)	(2.6.E-04)	(2.4.E-04)	(3.1.E-04)	(2.3.E-04)	(2.9.E+04)
Intervention	1.5.E-06★	1.3.E-06	1.7.E-06★	2.7.E-06★	1.9.E-06★	-2.8.E-06★★
	(2.5.E-07)	(1.1.E-06)	(3.5.E-07)	(1.3.E-06)	(3.3.E-07)	(1.2.E-06)
Liquidity	-4.6.E+08★	-4.3.E+08★	-7.1.E+08★	-1.2.E+08	-7.6.E+08★	-1.2.E+08
	(5.3.E+07)	(5.3.E+07)	(8.3.E+07)	(9.5.E+08)	(8.3.E+07)	(9.5.E+08)
Volatility	-2.65	10.54★	-12.9★	-11.4★	-7.86★	4.9★
	(2.03)	(0.81)	(2.58)	(0.46)	(1.99)	(0.43)
R^2	0.0140	0.0380	0.0260	0.0060	0.0350	0.0130
AIC	-9.099	-7.590	-8.485	-7.430	-8.515	-7.470

Note: ★/★★ statistically significant at $p < 0.01/0.05$ level. Standard errors in parentheses.

and significant for Phase 3. However, if we use a subsample that only covers Phase 1 (15 December 2010–31 October 2014), i.e. before the BOJ announced an increase in the intervention volume, the results are less clear.

As can be seen, the intervention parameters for TOPIX and 1320 ETF are positive, but the significant level and impact is lower. In fact, the parameter for 1321 ETF is negative, and the other results are not statistically significant. These results are consistent with previous studies, which indicates that the difference in our results compared to previous studies might relate to the fact that we use a more extensive dataset.

6.3 Impact on futures

Let us now turn to the impact on the TOPIX and Nikkei 225 futures contracts.

Table 8.8A shows the mean session returns for days when the morning returns are negative, and the BOJ intervenes in the market. As can be seen, during such days, both Nikkei 225 futures and TOPIX futures react positively. The mean morning-afternoon (ampm) returns are positive for Phase 1 and Phase 3.

We might expect that futures contracts contain some information about the intervention. Namely, if market participants sense the dynamics of returns during intervention days, they may attempt to profit from the (anticipated) intervention in the afternoon by buying Nikkei 225 or TOPIX futures contracts. As a result, the opening price of futures in the afternoon session may be higher if market participants anticipate an intervention. The opening price in the afternoon should reflect the market participants' expectation of the future stock price (i.e. afternoon stock price). The BOJ does not openly announce the criteria for an imminent intervention. However, market participants attempt to look for patterns, and the consensus view is that the BOJ tends to intervene when returns in the morning session are sharply negative. Interestingly, the mean afternoon returns for both futures contracts are negative. Thus, if futures contracts incorporate some information about the future price of the stock index, and if market participants anticipate an upcoming BOJ intervention, then the changes in futures prices ("NK1" and "TP1" in our analysis) might lead the stock prices as well.

Table 8.8B shows the mean return of the four ETFs and the two stock market indices in the afternoon – for days when the futures contracts react positively

Table 8.8A Morning-afternoon and afternoon mean returns (TOPIX and Nikkei 225 futures)

	$r_{NK1ampm}$	$r_{TP1ampm}$	r_{NK1pm}	r_{TP1pm}
TOPIX < 0				
Phase 1	5.5.E–03	5.4.E–03	–2.3.E–03	–1.6.E–03
Phase 3	3.7.E–03	3.6.E–03	–1.4.E–03	–1.3.E–03
Nikkei 225 < 0				
Phase 1	5.8.E–03	5.5.E–03	–2.5.E–03	–1.7.E–03
Phase 3	4.1.E–03	3.8.E–03	–1.6.E–03	–1.5.E–03

Table 8.8B Afternoon mean returns (1305 ETF, 1306 ETF, 1320 ETF, 1321 ETF, Nikkei 225 and TOPIX)

	r_{05pm}	r_{06pm}	r_{20pm}	r_{21pm}	r_{NKYpm}	r_{TPXpm}
$TP1_{ampm} > 0$						
Phase 1	-2.0.E-03	-1.6.E-03	-1.9.E-03	2.2.E-03	-1.1.E-03	-8.1.E-04
Phase 3	6.0.E-05	9.2.E-05	-2.7.E-04	1.2.E-04	-1.1.E-04	-6.5.E-06
$NK1_{ampm} > 0$						
Phase 1	-1.9.E-03	-1.5.E-03	-1.9.E-03	2.1.E-03	-1.1.E-03	-7.6.E-04
Phase 3	1.9.E-04	2.3.E-04	-2.1.E-04	9.2.E-05	-8.4.E-05	6.7.E-05

during the Tokyo lunch break (i.e. positive morning-afternoon returns). As can be seen, there are significant differences between Phase 1 and Phase 3. In Phase 1, mean returns in the afternoon session are negative (except for 1321 ETF). In Phase 3, afternoon returns for all asset classes are more substantial. When the Nikkei 225 future morning-afternoon return is positive, four out of six mean returns in the table are also positive. Therefore, we can infer that afternoon returns tend to be positive when the BOJ intervenes, and futures morning-afternoon returns are positive. This is particularly pronounced during Phase 3. In other words, the opening futures price in the afternoon session seems to reflect anticipation of an imminent BOJ intervention.

To further explore the impact of the futures, we conduct a Granger causality test for Nikkei 225, TOPIX and their respective futures contracts. We estimate models that have two autoregressive terms, with and without control variables. In this analysis, we pay attention to the impact of futures on stock indices. We then test the null-hypothesis $\beta_1=\beta_2=0$ in Equation (5). Equation (5) contains the lagged futures return, the corresponding morning-afternoon futures return ($r_{ifuturet-1}$) and the morning returns of the corresponding futures during the same day ($r_{ifuturet-2}$). We use afternoon returns of Nikkei 225 and TOPIX as r_{it}.

$$r_{it} = c + \alpha_1 r_{it-1} + \alpha_2 r_{it-2} + \beta_1 r_{ifuture\,t-1} + \beta_2 r_{ifuture\,t-2}$$
$$+ Controls\ (Liquidity, Volatility) + \varepsilon_t \tag{5}$$

Table 8.9 shows the result of the Granger causality test, which can tell us whether past data predict future values. As in the previous models, we use liquidity and volatility as control variables. After controlling for these, the causality structures are the same for both indices (TOPIX and Nikkei 225). Not only for the non-intervention sample but also the intervention sample, futures show Granger causality to their stock indices. In other words, futures prices have a significant impact on stock indices. The direction is mutual only during Phase 3. Therefore, we can confirm that futures prices have an effect on their underlying stock indices.

Put together, the results indicate that futures prices contain information about BOJ interventions, which may take place in the afternoon trading session. We

Table 8.9 Granger causality between TOPIX, Nikkei 225 and their futures contracts

	F stat.	P value	F stat.	P value		F stat.	P value	F stat.	P value
Whole sample			with control		Whole sample			with control	
$r_{NK1} \to r_{NKY}$	3233.81	0%	3189.30	0%	$r_{TP1} \to r_{TPX}$	351.40	0%	3007.85	0%
$r_{NKY} \to r_{NK1}$	4.707	0.9%	1.70	18.3%	$r_{TPX} \to r_{TP1}$	10.51	0%	7.97	0.04%
Non-intervention			with control		Non-intervention			with control	
$r_{NK1} \to r_{NKY}$	626.68	0%	2487.48	0%	$r_{TP1} \to r_{TPX}$	400.70	0%	2186.54	0%
$r_{NKY} \to r_{NK1}$	2.442	8.7%	1.12	32.6%	$r_{TPX} \to r_{TP1}$	1.56	21.1%	0.32	72.3%
Intervention			with control		Intervention			with control	
$r_{NK1} \to r_{NKY}$	909.78	0%	897.44	0%	$r_{TP1} \to r_{TPX}$	187.17	0%	991.60	0%
$r_{NKY} \to r_{NK1}$	1.974	14.0%	2.67	7.0%	$r_{TPX} \to r_{TP1}$	11.86	0%	1.31	27%
Intervention (Phase 3)			with control		Intervention (Phase 3)			with control	
$r_{NK1} \to r_{NKY}$	184.50	0%	157.96	0%	$r_{TP1} \to r_{TPX}$	84.12	0%	219.97	0%
$r_{NKY} \to r_{NK1}$	0.011	91.6%	11.36	0%	$r_{TPX} \to r_{TP1}$	5.40	0.5%	5.14	0.7%

Note: "Whole sample" covers all trading days during the studied period, and including both intervention and non-intervention days. F-statistics are calculated based on a Wald distribution.

cannot conclude that market participants are able to predict a market intervention and that the investment behaviour based on that anticipation will generate a rise in stock prices. Nonetheless, it is clear that many market participants are making an effort to predict an intervention, and that this is reflected in a regular futures price pattern. This pattern, then, contains information and leads the stock market in the afternoon session. In sum, the Nikkei 225 and TOPIX futures price movement provides support to the impact of BOJ intervention in the ETF market.

6.4   Impact on ETF price deviations from their underlying assets

Having analysed the impact of central bank intervention, we find a positive impact on afternoon returns – i.e. the possibility that market participants react before BOJ intervenes. Put differently, if market participants successfully anticipate the intervention, it does not surprise the market. Moreover, if arbitrage activities enable ETFs to track the underlying assets accurately, the difference between the ETF return and the returns of the underlying assets should be constant. If so, a BOJ intervention does not result in an ETF-deviation from the underlying asset price.

Four ETFs which track the stock market indices are discussed in this chapter: 1305 ETF and 1306 ETF (which track TOPIX), as well as 1320 ETF and 1321 ETF (which track Nikkei 225). In the first step, we estimate the difference of returns of TOPIX/Nikkei 225 and ETFs. In this step, after excluding the impact of liquidity and volatility, we use estimated error as the differences ($\hat{\varepsilon}$) in Equation (7). In the second step, we check the effect of intervention on these differences ($\hat{\varepsilon}$). If the intervention does not include any surprise content, ρ will be insignificant. We estimate both of Equation (6) and (7) with OLS.

$$r_{i\,pm} - r_{j\,pm} = c + \alpha \, \textit{Liquidity} + \beta \, \textit{Volatility} + \varepsilon \tag{6}$$

$$\hat{\varepsilon} = c + \rho \, \textit{Intervention (or Intervention Dummy)} + u \tag{7}$$

Table 8.10 Deviation of ETF returns from their underlying assets

Equation (6)	1305 ETF		1320 ETF	
	Whole sample	*Intervention*	*Whole sample*	*Intervention*
C	-1.6.E-05	-3.5.E-04	2.2.E-04	-4.0.E-05
	(1.7.E-04)	(3.9.E-04)	(0.00019)	(0.0004)
Liquidity	1.5.E+08	1.9.E+08	-1.4.E+08	4.0.E+08
	(1.5.E+08)	(3.2.E+08)	(1.6.E+08)	(3.1.E+08)
Volatility	1.61**	1.57*	-0.5	-0.5
	(0.82)	(0.3)	(1.06)	(1.0)
R^2	0.0093	0.02	0.003	0.0017

Equation (7)	1305 ETF			1320 ETF		
	Whole sample		*Intervention*	*Whole sample*		*Intervention*
C	-7.0.E-05	-2.0.E-04	-8.5.E-04*	-6.5.E-05	-9.1.E-05	-6.0.E-04
	(8.3.E-05)	(8.0.E-05)	(3.0.E-04)	(8.9.E-05)	(8.6.E-05)	(3.8.E-04)
Intervention dummy	2.6.E-04			2.4.E-04		
	(1.6.E-04)			(1.7.E-04)		
Intervention		9.8.E-07*	1.9.E-06*		7.8.E-07**	1.5.E-06**
		(3.1.E-07)	6.5.E-07		(3.4.E-07)	(6.9.E-07)
R^2	0.0014	0.0049	0.017	0.0009	0.0015	0.008

Note: */** statistically significant at $p < 0.01/0.05$ level. Standard errors in parentheses. Huber-White heteroskedasticity consistent standard errors and covariance are used. We show the results only for 1305 ETF and 1320 ETF as the results for the other ETFs are very similar in terms of the significance and sign of parameters.

where $i = 05, 06, 20$ or 21 and j = NKY or TPX and $(\hat{\varepsilon})$ is the estimated error from Equation (6).

The upper part in Table 8.10 shows the result of Equation (6) and the lower part shows the result of Equation (7). As can be seen, the ETFs tracking Nikkei 225, as well as TOPIX, deviate from their underlying asset returns after controlling for liquidity and volatility. All parameters for Equation (7) are positive but significant only for intervention. Thus, the higher the intervention volume, the greater the ETF-deviation. In other words, the volume of intervention can take the market by surprise, even if the intervention itself is anticipated. In other words, BOJ interventions are effective.

7 Impact on volatility

7.1 A comparison of volatility measures

Table 8.11 shows the mean of Garman and Klass volatility measures for different samples.

Table 8.11 Basic statistics of volatility

	$Volatility_{05}$	$Volatility_{06}$	$Volatility_{20}$	$Volatility_{21}$
Morning session				
Whole sample	2.72E–05	3.27E–05	3.03E–05	3.29E–05
Non-intervention	2.27E–05	2.82E–05	2.51E–05	2.74E–05
Intervention	3.93E–05	4.46E–05	4.40E–05	4.75E–05
Phase 3	4.54E–05	5.23E–05	5.38E–05	5.89E–05
Afternoon session				
Whole sample	2.75E–05	2.98E–05	3.45E–05	3.54E–05
Non-intervention	2.25E–05[++]	2.56E–05[++]	2.91E–05[++]	2.89E–05[+]
Intervention	4.07E–05[+]	4.11E–05[+]	4.89E–05[++]	5.29E–05[+]
Phase 3	1.5E–05[**+]	1.74E–05[*+]	1.84E–05[**+]	1.84E–05[**+]

	$Volatility_{NK1}$	$Volatility_{NKY}$	$Volatility_{TP1}$	$Volatility_{TPX}$
Morning session				
Whole sample	8.28E–05	3.22E–05	8.12E–05	2.99E–05
Non-intervention	6.75E–05	2.65E–05	6.72E–05	2.48E–05
Intervention	0.000124	4.75E–05	0.000118	4.35E–05
Phase 3	0.000126	5.95E–05	9.00E–05	4.88E–05
Afternoon session				
Whole sample	6.17E–05[*]	2.79E–05	5.04E–05[*]	2.45E–05
Non-intervention	5.37E–05[*]	2.47E–05	4.35E–05[+++]	2.11E–05
Intervention	8.3E–05[+]	3.66E–05[++]	6.88E–05[**+]	3.36E–05[++]
Phase 3	7.19E–05[++]	1.67E–05[*+]	6.82E–05[+]	1.45E–05[*+]

Note: [*]/[**] statistically significant at p < 0.01/0.05 level. [+]/[++] difference from returns of the whole sample in the afternoon session statistically significant at p < 0.01/0.05 level.

As can be seen, the volatilities are substantially higher for the intervention sample than those in the non-intervention sample (and the sample as a whole). However, for Phase 3, all volatilities are lower than those for the whole sample and their morning volatilities. Therefore, we cannot draw the conclusion that the BOJ interventions necessarily lead to lower market volatility.

According to the Mixture of Distribution Hypothesis (MDH) (see, for example, Clark, 1973; Epps and Epps, 1976), volatility co-moves with trading volume. To investigate the results in Table 8.11 further, we incorporate the trading volume on the Tokyo Stock Exchange (Table 8.12).

The average volume in the afternoon sessions for Phase 3 is significantly lower than the average volume for the whole sample. The MDH predicts that volatility will be lower when the trading volume decreases. Therefore, the lower volatility in the afternoon session is consistent with the MDH prediction.

After checking for stationarity of the volatility measures, we estimate a simple OLS model to investigate the impact of BOJ interventions on volatility. However, since Table 8.11 shows that the effect might be different

Table 8.12 Average trading volume in the afternoon sessions on the Tokyo Stock Exchange (number of shares)

Sample	Volume
Whole sample	1,070,000,000
Non-intervention	1,070,000,000
Intervention	1,090,000,000
Phase 3	869,000,000★

Note: ★ difference from the whole sample statistically significant at p < 0.01 level.

Table 8.13 Impact of intervention on volatility (1305 ETF, 1320 ETF, Nikkei 225 and TOPIX)

	$Volatility_{05pm}$		$Volatility_{20pm}$		$Volatility_{NKYpm}$		$Volatility_{TPXpm}$	
C	6.8.E-06	5.1.E-06	-5.4.E-06	-7.1.E-06	7.7.E-07	-1.7.E-07	6.2.E-06	3.4.E-06
	(5.9.E-06)	(6.0.E-06)	(4.6.E-06)	(4.6.E-06)	(2.4.E-06)	(3.2.E-06)	(3.3.E-06)	(3.3.E-06)
Intervention	-3.1.E-09	6.5.E-08	3.4.E-09	7.7.E-08★	-2.0.E-09	3.9.E-08★★	-2.7.E-09	5.1.E-08★
	(1.6.E-08)	(3.5.E-08)	(1.3.E-08)	(2.8.E-08)	(9.2.E-08)	(1.9.E-08)	(9.3.E-09)	(2.0.E-08)
Intervention × Phase3 Dummy		-8.0.E-08★★		-9.6.E-08★		-5.3.E-08★		-6.3.E-08★
		(3.7.E-08)		(3.0.E-08)		(2.0.E-08)		(2.1.E-08)
Liquidity	1.4.E+07★	1.4.E+07★	2.8.E+07★	2.7.E+07★	1.9.E+07★	1.8.E+07★	1.3.E+07★	1.3.E+07★
	(1.5.E+06)	(1.3.E+06)	(2.2.E+06)	(2.2.E+06)	(1.5.E+06)	(1.5.E+06)	(1.7.E+06)	(1.7.E+06)
R^2	0.012	0.014	0.07	0.078	0.07	0.077	0.029	0.03
F-statistic	12.115	9.65	77.99	55.75	79.14	55.19	30.44	23.45

Note: ★/★★ statistically significant at p < 0.01/0.05 level. Standard errors in parentheses. We show the results only for 1305 ETF and 1320 ETF as the results for the other ETFs are very similar in terms of the significance and sign of parameters.

for Phase 3, we include a new cross term (*Intervention × Phase3 Dummy*) as shown in Table 8.13.

As can be seen, the parameters of intervention are not statistically significant. However, if we add the cross term, both parameters become significant. During the period before 4 August 2016 (Phase 1 and 2), intervention has a positive impact on volatility. During Phase 3, however, intervention has a negative impact on volatility.

From this analysis, we can confirm that the impact of intervention differs throughout the studies period. From the beginning of BOJ interventions until August 2016, the effect is positive. However, during the latter period, intervention lowers the volatility in the markets. Given that the intervention volume has increased dramatically during Phase 3, we can conclude that BOJ intervention in the ETF market has come to play a crucial role in reducing volatility in the Japanese equity markets.

7.2　*Impact on volatility using an EGARCH model*

Next, we expand the basic analysis using an EGARCH model to explore the intervention impact. In a GARCH-type analysis, the conditional variance can be used as the proxy for volatility. We use Equation (3) and modify Equation (4) as follows:

$$\log(\sigma_t^2) = \omega + \sum \beta_j \log(\sigma_{t-j}^2) + \sum \alpha_i \left| \frac{\varepsilon_{t-i}}{\sigma_{t-i}} \right| + \sum \gamma_k \frac{\varepsilon_{t-k}}{\sigma_{t-k}} +$$
$$\rho_2 Intervention + \rho_2 (Intervention \times Phase3\ Dummy) \tag{8}$$

Thus, we incorporate the volume of intervention into the conditional error equation. From the discussion so far, we also use a Phase 3 dummy variable to check the impact of intervention during the latest BOJ intervention period.

Tables 8.14A and 8.14B show the impact of the BOJ intervention using an EGARCH model.

The term ρ_1 captures the impact of intervention on volatility. As can be seen, ρ_1 is significant and negative for all equations. Therefore, we can confirm that intervention has a negative impact on the volatility in these markets. When we

Table 8.14A Impact of intervention (EGARCH) (1305 ETF and 1320 ETF)

	r_{05pm}			r_{20pm}		
C	-4.0.E-05	-3.8.E-05	-4.8.E-05	3.1.E-04	3.1.E-04	3.5.E-04
	(1.4.E-04)	(1.5.E-04)	(1.5.E-04)	(1.8.E-04)	(1.8.E-04)	(1.7.E-04)
Liquidity	-3.7.E+08★	-3.9.E+08★	-4.1.E+08★	-4.9.E+08★	-5.2.E+08★	-5.1.E+08★
	(4.3.E+07)	(4.3.E+07)	(4.3.E+07)	(5.0.E+07)	(4.9.E+07)	(4.9.E+07)
Volatility	-0.12	-0.14	1.91	4.53★	4.2★	6.05★
	(0.42)	(0.51)	(0.42)	(0.38)	(0.33)	(0.46)
Intervention	1.6.E-06★	1.8.E-06★	1.8.E-06★	1.3.E-06★	1.4.E-06★	1.4.E-06★
	(1.8.E-07)	(2.2.E-07)	(2.3.E-07)	(3.4.E-07)	(3.8.E-07)	(3.8.E-07)
ω	-0.22★	-0.24★	-0.33★	-0.71★	-0.66★	-8.59★
	(0.019)	(0.021)	(0.024)	(0.064)	(0.06)	(0.24)
β	0.99★	0.99★	0.98★	0.95★	0.96★	0.23★
	(0.002)	(0.002)	(0.002)	(0.005)	(0.005)	(0.024)
α	0.19★	0.18★	0.173★	0.331★	0.621★	0.309★
	(0.01)	(0.01)	(0.01)	(0.016)	(0.017)	(0.017)
γ	-0.09★	-0.09★	-0.10★	-0.07★	-0.08★	-0.10★
	(0.01)	(0.01)	(0.01)	(0.01)	(0.01)	(0.02)
ρ_1		-5.8.E-05★	1.5.E-04		-8.7.E-05★	-2.7.E-03★
		(1.7.E-05)	(4.7.E-05)		(3.6.E-05)	(1.6.E-04)
ρ_2			2.2.E-04★			-3.7.E-03★
			(4.1.E-05)			(1.0.E-04)
R²	0.0095	0.0095	0.011	0.02	0.02	0.02
AIC	-8.01	-8.01	-8.01	-7.69	-7.67	-7.64

Note: ★/★★ statistically significant at p < 0.01/0.05 level. Standard errors in parentheses. We show the results only for 1305 ETF and 1320 ETF as the results for the other ETFs are very similar in terms of the significance and sign of parameters.

Table 8.14B Impact of intervention (EGARCH) (Nikkei 225 and TOPIX)

	r_{NKYpm}			r_{TPXpm}		
C	2.5.E-04★	2.2.E-04★	1.6.E-04★★	2.1.E-04★	2.0.E-04★	1.5.E-04★★
	(6.0.E-05)	(6.5.E-05)	(8.3.E-05)	(6.7.E-05)	(7.0.E-05)	(7.8.E-05)
Liquidity	-2.8.E+08★	-2.8.E+08★	-1.9.E+08★	-2.6.E+08	-2.7.E+08★	-2.0.E+08★
	(2.0.E+07)	(1.9.E+07)	(2.3.E+07)	(2.0.E+07)	(2.0.E+07)	(2.5.E+07)
Volatility	-5.79★	-5.76★	-1.84★	-2.53★	-2.51★	0.96★
	(0.34)	(0.34)	(0.29)	(0.41)	(0.41)	(0.33)
Intervention	4.9.E-07★	6.4.E-07★	4.7.E-07★	8.5.E-07★	9.3.E-07★	6.3.E-07★
	(1.0.E-07)	(1.4.E-07)	(1.8.E-07)	(7.4.E-07)	(1.4.E-07)	(2.0.E-07)
ω	-0.22★	-0.23★	-10.8★	-0.30★	-0.28★	-11.12★
	(0.032)	(0.034)	(0.35)	(0.034)	(0.034)	(0.385)
β	0.99★	0.99★	0.14★	0.99★	0.99★	0.13★
	(0.002)	(0.003)	(0.029)	(0.002)	(0.003)	(0.03)
α	0.195★	0.189★	0.486★	0.1889★	0.179★	0.541★
	(0.01)	(0.01)	(0.031)	(0.01)	(0.01)	(0.02)
γ	-0.12★	-0.12★	-0.09★	-0.119★	-0.121★	-0.166★
	(0.01)	(0.01)	(0.02)	(0.01)	(0.01)	(0.01)
ρ_1		-5.3.E-05★	2.6.E-03★		-3.9.E-05★	2.1.E-03★
		(1.9.E-05)	(1.0.E-04)		(2.3.E-05)	(1.0.E-04)
ρ_2			-3.2.E-03★			-2.5.E-03★
			(1.0.E-04)			(0.001)
R^2	0.0155	0.032	0.029	0.011	0.011	0.0091
AIC	-9.41	-9.41	-9.27	-9.51	-9.51	-9.39

Note: ★/★★ statistically significant at p < 0.01/0.05 level. Standard errors in parentheses.

incorporate an additional term (*Intervention × Phase3 Dummy*) into conditional variance equation, ρ_1 becomes positive, and ρ_2 is estimated negatively. From our results, therefore, intervention during Phase 3 reduces volatility, which is consistent with the results in Table 8.13.

The term β_j provides an insight into the impact of BOJ interventions on the volatility persistence. Lamourex and Lastrapes (1990) tested the impact of information inflow into the market on the GARCH effect (β_j). For testing this impact, they incorporated the trading volume into the conditional error equation. This is because trading volume can be used as the proxy of information inflow. They showed that β declined closer to zero when they included volume into the conditional variance equation. They concluded that information inflow might cause the persistence of volatility. Following Lamourex and Lastrapes (1990), we, therefore, explore the impact of intervention on volatility. When we incorporate this into the conditional variance equation, β in Table 8.14A and 8.14B remains more or less unchanged. However, if we include *Intervention × Phase3 Dummy*, β decreases (except for r_{05pm}). Following Lamourex and Lastrapes (1990), we can summarise the findings as follows. Intervention during Phase 3 may not only act to reduce volatility, but also reduce the volatility persistence.

8   Conclusions

Since the launch of Abenomics, the BOJ has promoted an aggressive monetary policy, including QQE, to reach the inflation target of 2%. Despite this, however, the target has not yet been met – resulting in regular interventions in the stock market via purchases of ETFs.

This is not the first time for the BOJ to intervene in the market. However, ETF interventions are a milestone in the sense that they are intended to stabilise the stock markets – and unlike any of the traditional interest rate-related monetary policy tools.

In this chapter, we have reviewed the ETF purchasing progress by the BOJ and outlined how it operates. Our empirical study covers the period from 15 December 2010 to 7 December 2018. It includes eight assets: the TOPIX and Nikkei 225 stock market indices and the futures contracts on these indices, as well as two ETFs tracking TOPIX (1305 ETF and 1306 ETF) and two tracking Nikkei 225 (1320 ETF and 1321 ETF). We use opening and closing prices in the morning and afternoon sessions and construct three returns: the return in the morning session, the return in the afternoon session, and return between the end of the morning session and the beginning of the afternoon session.

From studying the basic statistics for the whole period, the impact of interventions on stock prices is not clear. However, when we separate the period into three phases depending on the increasing intervention volume, revealing patterns begin to emerge. In particular, Phase 3, which covers the period after 4 August 2016 when the volume was more than doubled, is very different from earlier periods. Using an EGARCH model, and after controlling for liquidity and volatility, we find a positive and strong impact of central bank interventions on afternoon returns in the stock market. Furthermore, we find that the relationship between interventions and futures prices is less robust during Phase 1 and 2. However, when studying Phase 3, we observe that the opening futures price in the afternoon session seems to reflect anticipation of an imminent BOJ intervention. We also find that BOJ intervention tends to increase the deviation of the ETF price for that of the underlying assets. Thus, interventions seem to contain a surprise element that is transmitted to the market.

Put together, these findings suggest the following. The anticipation of an intervention by the BOJ may affect the stock prices through the investment behaviour of market participants. Even though the intervention is expected, a surprise factor remains – which has increased in line with the larger intervention volumes. Combining the results of the impact on prices, we document that BOJ interventions have a significantly positive influence on stock market indices – and that volume plays an important role. Our findings differ from previous studies, chiefly because we use a more extended dataset.

Finally, and in line with earlier studies, we also find that the BOJ has managed to reduce stock market volatility as a result of the regular ETF purchases.

This is particularly evident for Phase 3. What is more, not only the volatility but also the persistency of the volatility has been reduced through intervention.

There are, however, also limitations in this empirical study. For instance, we use four price snapshots per day. This captures intraday dynamics – but to a certain degree. In reality, traders may react to new information very fast, and if so, stock market indices and ETF prices may move within a few seconds or minutes after the BOJ intervention. To investigate this immediate impact, high-frequency data would be more appropriate. Thus, although we focus on intraday patterns, our results refer to a relatively long-term market impact. Furthermore, our primary focus in this chapter is on the impact on the financial markets. However, the ultimate goal of the BOJ interventions is to achieve a higher inflation rate, i.e. to meet the 2% target. From this perspective, our results can only give a partial evaluation of the monetary policy measures.

The question is: what might be the next phase for BOJ in terms of ETF interventions? The Japanese central bank has gradually increased its holdings of ETFs, and they now stand at 70–80%. This has prompted strong reactions by market participants, which are concerned about the market liquidity with such a dominant player. Could the BOJ holdings be sold back to the market as smoothly as in Hong Kong following the Asian Financial Crisis? We hope that this chapter can provide insights for the development in the ETF buying programme of the future.

Notes

1 Shinzō Abe assumed the post of prime minister in December 2012.
2 The BOJ adopted negative interest rates in January 2016. On 2 September 2016, the BOJ announced the introduction of "Qualitative and Quantitative Easing with negative interest rate".
3 ETF purchases began in 2010. During this period, Masaaki Shirakawa served as Governor of the Bank of Japan.
4 Another route to affect the real economy is via the wealth effect on consumption.
5 See Wong (2014) for a detailed analysis.
6 Moreover, from April 2016, the BOJ started a new category of ETFs that supports firms proactively to invest in physical and human capital. For data consistency, we do not use this ETF volume in our study.
7 Xu and Yin (2017) identify that ETF trading increases stock index efficiency.
8 Indeed, a private company provides the probability of a BOJ intervention on the Internet: https://nikkeiyosoku.com/boj_etf/. In our dataset, there are some days when the stock indices decline more than 1% in the morning session, and the BOJ intervened. However, these cases are very few.
9 Jiang et al. (2019) examine the Shanghai Stock Exchange (SSE) 50 index futures and SSE 50 ETF spot and options markets. Their tests cover the linear, nonlinear Granger causality, and lead-lag relationship. Using 1-hour data, significant lead-lag relationships are found from the results of a Granger causality test.

References

Amihud, Y. (2002) Illiquidity and stock returns: Cross-section and time series effects, *Journal of Financial Markets*, 5 (91), 31–56.

Bank of Japan (2010a) *Statement on Monetary Policy*, 28 October. Available from: www.boj. or.jp/en/announcements/release_2010/k101028.pdf [Accessed 28 October 2019].

Bank of Japan (2010b) *Statement on Monetary Policy*, 5 November. Available from: www.boj. or.jp/en/announcements/release_2010/k101105.pdf [Accessed 28 October 2019].

Bank of Japan (2011a) *Enhancement of Monetary Easing*, 14 March. Available from: www.boj. or.jp/en/announcements/release_2011/k110314a.pdf [Accessed 28 October 2019].

Bank of Japan (2011b) *Enhancement of Monetary Easing*, 4 August. Available from: www.boj. or.jp/en/announcements/release_2011/k110804a.pdf [Accessed 28 October 2019].

Bank of Japan (2012) *Enhancement of Monetary Easing*, 30 October. Available from: www. boj.or.jp/en/announcements/release_2012/k121030a.pdf [Accessed 28 October 2019].

Bank of Japan (2013) *Introduction of the 'Quantitative and Qualitative Monetary Easing'*, 4 April. Available from: www.boj.or.jp/en/announcements/release_2013/k130404a.pdf [Accessed 28 October 2019].

Bank of Japan (2014) *Expansion of the Quantitative and Qualitative Monetary Easing*, 31 October. Available from: www.boj.or.jp/en/announcements/release_2014/k141031a.pdf [Accessed 28 October 2019].

Bank of Japan (2015) *Statement on Monetary Policy*, 18 December. Available from: www.boj. or.jp/en/announcements/release_2015/k151218a.pdf [Accessed 28 October 2019].

Bank of Japan (2016) *Change in the Maximum Amount of Each ETF to Be Purchased*, 21 September. Available from: www.boj.or.jp/en/announcements/release_2016/rel160921c.pdf [Accessed 28 October 2019].

Bank of Japan (2018a) *Minutes of Monetary Policy Meeting on 30 and 31 July 2018*, 25 September. Available from: www.boj.or.jp/en/mopo/mpmsche_minu/minu_2018/g180731.pdf [Accessed 28 October 2019].

Bank of Japan (2018b) *Outline of Purchases of ETFs, Financial Markets Department*, 31 July. Available from: www.boj.or.jp/en/announcements/release_2018/rel180731h.pdf [Accessed 28 October 2019].

Bank of Japan (2019) *Purchases of ETFs and J-REITs*. Available from: https://www3.boj. or.jp/market/en/menu_etf.htm [Accessed 28 October 2019].

Barbon, A. and Gianinazzi, V. (2018) Quantitative easing and equity prices: Evidence from the ETF program of the Bank of Japan, *Swiss Finance Institute Research Paper*, No. 19–55.

Clark, P. K. (1973) Subordinated stochastic process model with finite variance for speculative processes, *Econometrica*, 41 (1), 133–153.

Epps, T. W. and Epps, M. L. (1976) The stochastic dependence of security price changes and transaction volumes: implications for the mixture-of-distributions hypothesis, *Econometrica*, 44 (2), 305–321.

Garman, M. B. and Klass, M. J. (1980) On the estimation of security price volatilities from historical data, *Journal of Business*, 53 (1), 67–78.

Harada, K. (2017a) BOJs ETF purchasing policy and the distortion of individual stock price average stock price, *Shokuen Review*, 57 (1), 135–150.

Harada, K. (2017b) The event study of the BOJ's ETF purchasing policy and the change of the composition of Nikkei 225, *The JSRI Journal of Financial and Securities Markets*, 100, 75–90, December.

Ide, S. and Minami, S. (2013) Is it true that BOJ's ETF purchasing policy distorts the market? *Gekkan Shihon Sijou*, 13–25, July.

Itzhak, B.-D., Franzoni, F. and Moussawi, R. (2017a) Do ETFs increase volatility? *SSRN Working Paper.*

Itzhak, B.-D., Franzoni, F. and Moussawi, R. (2017b) Exchange Traded Funds (TEFS), *NBER Working Paper Series,* No. 22829.

Ivanov, I. T. and Lenkey, S. L. (2018) Do leveraged ETFs really amplify late-day returns and volatility? *Journal of Financial Markets,* 41, 36–56.

Jiang, T., Bao, S. and Li, L. (2019) The linear and nonlinear lead – lag relationship among three SSE 50 Index markets: The index futures, 50ETF spot and options markets, *Physica A: Statistical Mechanics and Its Applications,* 525, 878–893.

JPX (2017) *ETF/ETN Factsheet 2017.* Available from: www.jpx.co.jp/english/equities/products/etfs/data/tvdivq0000004xpi-att/Factsheet2017EN.pdf [Accessed 28 October 2019].

Kobayashi, T. (2016) The effect of QQE on the ETF and J-REIT price, *JILI Journal (Special edition),* (1), 127–138.

Kobayashi, T. (2017) The effect of the quantitative and qualitative monetary easing on the returns and volatilities of Japanese stock and REIT markets, *Journal of Household Economics,* 46, 1–10.

Koyama, Y. (2012) Thinking about the Bank of Japan's purchase of JREIT, *Tochi Sogo Kenkyu,* winter, 19–29.

Lamourex, C. G. and Lastrapes, W. (1990) Heteroskedasticity in stock return data: Volume versus GARCH effects, *Journal of Finance,* 45 (1), 221–229.

Matsuki, T., Sugimoto, K. and Satoma, K. (2015) Effects of the Bank of Japan's current quantitative and qualitative easing, *Economics Letters,* 133, 112–116.

Serita, T. and Hanaeda, H. (2017) The impact of ETF on stock market, *Gekkan Shihon Sijou,* 387, 28–37.

Shirakawa, M. (2013) Central banking: Before, during, and after the crisis, *International Journal of Central Banking,* 9 (18), 373–387.

Statista (2019) *Development of Assets of Global Exchange Traded Funds (ETFs) from 2003 to 2018 (in Billion U.S. Dollars).* Available from: www.statista.com/statistics/224579/worldwide-etf-assets-under-management-since-1997/ [Accessed 28 October 2019].

Wong, H. Y. (2014) *An Empirical Study of the Hong Kong Tracker Fund and Its Relationship with Hang Seng Index and Hang Seng Index Futures,* PhD thesis, Hong Kong Baptist University.

Xu, L. and Yin, X. (2017) Does ETF trading affect the efficiency of the underlying index? *International Review of Financial Analysis,* 51, 82–101.

9 Quantitative and qualitative monetary easing, negative interest rates and the stability of the financial system in Japan

Etsuko Katsu

1 Introduction

Abenomics, which was introduced in December 2012 when the second Abe administration started with Shinzō Abe as a Prime Minister, entered its seventh year in 2019. So far, the Japanese economy has been expanding rapidly with a 52 trillion-yen increase in nominal GDP from FY2012 to FY2018, an increase of profits by corporations, and a stable Nikkei 225 stock market index above 20,000.

If the economic development continues in January 2019, it could surpass the longest economic expansion of the "Izanami boom" from February 2002 to February 2008 – the most extended economic recovery boom of 73 months in history after WW2. The unemployment rate reached a historic low of 2.3% in February 2019, when labour shortages could be seen in several sectors. It could be argued that the Japanese economy is entering into almost full employment without inflation. With this backdrop, it was decided to open up the labour markets to foreign blue-collar and middle-class workers with a more relaxed immigration inspection. However, the population has not felt the economic expansion, because wages have not risen for a long time, and a consumption tax hike was expected in October 2019. Nevertheless, a significant change is not expected in the monetary policy of the Bank of Japan (BOJ). Governor Kuroda, who started his second term in April 2018, initiated an aggressive unconventional monetary policy. However, he has not yet accomplished the Bank's inflation target of 2%, despite almost escaping a long and persistent deflationary period.

In contrast to Japan, the US enjoyed an immediate economic expansion under the Trump administration. With the tax reduction in the year of the interim election, the Federal Reserve (Fed) raised the federal funds rates four times in 2018. But in 2019, amid emerging uncertainty regarding the US–China trade war, Brexit, rising of US-Iran tensions, and possible regulatory reinforcement of mega global information companies (the four internet giants, Google, Apple, Facebook and Amazon, collectively known as "GAFA"), the US growth prospects have shrunk. Consequently, the Fed lowered the policy rate three times gradually in 2019. In Europe, the European Central Bank

(ECB) terminated a quantitative easing policy at the end of 2018, however, the European economy remains weak. Under these circumstances, it is widely believed that the monetary policy will remain soft for the foreseeable future.

This chapter investigates how Governor Kuroda's unconventional monetary policy, including the negative interest rate policy, affects financial markets and the behaviour of financial institutions – especially from the perspective of financial stability and monetary and fiscal policy coordination. The findings can be summarised as follows. Quantitative and Qualitative Easing (QQE) is found to have had a significantly positive impact on inflation expectations at first. Banks have pod their holdings from risk-free to riskier bonds, and lending by banks has picked up. However, the negative interest rate policy introduced in February 2016 has harmed the financial system. Furthermore, through an empirical study, it is shown that the negative interest rate policy, coupled with management efficiency, has influenced bank profitability and the return on equity of regional banks.

The chapter is organised as follows. Section 2 provides an overview of the monetary easing policy in Japan since the 1990s as well as the monetary policy under Abenomics. Section 3 assesses the negative interest rate policy launched in 2016. Section 4 examines the impact of unconventional monetary policy on financial markets, and the negative interest rate policy on the profitability of financial institutions. Section 5 focuses on regional banks. Following Petria et al. (2015) and Akbas (2012), the return on equity of regional banks is regressed on several variables that include the negative interest rate policy, to show the impact of that policy. The chapter concludes with an assessment of the BOJ's monetary policy and some policy implications.

2 Overview of the monetary policy in Japan since the 1990s

2.1 Zero interest rates policy and forward guidance

Back in 1994, when regulations of interest rates had been entirely abolished, the Bank of Japan changed its main policy instrument from discount rates to open market operations. From 1998, just after a revision of the BOJ law in 1997, they have decided on the usage of non-collateral overnight rates as a target interest rate. In 1999, when Japan suffered its severe financial crisis, the Bank of Japan introduced the so-called zero interest rates policy to keep overnight rates as low as possible. In April 1999, Governor Hayami informally expressed his view that the BOJ would maintain its zero interest rate policy until deflationary concerns had disappeared. This action came to be known as "forward guidance".

However, as the Japanese economy dropped into a severe deflation spiral, the Bank of Japan became the first central bank to introduce quantitative easing on 19 March 2001. The policy target was again changed from non-collateral overnight rates to current account balances at the Bank of Japan. At first, Japan's economic recovery was disappointing and the Bank of Japan provided ample liquidity. The uncollateralised overnight call rate was determined by the market at a certain level below the ceiling set by the Lombard-type lending facility. However, when the world economy expanded at an extraordinary high speed led by boom in China, the Bank of Japan removed its quantitative easing policy in March 2006. The target of monetary policy changed from the current account balance to the uncollateralised overnight call rate again.

Figure 9.1 shows that during the quantitative easing policy from March 2001 to July 2006, the outstanding amount in the non-collateral call market was squeezed at a very low level, because suppliers of funds did not invest in call markets due to the low return. Moreover, institutions did not specifically need the call market, as they could borrow directly from the BOJ at any time. Thus, they had a problem that the call market did not function well.

From the perspective of financial system stability, the quantitative monetary policy provided an opportunity for financial institutions to resolve their substantial non-performing loans accumulated during the 1990s financial crisis. During this period, the banks could clean up bad loans actively through the disposal of non-performing loans (NPLs). A consolidation period in the banking system followed (the number of city banks decreased from 12 in 1990 to 5 in 2019), and the financial system strengthened.

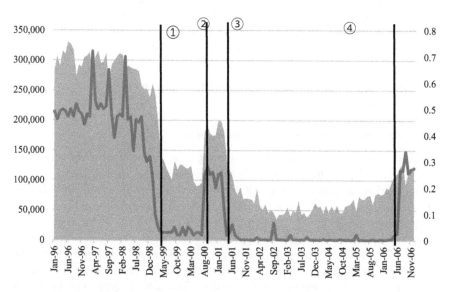

Figure 9.1 Call rate (%, RHS) and outstanding amounts in the non-collateral call market JPY 100 million, RHS)

Source: Bank of Japan. ① Introduction of zero interest rates in February 1999, ② Removal of zero interest rates in August 2000, ③ Introduction of first quantitative easing policy (QEP) in March 2001, ④ Removal of QEP in July 2006, 0.25% O/N rate.

2.2 Quantitative monetary policy after the Lehman Shock

Introduction of the complementary deposit facility

During the zero interest rate period from 2001 to 2006, the Japanese economy expanded due to the progress in resolving non-performing loans under the easing monetary policy, and the rapid growth of the Chinese economy. This expansion of the Japanese economy led the BOJ to hike policy rates again in July 2006, from 0 to 0.25%.

However, the sudden market turmoil after the Lehman Shock in September 2008 led to a downturn in the Japanese economy, affecting banks' balance sheets. Just after the Lehman bankruptcy, on 31 October 2008, the Bank of Japan decided to adopt a Complementary Deposit Facility (Bank of Japan, 2008). Usually, no interest rates are applied to reserve deposit balances in central banks. However, a positive rate (0.1%) was applied to the balances in excess of required reserves of the banks, and special reserve balances held by securities companies or money market brokers. Thus, after 2008, the BOJ followed the central banks in other advanced economies and in particular the Federal Reserve in offering interest on reserve deposits.

On 1 October 2008, with the Emergency Economic Stabilization Act of 2008, the Federal Reserve decided to pay interest on required reserve balances (IORR) and on excess reserve balances (IOER). The reason why they introduced IORR was to effectively eliminate the implicit tax that reserve requirements used to impose on depository institutions.[1] The Bank of Japan followed this Fed action to make its monetary policy easing more effective. The objective of the introduction of the Complementary Deposit Facility in Japan was to keep current account balances at a high level. This would increase the money stock circulating in the whole economy and spur on the Japanese economy. During the quantitative easing policy from 2001 to 2006, money markets did not work well, and the market volume continuously declined (as mentioned earlier). One of the reasons why the BOJ introduced the Complementary Deposit Facility in 2008 was also to stimulate the money market to function well and to normalise trading.

Comprehensive Monetary Easing in 2010

Although the Japanese economy showed signs of a moderate recovery in 2010, the pace of recovery was slowing down partly due to the slowdown in overseas economies led by the global financial crisis, the EU sovereign debt crisis, and the effects of the appreciating Japanese yen. Based on the earlier assessment of economic activity and price developments, the Bank judged it necessary to enhance monetary easing further as follows.

First, the Bank of Japan encouraged the uncollateralised overnight call rate to remain at around 0 to 0.1%. Second, the Bank intended to maintain the virtually zero interest rate policy until it would judge, based on the "understanding of medium- to long-term price stability", that price stability was in sight. Third, it introduced an Asset Purchase Program on its balance sheet. This involved purchasing various financial assets, such as government securities, commercial papers (CPs), corporate bonds, exchange-traded funds (ETFs) and securities issued by Japan real estate investment trusts (J-REITs) (Bank of Japan, 2010). This was similar to the security-purchasing programme implemented in the US. However, the size of the Asset Purchase Program in Japan was more limited.

Just after the Lehman Shock in 2008, one of the failures of the Bank of Japan's policy was not to implement further quantitative easing policy as quickly as the Fed or the ECB. Figure 9.2 shows the comparative trend of the monetary base of the Fed and the BOJ since 2008. It illustrates that the Bank of Japan's response to the shock was very delayed in comparison to the Fed and the ECB. The Federal Reserve introduced its first quantitative easing programme (QE1) in October 2008 (just after the Lehman Shock). But Japan had to wait until the BOJ introduced QQE in April 2013.

The different responses by the Fed, the ECB, and the BOJ resulted in tremendous "yen-daka" (yen appreciation), which hurt the profits of the Japanese export-oriented industry. It was also negative for stock prices, as foreign profits denominated in yen decreased if yen appreciated. Combined, this made it difficult for the whole economy to exit from deflation. Just before the launch of Abenomics, the yen exchange rate reached 80 yen per dollar, and the Nikkei 225 was around 8,000.

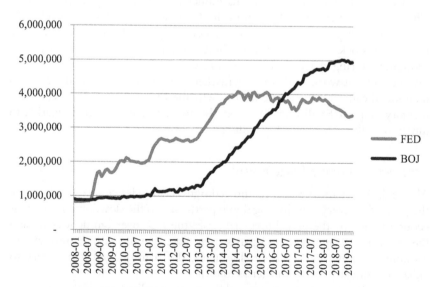

Figure 9.2 Monetary base after the Lehman Shock (BOJ: JPY 100 million, FRB: USD million)

Sources: FRB, Bank of Japan

2.3   Abenomics and QQE in 2013

Introduction of QQE in 2013 as one of the arrows of Abenomics

In April 2013, Haruhiko Kuroda, former President of the Asian Development Bank (ADB) and Vice Minister of the Ministry of Finance (MOF), was appointed as Governor of Bank of Japan, and immediately introduced QQE (Quantitative and Qualitative Easing monetary policy) as one of the three arrows of Abenomics. This unconventional monetary policy was seen as a powerful method to exit from the deflationary spiral.

QQE consisted of two parts. First, it raised inflation expectations through the Bank's strong commitment to achieving the price stability target of 2% in terms of the year-on-year rate of change of the consumer price index (CPI) at the earliest possible time (at first within two years). The increase of expected inflation rates was a main driver to push up Nikkei stock prices and depreciate yen exchange rates drastically.[2] Second, QQE exerted downward pressure not only on short-term nominal interest rates but on the entire yield curve through massive purchases of Japanese government bonds (JGBs). Consequently, both short- and long-term real interest rates could be lowered (Kuroda, 2016).

The policy under Kuroda entered a new phase of monetary easing – both in terms of quantity and quality. It doubled the monetary base and the amounts outstanding of JGBs and ETFs in two years, and more than doubled the average remaining maturity of JGB purchases. At first, the BOJ increased the monetary base at an annual pace of about 60–70 trillion yen, but in 2016, raised this annual increase to approximately 80 trillion yen.

QQE2 in October 2014

On 31 October 2014, Governor Kuroda announced an expansion of the quantitative and qualitative monetary easing policy (QQE2). First, the Bank would conduct money market operations so that the monetary base would increase at an annual pace of around 80 trillion yen from approximately 60 trillion yen. Second, the Bank would extend the average remaining maturity of the Bank's JGB purchases from 7 years to about 7–10 years. Third, the Bank of Japan trebled the amounts of the annual pace of purchases of ETFs and J-REITs (3 trillion yen and 90 billion yen respectively). Moreover, the Bank made ETFs that track the JPX-Nikkei Index 400 eligible for purchases, to contribute to the corporate governance of Japanese companies as an additional effect of the policy.

At the time, the Japanese economy had continued to show a moderate recovery trend and was expected to continue growing at a pace above its potential. However, the increase in the consumption tax in April 2014 weakened aggregate demand, and a substantial decline in crude oil prices put downward pressure on inflation.

On 31 October 2014, the same day as the decision on QQE2, the Government Pension Investment Fund (GPIF) announced that it would change its

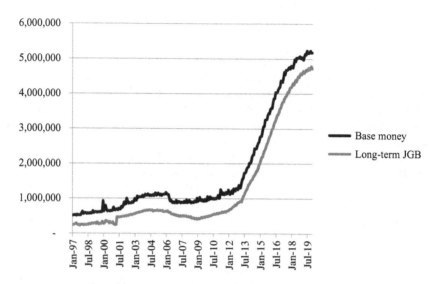

Figure 9.3 Base money and JGB holdings by the BOJ (JPY 100 million)

Source: Bank of Japan

portfolio structure and introduced a new asset allocation policy. As for domestic bonds, which were mainly JGBs, GPIF reduced their share from 60% to 35%. Instead, the percentage of domestic stocks increased from 12% to 25%, foreign bonds from 11% to 15%, and foreign stocks from 12% to 25%. The timing of the announcement (coinciding with the decision by the BOJ) meant that the decrease in JGB purchases by the GPIF was compensated by BOJ's actions to protect budget sustainability and to ease the tensions in the bond market (Noguchi, 2014).

3   Negative interest rate policy in 2016

3.1   *Introduction of negative interest rates*

On 29 January 2016, the Bank of Japan unexpectedly announced that it would introduce negative interest rates called "QQE with negative interest rates". The first countries to introduce negative interest rates were Denmark in July 2012, Switzerland in December 2014, Sweden in February 2015, and Hungary in March 2016. The Eurozone introduced negative interest rates in June 2014. In the case of European countries, if neighbouring countries cut their policy interest rates, this could directly cause the domestic currency to appreciate. This motivated central banks in small open European countries to implement negative interest rates policy in a chain (see Jobst and Lin, 2016).

If we assume that optimal policy rates are determined by the Taylor rule as follows, the natural rate of interest plays a crucial role.

$$i_t^* = \pi_t + r_t^* + \alpha(\pi_t - \pi) + b\hat{y}_t \tag{1}$$

where i_t^* is the optimal policy rate, π_t is the inflation rate, r_t^* is the natural rate of interest, π is the central bansk's inflation target, and $\hat{y}_t$ is the output gap. The natural rate of interest is the real interest rate, which applies to full employment.

In Japan, the expected decrease in the labour force, the ageing society, the increase in inequality, and the stagnation of innovation has decreased the natural rate of interest. This equation implies that when the natural rate of interest is negative, it is rational to introduce a negative policy rate. Several academic articles had pointed out that the natural rate of interest is calculated to be negative.[3] According to Okazaki and Sudo (2018), based on a DSGE model, the natural rate of interest in Japan fell below zero after 2008.

The primary purposes of the introduction of negative interest rates were as follows (Bank of Japan, 2016). First, it leads to a downward shift of overall interest rates, which should spur the economic activity of all entities to increase the inflation rate towards the targeted 2%. Second, when the Eurozone and several other countries introduced negative interest rates, their currencies depreciated. Hence, the BOJ could avoid further appreciation of the yen. Third, in 2016, the Chinese economy began to slow down after the Chinese stock market turbulence in 2015. Oil prices and stock markets around the world also declined. To avoid a similar development in Japan, the BOJ wanted to surprise the markets. Indeed, during the day of the announcement, stock prices increased dramatically. However, the day after, stock prices fell sharply – led by a decline in banking stocks due to the expectation of lower profits in the banking sector.

3.2 The 3-tier system of negative interest rate policy

In Japan, when BOJ introduced "QQE with a Negative Interest Rate" in January 2016, the Bank of Japan launched a 3-tier system, which applied a negative interest rate only to the current accounts of "policy-rate balances" at the BOJ.

In the Eurozone, the ECB had introduced a corridor system from its establishment in 1999, consisting of a marginal lending facility, the main refinancing operation and a deposit facility (excess reserve facility). The interest rate on the marginal lending facility usually provides a ceiling for the overnight market interest rate, and the interest rate on the deposit facility offers a floor for the overnight market interest rate. In the case of the ECB, only interest rates on the deposit facility turned out to be negative (-0.4%). In the case of Japan, the central bank divided reserve requirements into three tiers, which had a positive interest rate, zero interest rate, and a negative interest rate applied, respectively (see Figure 9.4) (Bank of Japan, 2016).

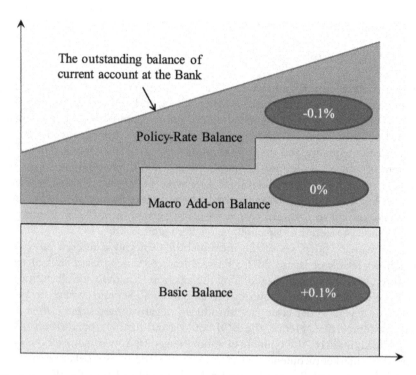

Figure 9.4 Tier system of the current account in Japan

Source: Bank of Japan

The aim of the introduction of the 3-tier system was, apparently, to support the profitability of banks. Negative interest rates contribute to a further decline in long-term interest rates and thus act to decrease home loan and overall lending rates. However, they also lower the margin of profit on lending by banks, because Japanese commercial banks are not able to introduce negative deposit rates (as some European countries could). In the case of ECB, negative interest rates are applied to more than 80% of the whole reserve requirement. This stands in sharp contrast to around 5% in the case of BOJ (Figure 9.5).[4]

After the introduction of negative interest rates, long-term interest rates and overnight call rates all fell below zero (see Figure 9.6). However, this created several issues. First, banks, insurance companies, and pension funds suffered from a further decline in bond yields and a flattening of the yield curve. Second, as city banks, regional banks, foreign banks, and cooperative banks have different positions in the money markets, they started to arbitrage between themselves to make profits using the 3-tier system.

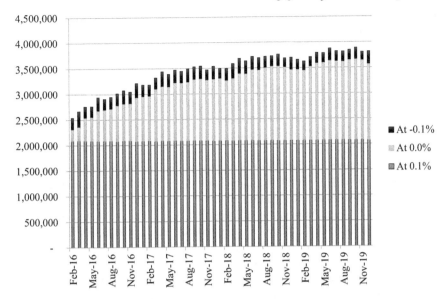

Figure 9.5 Outstanding balance of the current account at the BOJ (JPY 100 million)

Source: Bank of Japan

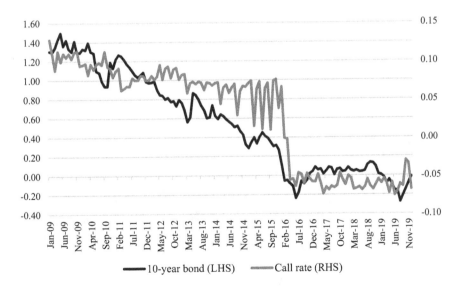

Figure 9.6 Long-term interest rates and non-collateral overnight rates (%)

Source: Bank of Japan

3.3   Arbitrage trading among the banks and the functioning of the money market

After the introduction of the 3-tier system of the current account balance at the BOJ in 2016, arbitrage trading started between depository institutions. Usually, we can divide the institutions into two groups. The first group consists of money centre banks (city banks) and foreign banks, which are cash-deficient and depend on the money market normally. The second group includes trust banks, post banks, and regional banks, which have abundant deposits and act as providers of money.

Figure 9.7 shows the 3-tier current account holdings of financial institutions as of the end of January 2019. City banks,[5] regional banks (member banks of the Regional Banks Association of Japan), and regional II banks (member banks of the Second Association of Regional Banks) do not have a policy rate account applied at -0.1%. However, post banks, trust banks, and foreign banks have a certain amount of negative-rate balances.

If we study the time series data of 3-tier balances held by financial institutions, we can see an increase in the policy rate account applied at -0.1% by foreign banks and trust banks. However, a significant decrease is shown for post banks. Post banks have recently drastically changed their strategy from a traditional "JGB buy and hold" stance to a more active and alternative investment strategy, which includes private equity, investment in fund-of-funds and fee-based selling of financial products to individuals.

Using the 3-tier system, financial institutions can conduct arbitrage trading to make profits. For example, major banks, which have scarce money, obtain

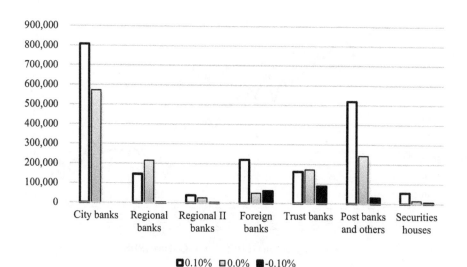

Figure 9.7 3-tier holdings by financial institutions (JPY 100 million)

Source: Bank of Japan

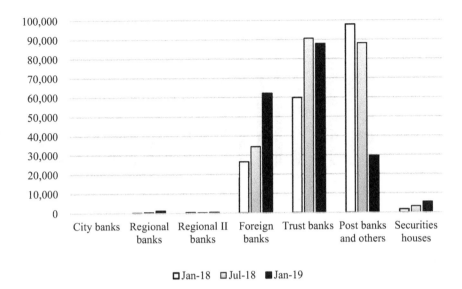

Figure 9.8 Holdings of special policy account with negative interest rates (JPY 100 million)
Source: Bank of Japan

funds from the interbank market with negative interest rates around -0.05% and place deposits at 0.1% using the Complementary Deposit Facility at the Bank of Japan. This way, a risk-free profit is generated.

As described previously, when the BOJ first introduced quantitative easing in 2001, banks, which invested in the money market, could not get any interest after deducting broker commissions, and trading volume decreased. But this time, the 3-tier system and the 0.1% of Complementary Deposit Facility kept the amounts outstanding in the money market at a certain level, avoiding the ill-functioning of the short-term money market as seen in 2001.

3.4   QQE with yield curve control (YCC)

In September 2016, the Bank of Japan introduced QQE with yield curve control (YCC), a framework controlling the entire yield curve (Bank of Japan, 2016). The new programme targeted long-term interest rates, in part to resolve issues created by negative interest rate policy, which flattened the yield curve. At the same time, the Bank of Japan changed its operational variables from the monetary base to interest rates again. The aim of YCC was to keep 10-year JGB yields stable around 0% to stimulate lending by financial institutions without damage to their profitability. Figure 9.9 shows the yearly change of JGBs held by BOJ. It shows that the BOJ kept 80 trillion yen to

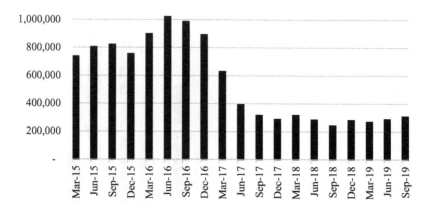

Figure 9.9 Tapering of JGB purchases by the BOJ (yearly change of outstanding JGBs held by the BOJ, JPY 100 million)

Source: Bank of Japan

buy JGBs each year. However, after September 2016, it started to taper the JGB purchases.

It has generally been thought that the central bank can control short-term interest rates, but cannot and should not control long-term interest rates. However, Amamiya (2017) points out that this kind of policy has existed in the past. Examples include the interest rate cap policy before WW2 in the UK, the government bond price supporting system in the UK in the 1970s, the "bills only" policy in the US in the 1950s and the controversial operation twist policy in the 1960s. These policies worked well from a fiscal policy perspective. However, from a monetary policy point of view, they shared several problems (such as monetising the fiscal deficit). Amamiya (2017) argues that the BOJ policy is different from those in the past. Nonetheless, it demonstrates the limits of monetary policy, and there should make difficult for future exit from unconventional monetary policy.

4   Impact of unconventional monetary policy on financial markets

4.1   The ETF market

From 2013, the Bank of Japan's holdings of securities issued by exchange-traded funds (ETFs) and real estate investment trusts (REITs) increased sharply. The purchase of ETFs by the Bank of Japan dates back to October 2010, when Masaaki Shirakawa was governor. In the beginning, the central bank kept its purchasing value below 450 billion yen per year. However, from 2013, the BOJ aggressively increased their possession of ETFs. The aggregate outstanding of ETFs held by the Bank of Japan rose to over 23 trillion yen at the end of January 2019 (two-thirds of the total ETFs outstanding of 35.72 trillion yen). This equates to around 4% of the whole market capitalisation of the Tokyo Stock Exchange. At first, it was believed that this would spur the economy (by keeping the Nikkei 225 index above 20,000). However, as the Bank of Japan increased its ETF holding, concerns started to arise. These concerns primarily related to the impact on market liquidity and a possible distortion of the price formation.

First, with the BOJ's buy-and-hold strategy, the central bank absorbs stocks that are less traded in the market and thereby distorts the price formation. Second, the ETF purchase increases the price/earnings ratio, but this effect is temporary. Third, this policy leads the BOJ to become a major shareholder of private enterprises, which could weaken the corporate governance of Japanese corporations. Fourth, the BOJ already possesses many risky assets in its inflated balance sheet, and market shocks could have a more negative impact on their balance sheet.

According to a Nikkei estimate in April 2019 (Nikkei, 2019), the Bank of Japan would hold more assets than the Government Pension Investment Fund and become the largest shareholder on the Tokyo Stock Exchange by the end of 2020, if the BOJ continued buying stock at its current pace. With its passive investor style, this could harm the stock market liquidity and weaken the corporate governance further.

4.2   The JGB market and the portfolio rebalancing effect

The government bonds held by the Bank of Japan have increased rapidly. According to flow of funds statistics, JGBs held by the BOJ have increased approximately four-fold within five years, from 93.9 trillion yen (a holding share of 13.5%) at the end of March 2013, to 445.9 trillion yen (49.6%) at the end of June 2018. Not only the volume but also the maturity of the JGBs has increased. At first, 10-year bonds were the focal point but then extended to 40 years in the QQE process, which flattened the yield curve to make monetary policy more effective.

On the other hand, the strong influence of the central bank in the government bond market is a cause for concern. First, market liquidity is negatively affected. Government bonds held by the Bank of Japan are essentially a long-term possession (buy and hold), which diminishes market liquidity and harms the price formation. Second, the market-making function is affected by a reduction in the number of intermediaries in the government bond market. Usually, banks hold JGBs as collateral for funding. However, if the BOJ increases its influence and control over JGB prices, the market-making function is distorted. Third, a decrease in government bond yields leads to a reduction of related lending rates by banks. This lowers the profitability of banks, as well as institutional investors such as pension funds or insurance companies.

The most significant impact of QQE is the portfolio rebalancing effect. The banks increased their government bonds holdings significantly throughout the 2000s, reaching a peak of 321 trillion yen (share 46.2%) at the end of March 2013. Since, however, the holdings of JGBs by banks have decreased by more than half to 153 trillion yen (share 15.1%) at the end of December 2018 (see Figure 9.10). This relates to the introduction of the Complementary Deposit Facility in 2008 (mentioned previously) and the active buying by the Bank of Japan since the launch of QQE in 2013. For banks, this was no problem as the Complementary Deposit Facility provides a 0.1% deposit rate (higher than JGB nominal coupon rates of around 0%).

Because of the BOJ's massive purchases of JGBs, investors and financial institutions have shifted from JGBs to higher-yielding assets such as foreign bonds, corporate bonds, stocks, and loans. During QQE1, large banks were the primary sellers of JGBs to the central bank, and the "big three" banks vigorously reduced their JGB portfolios during this period. The decline in holdings of government debt by the major banks weakened the bank-sovereign linkage, as pointed out by Arslanalp and Lam (2013). As of December 2018, BOJ held around 46.0% of the JGB market, and is likely to increase to around 50% by the end of 2019. JGB purchases by the Bank of Japan first took place from city banks, then regional banks, and recently by post banks. Since January 2019, the BOJ has been tapering their JGB purchase, but it is still the largest holder of JGBs in the market (Figure 9.11).

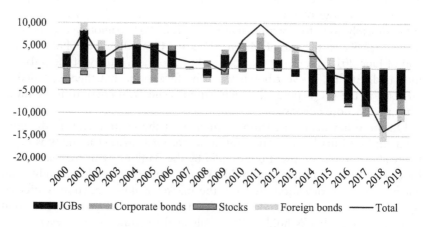

Figure 9.10 Change in bond holdings by banks in Japan (JPY 100 million)

Source: Bank of Japan

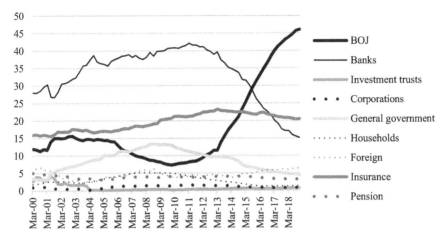

Figure 9.11 Share of JGB holdings by financial institutions (%)

Source: Flow of funds data, Bank of Japan

4.3   Unconventional monetary policy and financial institutions

As discussed so far, unconventional monetary policy had an impact on the economy, but also created some market distortions. The negative interest rate policy cast a deep shadow over the banking sector. QQE led to an increase in lending by Japanese banks. However, since the introduction of the negative interest rate policy, the situation has changed.

Lending market

1 STRUCTURE OF THE BANKING SYSTEM IN JAPAN

The Japanese banking sector consisted of 137 banks at the end of 2018, which included 5 city banks, 14 trust banks, 64 regional banks (members of the Association of Regional Banks in Japan) and 39 regional II banks (members of the Second Association of Regional Banks). Cooperative financial institutions (including 259 Shinkin and 146 Shinso, which are cooperative financial institutions with membership composed of local residents and small companies with less than 300 employees), and 17 other financial institutions (including post banks). In the loan market, city banks are dominant. However, the share of regional banks is almost the same as city banks (see Figure 9.12).

2 DOMESTIC LENDING

After the introduction of QQE in 2013, lending by all categories increased, and this was especially led by regional banks (Figure 9.13).

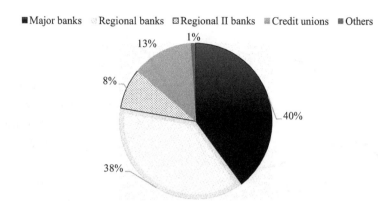

■Major banks   ░Regional banks   ⊠Regional II banks   ▓Credit unions   ■Others

Figure 9.12 Loan market in Japan at the end of 2018 (%)
Source: Bank of Japan

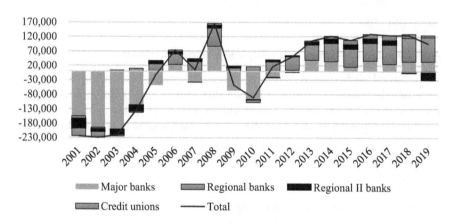

Figure 9.13 Change in outstanding loans (by bank category, JPY 100 million)
Source: Bank of Japan

Regional bank loans to small firms increased, these focus on real estate lending, medium-risk markets, and dollar-denominated foreign bonds. However, after negative interest rates were introduced in 2016, and geopolitical risks increased, this process has slowed down. The speed of the increase of domestic loans by major banks has decreased among all bank categories. Their expansion of domestic loans increased in 2017 due to merger and acquisition-related lending to large corporations, and because banks have shifted some of their activities to fee-based services and increased their lending volumes to offset declining interest revenues. Since 2018, they have decreased housing and individual loans. Regional II banks and credit associations (shinkin), which specialise in small-scale and community lending, have slowed their rate of increase of loans after 2017 (see Figure 9.14).

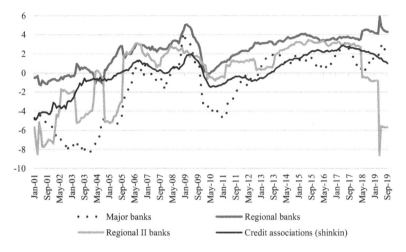

Figure 9.14 Lending by banks (by bank category, y/y change in %)
Source: Bank of Japan

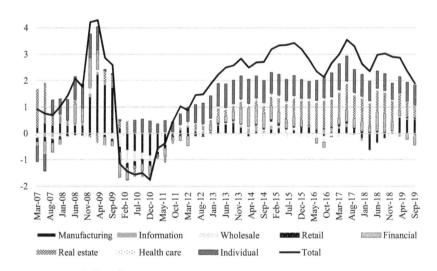

Figure 9.15 Share of lending by category (all banks, %)
Source: Bank of Japan

As for bank lending by industry category, lending in the areas of real estate and financial institutions has increased recently (see Figure 9.15). This reflects the trend of small and medium-sized banks' lending to rental housing businesses. The latest financial report by the BOJ in April 2019 pointed out that even in comparison with the bubble period, real estate lending in terms of

GDP is overheating and growing faster than its trend. Especially regional banks have been actively extending loans to middle-risk firms with relatively low creditworthiness. For such loans, however, local financial institutions have continued to face difficulties in securing profit margins commensurate with the risks involved. It is thus necessary to pay attention to financial institutions' vulnerability to future rises in credit costs (Bank of Japan, 2019).

3 INTERNATIONAL LENDING

As mentioned earlier, in the domestic market, city banks and regional banks have decreased their speed of lending. By contrast, major banks have increased their international lending, where interest income is increasing due to the continuing economic expansion in emerging markets and the US. Japanese banks are very active in the Asian market in particular, and this includes mergers and acquisitions of local banks to acquire liquidity denominated in local currencies. As a result, more than 35% of the profits of major banks came from international business in 2018 (Figure 9.16).

After the Lehman Shock in 2008, the Bank for International Settlements strengthened the Basel Accord. Consequently, city banks active in international business tried to meet the new requirements, which made their financial base stronger than ever before and enabled them to expand internationally. By contrast, regional banks and community banks, whose business is mainly in

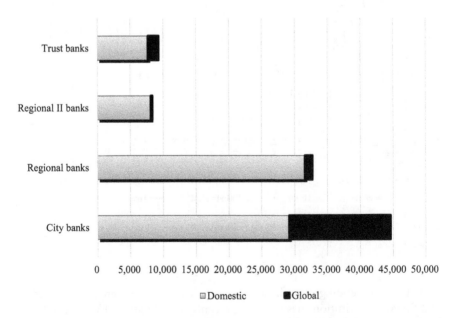

Figure 9.16 International and domestic profits by bank category (FY2018, JPY 100 million)
Source: Japanese Bankers Association

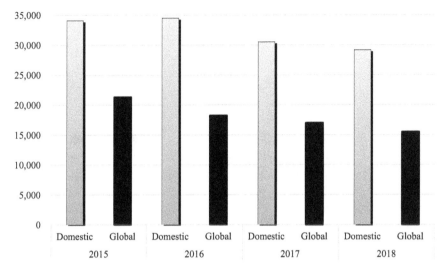

Figure 9.17 Domestic and global profits by city banks (JPY 100 million)
Source: Japanese Bankers Association

the domestic market and with limited loans overseas, suffer from decreasing margin profits as a result of the negative interest rate policy. Although profits from overseas business have been decreasing in recent years due to increasing funding costs, city banks remain very active in international business through M&As as described earlier.

4.4 Negative interest rate policy and Japanese bank profits

Japanese bank profits

The negative interest rate policy has therefore mainly hit the banking industry in Japan. According to the data from the Japanese Bankers Association, ordinary profits of all (115) banks were 2.23 trillion yen at the end of September 2018 (a decrease by around 4.5% from the previous year). Ordinary profits of five city banks increased by approximately 6.5% to 1.35 trillion yen. The regional banks and regional II banks reported a decrease by 26.8% to 489 billion yen and 19.1% to 95 billion yen, respectively. Figure 9.18 shows ordinary profits of each bank category from 2014 to 2018.

Net interest profits of city banks increased by 7.7% in September 2018. However, net interest profits of the larger regional banks and smaller regional II banks decreased by 1.0% and 1.3%, respectively. As for fees and commissions from the selling of mutual funds or insurance instruments (which became mainstream in the movement "from savings to investment"[6]), an increase of

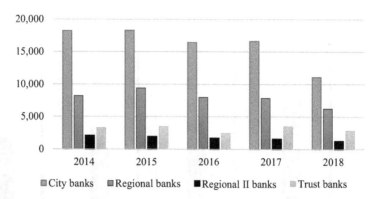

Figure 9.18 Bank profits

Source: Japanese Bankers Association

2.3% and 1.0%, respectively, is reported. Here, the rise for city banks is considerably more significant than for regional banks. To compensate for the decline in interest income, regional banks have focused on investments in bonds and stocks, especially dollar-denominated government bonds, real estate lending, and medium-risk lending. However, an increase in federal funds rates, coupled with geopolitical risks, reduced the profits of regional banks in 2018 – and this trend could continue for the time being.

Reduction of loan profit margins

Negative interest rates had a severe impact on loan profit margins. Deposit rates stopped responding to policy rates once they became negative. In some cases, bank lending rates increased, rather than decreased, in response to policy rate cuts (Figure 9.19). Thus, loan profit margins, which are critical to regional banks, contributed to an overall reduction in bank profits.

According to data from the Japanese Bankers Association, it is clear that profits of all bank categories decreased after the introduction of the negative interest rate policy. Among the three groups, the speed of decrease in profits of regional banks and smaller regional II banks is more pronounced than of major banks. The profits of regional banks have continued to decline, reflecting the persistent downward trend in deposit-lending margins and decreasing domestic net interest income.

5   Financial stability of regional banks

As mentioned already, the negative interest rate policy has had adverse effects on financial intermediaries – and particularly deposit-dependent banks such as regional banks in local areas. This section focuses on the financial stability of

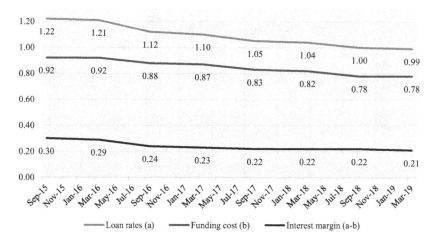

Figure 9.19 Average interest income by banks in Japan (%)

Source: Japanese Bankers Association

regional banks, and consists of an analysis of asset size, return on equity (ROE), and demographics.

5.1 Regional bank profits

The profits of regional banks have increased from 2010. However, after 2016, regional banks registered three consecutive years of decrease in their profits (Figure 9.20).

For the 2018 fiscal year, among 79 regional banks and regional II banks, 55 institutions experienced lower profits, and three banks sustained losses. The losses mainly stemmed from trading of foreign bonds (with the increase in interest rates in the US) and non-performing loans (due to the collapse of small and medium-sized corporations and the shrinking regional economy in Japan).

In Japan, capital and human resources are concentrated in the metropolitan area. In local areas, the working population is shrinking, and ageing faster than in the metropolitan areas. The number of corporations in the regions is decreasing, and these structural factors (coupled with cyclical reasons) make it difficult for regional banks to be profitable. In addition, regional banks were hit by negative interest rates, since they rely heavily on net profit margins. Finally, and as mentioned previously, regional banks have also been affected by higher interest rates abroad and geopolitical instability.

5.2 Consolidation of regional banks in Japan

Lower profitability and, naturally, losses hurt financial stability. As a result of the declining profits of regional banks, a string of mergers and acquisition have

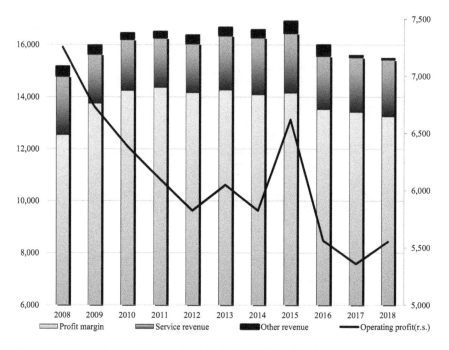

Figure 9.20 Operating profit by regional banks (JPY 100 million)

Source: Association of Regional Banks. Notes: 64 banks, interim results.

followed. This is an effective way for the banks to consolidate and reconstruct their earnings capacity through more efficient resource allocation and rationalisation of management.

Table 9.1 shows the number of banks and cooperative financial institutions in Japan. It shows that the number of banks has halved during the last 30 years.

In the 1990s and 2000s, city banks were involved in mergers and acquisitions. This resulted in a reduction from 13 to 5 banks, a stabilisation of their financial base, and a rationalisation of their resource usage. Especially after 1995, when the financial crisis became more severe, city banks preferred to consolidate to protect themselves and to avoid injections of public funds. In the 2010s, however, the main M&A activity has involved regional banks. This has resulted in a dramatic reduction of regional banks and community banks.

There are several types of mergers and acquisitions in the regional banks' consolidation process. First, there is consolidation within the same prefecture. These are common, and the objective is mainly to rationalise management and to cut IT and labour costs using economies of scale. The second type encompasses larger regional areas, whereby a bank can expand its business area through its brand. The third type involves consolidating agriculture and SME lending. The consolidation of regional banks mainly involves holding

Table 9.1 Number of Japanese banks by category

	City banks	Regional bank	Regional II	Trust banks	Long-term banks	Total banks	Shinkin	Shinso	Roukin	Rengou	Total
1990	12	64	68	16	3	163	451	408	47	0	1069
1995	11	64	65	30	3	174	416	370	47	0	1007
2000	9	64	57	31	3	167	372	281	40	3	863
2005	6	64	47	21	1	148	292	172	13	3	628
2010	6	63	42	18	0	145	271	158	13	3	591
2015	5	64	41	16	0	141	265	151	13	3	572
2018	5	64	39	14	0	137	259	146	13	3	559

Source: Deposit Insurance Institution

companies. As of the end of 2018, there were 12 regional financial groups, to which 18 regional banks and 7 regional II banks belong. The reason why the number of regional banks and regional II banks remains unchanged during the past years is that they are counted as individual banks, already under their holding companies.

5.3 Asset size and return on equity

Figure 9.21 and Figure 9.22 are scatter diagrams of ROE and asset size of 64 regional banks and 12 holding companies in 2018. These figures show that asset size and ROE are positively correlated. It is even more apparent when we study the scatter diagram of the 12 regional holding companies of regional banks. The correlation coefficient R^2 is 0.2495 in Figure 9.21 and 0.5871 in Figure 9.22. This demonstrates that the correlation between asset size and ROE is more significant for holding companies and that the consolidation among regional banks benefits from economies of scale.

5.4 Structural problems of regional banks

As already mentioned, the low profitability of regional and community banks is due to two reasons.

First, the working-age population in rural areas is declining, and resources are concentrated in the metropolitan areas of Tokyo, Osaka, and Nagoya. Figure 9.23 shows that the GDP correlates with the lending volume of each prefecture. This means that when the population of an area decreases rapidly, the lending volume could be affected. Moreover, during the last 20 years, the number of corporations in Japan have decreased from 5 to 4 million, which has also led to a decline in lending in rural areas. Second, ultra-low interest rates and stiff competition have affected the banking sector. As a result, regional banks tend to expand their business base into other prefectures. Here, they not only face competition from other regional banks but also from other financial institutions.

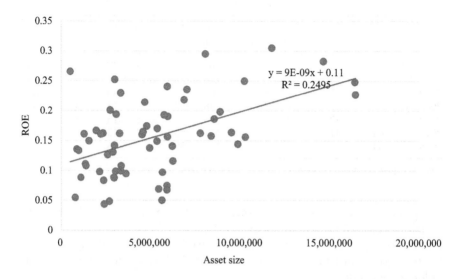

Figure 9.21 Correlation between asset size (JPY million) and ROE (%), regional banks except Tokyo and Nagoya

Source: Association of Regional Banks

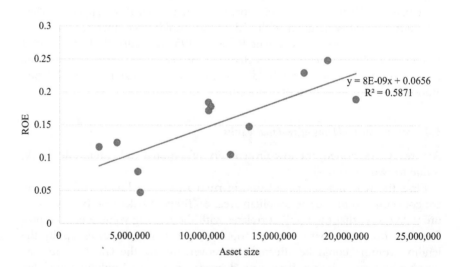

Figure 9.22 Correlation between asset size (JPY million) and ROE (%), holding companies

Source: Association of Regional Banks

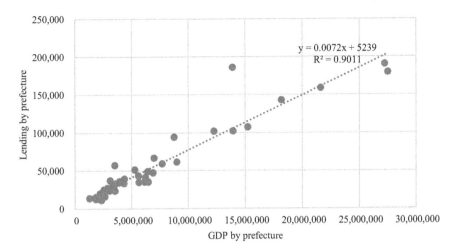

Figure 9.23 GDP and lending by prefecture (excluding Tokyo and Osaka) in JPY 100 million
Sources: Cabinet Office, Bank of Japan

There are three broad views on competition in the financial sector: the "competition-fragility view", the "competition-stability view", and the "mixed view". Keeley (1990) and Saunders and Wilson (1996) support the competition-fragility view using US banking data, and so do Salas and Saurina (2003) using Spanish banking data. The competition-fragility view is dominant in Japan, where severe competition acts to narrow the interest rate gap and thereby lower profits. The Japanese Financial Service Agency (JFSA) shows that the expected default ratio in Japan has been increasing since 2010 (FSA, 2018), and that (regional) banks have been affected by weak demand for funds in regional areas. This is in line with a decrease in the profit mark-up (competitive index), as calculated by the Bank of Japan. This has several policy implications in terms of supervision of regional banks. Monetary policy and oversight of regional banks are not sufficient. It is also necessary to strengthen the local economy itself – in line with "Regional revitalisation" within one of the three arrows of Abenomics.

5.5 Empirical study

Let us now try to identify the main factors that affected the profitability of regional banks and city banks from 2008 to 2017. Assume that profitability is critical for financial stability as a whole, and that bank ROE is used as an indicator for profitability. We then estimate the following equation:

$$ROE = \alpha + \beta_1 Concentration + \beta_2 Crisk + \beta_3 Efficency + \beta_4 NegativeIR + \varepsilon \quad (2)$$

Table 9.2 Regression result

Dependent variable: ROE	Regional banks	Regional II banks	City banks
Independent variable			
Concentration	-3.406413	-0.382817	-0.059931
	(-1.040129)	(-1.723305)	(-1.010303)
Credit risk	2.572435	-0.860854	0.71437
	(-0.267411)	(-1.92944)	(1.539169)
Efficiency	-0.100402**	-2.497873*	-0.057173***
	(-3.10527)	(-2.369784)	(-4.433223)
Negative IR	-0.193434**	-0.006649*	-0.003366**
	(-2.896471)	(-2.15903)	(-3.007704)
Adjusted R²	0.758826	0.879577	0.813915
Prob. (F-statistic)	0.020798	0.003858	0.011139

Note: */**/*** statistically significant at p < 0.10/0.05/0.01 level.

Where *Concentration* is the share of the working-age labour force of Tokyo in logs, *Crisk* is credit risk (impaired credit divided by gross loans), *Efficiency* is costs divided by deposits, *Negative IR* is a dummy variable for negative interest rates, and ε is error terms.

In this regression, yearly data for three groups of banks are used for the period 2009–2018. The three groups are city banks, regional banks, and second regional banks (aggregated). The bank variables are from the Japanese Bankers Association. The GDP/prefecture data series is from the Cabinet Office database.

The results are shown in Table 9.2.

It seems that the concentration in Tokyo does not influence ROE, and the estimated coefficient has a weak statistical significance for all three banks. Moreover, credit risk (measured as the ratio of non-performing loans to all loans) does not have a statistically significant impact on bank performance.

As for efficiency (measured as a cost ratio), the coefficient has the expected (negative) sign and, in this case, it is significant. However, the relative effect of efficiency is more pronounced for regional II banks and regional banks. Job and branch reductions have had an impact on the performance of regional banks and city banks. The most significant influence on ROE has been negative interest rates. All categories have been affected, but regional banks in particular.

5.6   Supervision, regulation, and the banking system

As mentioned earlier, regional banks have increased real estate financing, medium-risk financing, and US dollar bond investments in an environment of weak funding demand in local areas. Net profits from traditional core businesses have decreased, and the US bond holdings are sensitive to potential interest rate hikes by the Fed. In addition, with decreasing profit margins, regional banks have prolonged their lending. This makes them vulnerable to interest rate and maturity risks should government bond prices fall in the process of a future exit from the unconventional monetary policy by the Bank of Japan.

In March 2019, the Financial Services Agency announced that they would reinforce the interest rate risk regulation of major banks, and extend it to regional banks. A small set of Japanese banks has purchased a significant portion of AAA-rated collateralised loan obligations (CLOs) in search of higher yields in the environment of ultra-low interest rates in Japan. However, small regional banks, in particular, tend to buy CLOs without detailed assessments of the underlying risks.

An exit by the BOJ from its unconventional monetary policy, and the next cyclical downturn could come soon. As a result, it will be necessary for local banks to strengthen their capital base and prepare for another economic downturn and for the regulator to monitor them to keep pace with the government policy of regional revitalisation.

During the autumn of 2019, the Japanese internet company SBI Holdings made large-scale investments in two regional banks (Shimane bank and Fukushima bank), which had suffered continuing losses in their core businesses. SBI Holdings declared to launch a regional bank union initiative to provide FinTech know-how and financial products together with 10 regional banks, introduce a management rationalisation programme, lower IT costs, and increase synergy effects. The JFSA welcomes these moves and sees them as regional economy stabilisers.

6   Concluding remarks

This chapter has investigated the effects of monetary policy under Abenomics on the markets and the stability of financial institutions. After analysing the main determinants of the profitability of regional banks, we can conclude that the empirical findings are consistent with the expected results. Negative interest rates and management efficiency have had an influence on bank profitability and the return on equity of regional banks. At first, the unconventional monetary policy worked very well to increase inflation expectations. However, the negative interest rate policy has cast a shadow on financial intermediaries, especially outside the large urban areas.

Notably, the Tokyo Stock Exchange (TSE) plans to reduce the number of companies listed on its First Section by up to 30%. The First Section currently includes over 2,100 companies. If they use a market capitalisation of 50 billion yen as a criterium (now 2 billion), 38 regional banks would be excluded from the TSE First Section. This would have another negative effect on small and medium-sized regional banks in the future.

Monetary policy under Abenomics implies a close collaboration between the Ministry of Finance and the Bank of Japan. From this perspective, in the future when more JGBs will be held by non-resident entities, the current account in Japan turns into deficit, and the purchase of JGBs by the Bank of Japan reaches its limit, a sudden crisis could break out with a spike in long-term interest rates. Japan has to prepare for such threats, and the Bank of Japan should seek a smooth exit policy instead of cutting deep the negative interest policy rates.

Notes

1 According to the minutes released recently, the BOJ policy commission introduced temporary measures under which the Bank paid interest on excess reserve balances (complementary deposit facility) at 0.1%, in order to prevent the uncollateralised overnight call rate from falling well below its targeted level and to facilitate money market operations (BOJ, 2008).
2 The Fisher equation tells us that when the expected inflation increases, real interest rates will decrease. This pushes up stock prices and the exchange rate depreciates. $i = r + \pi^e$, where i = nominal interest rate, r = real interest rate, π^e = expected inflation rate.
3 See Iiboshi et al. (2017) for Japan, Barsky et al. (2014) and Del Negro et al. (2015, 2017) for the US, and Hristov (2016) for the euro area.
4 BOJ can control the amount of the policy-rate balance to which negative interest rates are applied, and has sometimes adjusted the balances.
5 Mizuho Bank, MUFG Bank, Sumitomo Mitsui Banking Corporation, Resona Bank, and Saitama Resona Bank.
6 The slogan by the government refers to promoting more investment from savings to boost the economy (including tax incentives on stock investments).

References

Akbas, H. E. (2012) Determinants of bank profitability: An investigation on Turkish banking sector, *Öneri Dergisi*, 10 (37), 103–110.
Amamiya, M. (2017) History and theories of yield curve control, *Keynote Speech at the Financial Markets Panel Conference to Commemorate the 40th Meeting*, Bank of Japan, January 11. Available from: www.boj.or.jp/en/announcements/press/koen_2017/data/ko170111a1.pdf [Accessed 12 November].
Arslanalp, S. and Lam, W. R. (2013) Outlook for interest rates and Japanese banks' risk exposures under Abenomics, *IMF Working Paper*, No. 13/213.
Bank of Japan (2008) *Minutes of the Monetary Policy Meeting*, October 31. Available from: www.boj.or.jp/en/mopo/mpmsche_minu/minu_2008/g081031.pdf [Accessed 12 November 2019].
Bank of Japan (2010) *Comprehensive Monetary Easing*, October 5. Available from: www.boj.or.jp/en/announcements/release_2010/k101005.pdf [Accessed 12 November 2019].
Bank of Japan (2016) *Comprehensive Assessment: Developments in Economic Activity and Prices as Well as Policy Effects Since the Introduction of Quantitative and Qualitative Monetary Easing (QQE) – The Background Note*, 21 September. Available from: www.boj.or.jp/en/announcements/release_2016/k160921b.pdf [Accessed 12 November 2019].
Bank of Japan (2019) *Financial System Report, Bank of Japan Research Papers*, April. Available from: www.boj.or.jp/en/research/brp/fsr/data/fsr190417a.pdf [Accessed 12 September 2019].
Barsky, R., Justiniano, A. and Melosi L. (2014) The natural rate of interest and its usefulness for monetary policy, *American Economic Review*, 104, 3743.
Del Negro, M., Giannoni, M. P., Cocci, M., Shahanaghi, S. and Smith, M. (2015) Why are interest rates so low? *Federal Reserve Bank of New York, Liberty Street Economics* (NY Fed Blog), 20 May.

Del Negro, M., Giannone, D., Giannoni, M. P. and Tambalotti, A. (2017) Safety, liquidity, and the natural rate of interest, *Federal Reserve Bank of New York, Staff Report*, No. 812.

Financial Service Agency (2018) Challenges of regional banks and their competition (in Japanese), *Committee of Intermediation Reform*.

Hristov, A. (2016) Measuring the natural rate of interest in the Eurozone: A DSGE perspective, *CESifo Forum*, 17 (1), 86–91.

Iiboshi, H., Shintani, M. and Ueda, K. (2017) Estimating the nonlinear new Keynesian model with the zero lower bound for Japan, *Mimeo Working Paper*.

Jobst, A. and Lin, H. (2016) Negative Interest Rate Policy (NIRP): Implications for monetary transmission and bank profitability in the Euro Area, *IMF Working Paper*, No. 16–72.

Keeley, M. C. (1990) Deposit insurance, risk and market power in banking, *American Economic Review*, 80 (5), 1183–1200.

Kuroda, H. (2016) Overcoming deflation: Theory and practice, *Speech at Keio University in Tokyo*, Bank of Japan, 20 June. Available from: www.boj.or.jp/en/announcements/press/koen_2016/ko160620a.htm/ [Accessed 12 September 2019].

Nikkei (2019) BoJ, the largest shareholder of Japanese stocks (in Japanese), *Nikkei*, 16 April. Available from: www.nikkei.com/article/DGXMZO43792260W9A410C1EA2000/ [Accessed 12 November 2019].

Noguchi, T. (2014) *Mizuho Insight*. Research Institute of Mizuho Bank.

Okazaki, Y. and Sudo, N. (2018) Natural rate of interest in Japan: Measuring its size and identifying drivers based on a DSGE model, *Bank of Japan Working Paper Series*, No.18-E-6.

Petria, N., Capraru, B. and Iulian Ihnatov, I. (2015) Determinants of banks' profitability: Evidence from EU 27 banking systems, *Procedia Economics and Finance*, 20, 518–524.

Salas, V. and Saurina, J. (2003) Deregulation, market power and risk behavior in Spanish banks, *European Economic Review*, 47 (6), 1061–1075.

Saunders, A. and Wilson, B. (1996) Bank capital structure: Charter value and diversification effects, *New York University Salomon Center Working Paper*, No. S-96-52.

Index

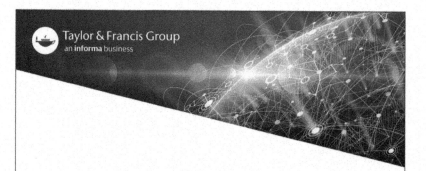